Our land, the first garden of Liberty's tree,
It has been, and shall yet be, the land of the free.
— THOMAS CAMPBELL

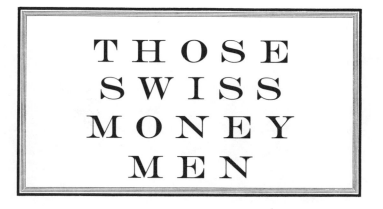

THOSE SWISS MONEY MEN

RAY VICKER

Charles Scribner's Sons
New York

The author wishes to thank the two score Swiss bankers and monetary authorities who graciously cooperated in preparation of this book through extensive interviews and the checking of portions of this work for accuracy. Their cooperation and helpfulness in presenting the facts refuted those innuendos about Swiss bankers which have characterized them as secretive, soulless Gnomes of Zurich. Thanks also to my wife, Margaret, who served as secretary, editor, and critic in preparation of this work.

CONTENTS

PART I

PART II

PART III

THOSE SWISS MONEY MEN

PART I

CHAPTER I

RASCALS OR PARAGONS, THE MYTH AND THE REALITY

Lord George Brown, Britain's Labor peer and one-time foreign minister, popularized the term "Gnomes of Zurich" for Swiss bankers. He didn't mean it as a compliment. Lord George Brown seldom has a compliment for any banker, least of all for any from Switzerland. This was his way of labeling them as scrooges and cold-hearted reprobates, in other words, the type of characters who wouldn't loan a dime to a British Labor government.

Robert M. Morgenthau, one-time United States attorney for the Southern District of New York, didn't have any good to say about Swiss bankers either. He told the House Banking and

Currency Committee in Washington that "Numerous banks in Switzerland are owned and controlled not only by Americans, but in some cases by American hoodlums."

The committee was conducting one of those innumerable Washington investigations which help get congressional names into hometown newspapers, while irritating only foreigners who won't be voting in forthcoming elections anyway.

In Switzerland, you hear something different along with the yodeling lieders on juke boxes and the tinkle of cow bells in high mountain pastures. If motherhood and dogs are sacred in America, banks and money are deified in Switzerland. The former are the temples of the latter. Swiss bankers are the high priests performing their pecuniary ceremonies behind glass cages or in small offices so private that the client may feel embarrassed by the presence of a mirror.

Swiss banks allied with gangsters? "This is grotesque," says one rebuttal of Swiss Credit Bank, Zurich, one of the country's Big Three banks.

Swiss Credit Bank is also known as Credit Suisse (French), Schweizerische Kreditanstalt (German), and Credito Svizzero (Italian) in this multilingual country of Switzerland. Sometimes, too, it seems as if different languages are being used by different people to describe Swiss banks.

The truth?

You can find something somewhere to justify everything that has ever been said about Swiss bankers. There are staid, respectable operators who go to church every Sunday, spout platitudes about the incorruptibility of Swiss banks and who really do regard the money of others as sacred, even when they have their hands on it. There also are fast-buck operators who can devalue your dollars faster than could any Group of Ten meeting in Washington.

Bernard Cornfeld, the one-time Swiss-based mutual-fund king, used to promote his funds with the question: "Do you sincerely want to be rich?" He was asking the question of salesmen hired to sell his funds, not of the customers who flocked to invest in them.

American Express, Inc., the travel giant whose offices often are homes away from home for overseas Americans, has a cer-

tain amount of financial acumen, even competitor Thomas Cook
& Son will admit. Yet, it was in Switzerland that it was taken
for several hundred thousand dollars in a deal involving Allied
Fund for Capital Appreciation.

Big Swiss banks err, too. Penn Central floated a $59 million
loan in Switzerland just before the railroad went bankrupt. The
deal was negotiated through a Zurich bank. United California
Bank, Los Angeles, is a major American bank. Yet, it has the
dubious distinction, too, of being involved in the biggest bank
failure ever to occur in Switzerland, a $50 million debacle.

Nevertheless, billions of dollars do flow into Switzerland
for safekeeping and investment annually. This indicates that
either the bulk of Swiss bankers are monetary puritans or the
world is peopled by fools. The first interpretation is more logical, since fools usually are parted from their money before they
can shift it to Switzerland.

Around the world, when people worry about their money,
they rush it to Switzerland, even when domestic laws forbid it.
Switzerland never seems to have any trouble which would adversely affect the value of its currency or the safety of the money
entrusted to its bankers. Even in World War II, when Hitler's
powerful army conquered most of the continent, Switzerland
mobilized its defense forces and discouraged Nazis from launching an invasion.

Swiss Credit Bank was worried enough that in 1940 it established a branch in New York, aiming to shift the bank's headquarters there were Switzerland overrun. It didn't happen,
though. Switzerland emerged from World War II with its reputation enhanced as a money refuge.

In 1971, a bad year for the U.S. dollar and the monetary
system generally, the Swiss franc's parity value increased by
over 13 percent. Meanwhile, the dollar's value fell by nearly 10
percent. Truly, little Switzerland showed that it knew how to
take care of its own money, as well as somebody else's.

Today, Switzerland manages about $75 billion worth of
portfolio funds for South American millionaires, for oil-rich
Mideastern Arabs, for Indian potentates, for European businessmen, and for thousands of less important folk. In recent
years, Americans who have been worried about the declining

value of the dollar have joined the parade of international depositors who realize that Switzerland is much more than an Alpine resort land.

Swiss banks in 1972 had about $52 billion worth of assets on their books above that portfolio total. Thus, in all, Swiss bankers had around $127 billion under their control, a staggering figure when the small size of this nation is considered. This is equivalent to about $20,000 each for every man, woman, and child in this 6.3 million population country. U.S. banks would control over $3 trillion if they maintained the same relationship.

Swiss bank selling points include:
—Political and economic stability in a capitalistic society.
—Swiss internationalism.
—Geographic advantages.
—Facilities and banking know-how.
—Bank secrecy.

Neutral Switzerland has not been in a war since the time of Napoleon. It is a land with few natural resources except for water and picturesque scenery. So it has always had to depend upon shrewdness in dealings with neighbors.

"Money is in our blood," one Basle banker said not long ago when talking about his family's long banking history. He voiced the word money reverently, as if he were making a mental sign of the cross before one of his private gods.

Swiss bankers aren't ashamed of being capitalists. They glory in it. Money, whether in the concrete or abstract, arouses no guilt complexes about starving Armenians or unshod Bengalis. Here, money often seems not only a means to an end, but the end itself. Paraphrasing McLuhan, money is the message. Swiss banks are the media for carrying that message.

One Swiss banker with a sense of imagery likens the Swiss money system to a railroad. Trains enter and leave a terminal all the time, few remaining long. So money arrives from the Mideast, from South America, from North America. That money doesn't remain long. It departs for the American stock market, for the eurodollar market, for Kaffirs (that South African mining market with its quaint, racist name), and for anything else that provides a return.

General Motors Corp? Swiss banks certainly own pieces of

that. Ditto for International Business Machines Corp. Virtually every major corporation in the world has some of its shares in Swiss portfolios. Customers include thousands of individuals who, for their own reasons, prefer to invest from behind the façades of Swiss banks.

In any Swiss bank, arriving telex messages may be from Hong Kong, from New York City, from Tokyo, from San Francisco, from London, or from a score of other places. Messages will detail buy or sell orders, deposits, withdrawals, ask advice.

Swiss bankers are worldwide operators, but in a peculiarly Swiss way. They use foreign branches and links as conduits for streams of money into Switzerland, not as deposit and loan centers in foreign lands. No matter how international they get, Swiss bankers are first of all Swiss. And Swiss bankers may be encountered almost anywhere. One official of a Big Three bank was met in the lobby of the President Hotel in Johannesburg, South Africa, a high-rise hotel with deluxe accommodations.

Was he on business or pleasure, he was asked.

"A combination of both," he said. "As you know, we have a South African investment trust, mutual fund you Americans would call it, and we do handle a fair amount of South African gold."

Indeed they do, and you may encounter another Swiss banker in Dubai on the Persian Gulf selling some of that gold. Big Three banks have a good share of this profitable Dubai business. One Zurich banker makes trips twice a year to Rio de Janeiro, Buenos Aires, and Caracas where some bank customers are located. Swiss Bank Corp., Basle, another of the country's Big Three, recently opened a new branch in Tokyo. Other Swiss banks eye this same market.

When the Group of Ten met in Washington in the red brick Smithsonian Institution building December 17–18, 1971, to realign the world's currencies, Dr. Edwin Stopper, president of Swiss National Bank, occupied one of the seats. The Group of Ten is a prestigious monetary group composed of the ten leading industrial nations of the world. Actually, it is a Group of Eleven, for Switzerland attends, though officially listed as only an observer.

Switzerland's importance in monetary affairs should not be

underrated. During the near-panic 1971 monetary crisis, four nations emerged as strong currency countries. They were West Germany, Switzerland, Japan, and Britain. Other countries played roles. But those four attracted most of the money when people around the world sought to rid themselves of U.S. dollars.

Such importance in the monetary field is why Swiss bankers sometimes are called Gnomes of Zurich. It is a title they do not like. It connotates Machiavellian schemers trying to upset a currency, or to hike gold's price to a fantastic level.

"Rumors concerning possible currency devaluations or increases in the price of gold do not originate in Switzerland, but, as a rule, in the countries concerned, and are then carried across the border by the doubtful, the dissatisfied, or speculators," said F. W. Schulthess, chairman, Swiss Credit Bank, Zurich.

Sometimes Switzerland actually helps to prop a weak currency. In October, 1967, when Britain needed quick help to bolster its sagging pound sterling, Sir Leslie O'Brien, governor of the Bank of England, flew to Zurich. Sir Leslie is a silver-haired, placid gentleman who could reverse his collar and pass for a clergyman on a mission to save souls. This time the goal was more worldly.

Dr. Alfred Schaefer, chairman of Union Bank of Switzerland, the country's biggest bank, hurriedly arranged a luncheon with officers of the Big Three and the chairman of Swiss National Bank. Quickly, a loan of 450 million francs (over $100 million at the applicable exchange rate) was arranged for Britain. It proved to be an expensive lunch. Britain had to devalue the next month, anyway.

Switzerland has more reason than most countries for wanting currency stability, not only for its own franc, but for the foreign currencies of other nations. As a major foreign investor, Switzerland always has substantial sums in the U.S., Britain, and elsewhere, funds which cannot be transferred ahead of every currency crisis.

"Switzerland is more heavily exposed to psychological influences in the monetary field than any other country in the world," said Dr. H. J. Mast, chief economist, Swiss Credit Bank, a man who is one of the most informed persons in the country on banking affairs. "Since its foreign assets represent a greater proportion of its national income than is true anywhere else, measures which shake people's confidence in the stability of the international monetary system must inevitably create very special problems for Switzerland."

Switzerland certainly was involved in the monetary crisis of 1971, as later chapters will show. The dollar crisis was a Swiss crisis, just as it also was a German crisis, a Japanese crisis, and a British crisis. But Switzerland's role was akin to that of a cog in a machine rather than that of the driving force, even if Swiss National Bank's reserves did jump from $5.1 billion at the start of 1971 to just under $7 billion at year-end.

No amount of promoting would bring such a flood of money, were it not for the mystique which envelops Swiss banking. Money rushes into the country from all parts of the world because so many people everywhere believe that the Swiss can take good care of somebody else's money.

Geography plays a role in Switzerland's attractiveness. It sits in central Europe, easily accessible by rail, plane, or road. For decades, Frenchmen have vacationed in Switzerland and used that time to check bank accounts in the country. Arabs like Geneva at almost any time of the year for the same reason. Some Americans, in recent years, have been combining winter ski vacations with visits to Zurich's Bahnhofstrasse or to Geneva's rue du Rhône where there are banks to suit every taste.

Swiss are conservative, no matter how progressive they might be in the mechanical handling of your account. The typical Swiss banker believes that his first duty is to preserve your capital against the vagaries of financial fluctuations. His second obligation is to seek appreciation. So go-go money management is viewed with suspicion verging on hostility.

Swiss banks are really department stores of financial services. They take simple demand and time deposits. They handle stock transactions as might any broker in the United States. They float bond issues. They deal in commodities and in foreign exchange. They sell certificates of deposits in eurodollars, sterling, deutsche marks, and other currencies. If you open an account with dollars, the account may be designated as you wish, in dollars, in Swiss francs, in German marks, in pounds sterling.

You can transfer back and forth, though you pay the foreign exchange commission each time. In fact, you pay for every service in a Swiss bank, for the Swiss operate to make money for themselves, too.

This ability to shift accounts from one currency to another fast means that Switzerland caters to speculative movements of currencies across borders in any monetary crisis. In justice to Switzerland, however, it should be said that big multinational American companies have been the main actors in some of the past currency crises, often using Swiss accounts to juggle money back and forth from a weak currency into a strong. President Nixon terms this speculation. The big corporations aver that they merely try to safeguard funds entrusted to managements by stockholders.

In any case, a Swiss account provides a versatility for the holder that is difficult to match anywhere else in the world. The client can buy or sell shares for his portfolio from the American stock market, from the London market, from Johannesburg, from Tokyo, from Australia, and from a dozen other exchanges. The bank handles all transactions, keeping them in bearer accounts. This means the bank's name, not yours, is listed as the owner of those shares. Naturally, you have your bank receipts to verify accounts with the bank, and to identify profit and loss for U.S. taxes.

Should you care to plunge into cocoa futures or to gamble on the foreign exchange market, the bank can handle those transactions, too. (You will find that the conservative banker does nothing to encourage this type of investing.) Bonds of literally hundreds of companies around the world are at your fingertips, if you have the cash in your other hand. Swiss bankers like bonds. They will encourage you to hold some of them. If a straight interest return is desired, then, the bank can invest your money in certificates of deposit. Bank deposits paid only 1.5 percent for time accounts in early 1972 and had a negative interest rate of 8 percent annually in the second half. CD's were paying 4 to 5.88 percent. At certain times, the latter have paid 10 and 11 percent.

Clients can speculate in silver, or even buy gold bars. These may be hauled from the bank in bars the size of a cigarette lighter up to bricks weighing five hundred pounds. Most gold speculators, however, leave their purchases in vaults of a bank, preferring to depart with a paper slip which confirms the purchase.

But, remember *it is illegal for an American to hold or to trade in gold.* This you may be told by a Swiss bank; then again, you may not. In any case, whether or not the Swiss bank says anything, you will be breaking American law if you speculate in the yellow metal.

Consider I.O.S. Ltd., the big mutual fund and financial services company, for example. This author remembers sitting down in Geneva with C. Henry Buhl III, a key investing official of I.O.S., some years ago in the mutual fund's headquarters along Lake Geneva's promenade. Buhl is a slight-of-build aristocrat of money who comes from a Detroit family that has always had it. On this day, he was in excellent humor, having just received news of a market development which assured I.O.S. of a tidy profit.

"The free gold price is jumping," said Buhl, voice sounding as if he were watching his favorite horse circling a track. Then, he added quickly: "And we have taken a heavy position in gold."

He mentioned figures which suggested literally tons of the yellow metal, about $30 million worth.

"I thought Americans couldn't own gold," said this author. There had been no news of Buhl or Bernard Cornfeld giving up American citizenships.

"I.O.S. is a Panamanian company located in Switzerland," explained Buhl. "The American law has nothing to do with us."

"Oh," said this author. Few people are sidewalk lawyers able to decipher the legalities of a situation on the spot. This certainly must have applied to Buhl, too, else he would not have been talking so freely about gold to an outsider.

His remarks were duly swept into a story about the I.O.S. gold coup. This was dispatched within the hour via the Palais des Nations telex in the United Nations Headquarters press room to the Dow Jones Wire Service and the *Wall Street Journal* in New York.

In December, 1971, the U.S. government wrote the sequel to this little tale. It brought charges against Bernard Cornfeld and

I.O.S. seeking a double penalty of over $60 million for the group's dealings in gold. That gold isn't glittering very brightly for I.O.S. any longer.

Swiss bankers learned the value of discretion long ago. They enshrined it in law in their bank secrecy. If you have an account in Switzerland, you can be fairly sure the news won't get around. Information about your bank account is as confidential as your psychiatrist's report of why you have been acting odd lately.

Article 47 of the Swiss banking law reads:

Whoever knowingly
a) in his capacity as auditor or in assisting an audit willfully violates his duties in connection with the preparation or rendering of an auditor's report, omits to remind, as prescribed, the bank under audit to take the required measures or does not submit the prescribed reports to the Banking Commission,
b) as member, official or employee of a bank, as auditor or assistant auditor, as member of the Banking Commission, as official or employee of its staff, violates the obligation of secrecy or of professional secrecy or who causes or attempts to cause its violation, is liable to a fine up to Sfr 20,000 or to a prison term not exceeding 6 months. Both penalties can be imposed concurrently. If the violation is due to negligence, the penalty is a fine up to Sfr 10,000.

That Sfr 20,000 fine is equivalent to about $5,200. Moreover, Swiss society being as it is, any bank employee convicted under this act stands little chance of ever obtaining a job in Swiss banking again.

In plain English, nobody in a bank may talk about your account to anybody, not even to a tax collector. The essence of that law permeates to the lowest level in a bank. It is such a part of the social credo that any question about an account is viewed with horror, as if you might be hinting that you want to rob the bank.

Swiss have developed a device to carry this secrecy even further—the numbered account.

Bank secrecy applies to every account, whether numbered

or not. But there's always a chance that a disloyal bank employee may leak information about an account. Hence, the numbered account, which is exactly what it sounds like. The name of the client is known only to one or two top employees of the bank. Only a number appears on all records of transactions, and on files of that account.

The holder of such an account may forward deposits for that numbered account, without signing his name. If the letter is intercepted by police, secret service investigators, the KGB, or by anybody else enroute, there would be nothing to implicate the account holder. Numerous people of consequence in Communist countries have such numbered accounts in Switzerland, along with thousands of people from elsewhere in the world. In the 1930's, many German Jews had secret accounts, the only way they could safeguard assets. Anonymity might mean the difference between life and death for many a numbered account holder.

But you can't open a numbered account anonymously. You must identify yourself when the account is established, and the bank may ask for references. Thus, the picture of a numbered account holder being only a number to the bank is false. He is known—but only to a limited number of people at the bank.

Abuses may develop under such a system. Legend has it that Juan Peron, ex-dictator of Argentina, had $200 million in Swiss numbered accounts when he left Buenos Aires for exile. Moïse Tshombe, the late president of Zaïre, reportedly salted so much money in various Swiss accounts that he could finance rebellions in what used to be called the Congo. Kwame Nkrumah, Ghana's first president and one-time darling of the liberals, allegedly funneled enough from his country's treasury into Swiss accounts to guarantee himself a regal lifestyle until his untimely death.

Legends can't be confirmed. Reputable Swiss bankers bridle at the suggestion that such cases are representative. They claim that responsible banks refuse clients whose personal or business backgrounds appear dubious.

Still, a member of New York's or Chicago's Mafia may look very much like a reputable businessman. Identity documents may be forged easily. Bank secrecy can sometimes be a shield for the criminal no matter how high the ethical standards.

Swiss bank secrecy has a long history of tradition and common law behind it. This was defined in law in 1934 as a counter to attempts by German Nazis to trace Jewish money held in Switzerland.

In Berne, Switzerland's capital, one government spokesman said: "It was to protect unfortunate victims of persecution that Switzerland enacted this legislation."

Discretion is at the root of all banking activity whether in Switzerland, in America, or almost anywhere else. Swiss banking secrecy, however, diverges sharply from American policy in a key sector. Secrecy applies to nearly everybody, including government investigators. If a crime is committed, a court may order an account to be opened. Proof of that crime must be clear cut, whether presented by investigators from inside Switzerland or from a foreign land. This precludes fishing expeditions where investigators examine personal accounts hoping that these will provide the evidence for a criminal prosecution against somebody.

In Switzerland, a crime is a crime only when it happens to be a crime in the country, regardless of how a foreign nation may characterize the act. Tax evasion is not a crime in Switzerland. Therefore, nobody in or out of the country can breach bank secrecy provisions in a tax evasion case.

"The Swiss authorities have always in principle rejected the requests of foreign countries for legal assistance in fiscal matters," says one official of Swiss Credit Bank, Zurich.

Swiss are good at lecturing anyone who pushes this matter very hard. They will tell you, for instance, that if America's taxes are so high that they encourage tax evasion, perhaps America should reduce its taxes to the point where compliance is achieved instead of looking to Swiss for help. That's a bit of advice which probably would be applauded in Union League Clubs around America. It brings sour expressions to faces of American government officials who periodically visit Switzerland seeking information about certain characters.

The U.S. has tried again and again to persuade Switzerland to relax its stand. The Swiss stubbornly refuse to oblige, except

in those cases where crimes are clearly evident. A new Mutual
Judicial Assistance Treaty, however, could help.

Listen to Swiss bankers in their clubs when they talk as
freely as Swiss bankers ever do, and their positions certainly
sound logical, from the Swiss view. Swiss realize that this nation
has become a money center because of the country's stability, its
absence of wars, its capitalistic society, and because of its bank
secrecy. They aren't going to change such a profitable situation,
not even for Uncle Sam's tax collectors. On the other hand,
there is a growing readiness on the part of Switzerland to impart
information about American tax offenses coming under the
heading of the fight against organized crime.

Certainly, there may be gangsters' bank accounts in Switzerland, and some may rival the gross national products of ba-
nana republics. At Zurich Airport, not long ago, one well-
dressed money courier for Meyer Lansky was observed
debarking at the terminal carrying an attaché case and the har-
ried air of an overworked businessman who already is late for
an appointment. Lansky often is mentioned as an underworld
lord by United States government investigators, though they
have never been able to convict him of anything. On this day,
was some money going into a Lansky secret numbered account
in Switzerland? The U.S. government would like to know the
answer to such questions, but is stymied by Swiss law from
learning the truth.

Still, the presence of some crime money does not indicate
that this is typical, nor that Swiss bankers go looking for it.
Switzerland has brilliant and honest investment managers who
can invest your dollars for your benefit, and literally return two
for every one over a period of years. If there also are tax advisors
here who can show you how to gyp Uncle Sam of his legitimate
lien on your gains, they are unlikely to be working for a bank.

It is this capacity for fiscal skullduggery by depositors plus
benign neglect in such matters by bankers which irritates Uncle
Sam's tax collectors. Swiss bankers are so secretive about their
clients that the U.S. Internal Revenue Service develops headaches everytime money strands in tax cases lead like long-dis-
tance electrical wires into the shuttered offices of Swiss banks.
Some revenue agents now act as if they feel that an American

would not have a Swiss bank account unless he wanted to gyp
the U.S. government.

Why do Americans have Swiss bank accounts? Fears of
inflation and of more dollar devaluations are key reasons. Desire
to invest in Europe is another. Then, there are thousands of
expatriate Americans who live and work in Europe. They often
find it convenient to bank in Switzerland. U.S. corporations use
Swiss banks as collection and disbursal points for international
financial operations.

Recently, one Swiss banker provided an insight into the
types of Americans who hold Swiss accounts. After being assured of anonymity, he leaned back in his chair, thought for a
moment, then said: "A personal friend works for an American
oil company in the Mideast. He has two children who are attending school in this country. He keeps a bank account here to
finance their education."

Almost as an afterthought, he added: "The money which
goes into this account comes from a bank in New York City, so
everything is open and aboveboard, just as are most of the
American accounts we have."

Over the next few minutes he cited the following examples
of American bank account holders:

—A Detroit dentist who is worried about the stability of
the dollar.

—A locally based official of an American company.

—A New York financier who prefers to invest in European
stock markets through his Swiss account.

—A retired American now living in Switzerland.

—A New York City divorcee who is seeking to keep certain
assets from her ex-husband, through a complex trust arrangement.

—A wealthy Middlewestern American who believes in
diversifying his holdings.

—The president of an Eastern seaboard advertising agency
which does business on both sides of the Atlantic.

—An executive of a multinational firm based in New York,
who opened a Swiss bank account years ago when working
abroad.

—A Middlewestern couple who spend every summer in

Europe, who opened an account as a safety deposit box for future vacations.

Whether or not these people were avoiding U.S. taxes on unearned income in Switzerland did not concern this banker. That was a matter for the taxpayer and the U.S. government.

It is perfectly legal for an American to have a Swiss bank account. An estimated 150,000 Americans do have them. As long as they pay U.S. taxes due, they need not hang their heads in shame nor slink furtively to the nearest mailbox when dispatching deposits to Geneva, Zurich, or Chiasso.

Swiss bankers say many more thousands of Americans are interested in learning something about Swiss bank accounts, how they can be established, how bankers handle money, how American law applies to them, and other factors about the allegedly mysterious Gnomes of Zurich. President Nixon's devaluation of the dollar in December, 1971, undoubtedly intensified the concern many Americans have for their money.

Seen up close, the Swiss banker is nowhere near as mysterious as those dramatic tales about him might imply.

CHAPTER II

BANKERS FOR THE WORLD

In Basle, justice authorities recently ordered an unidentified young man to stand trial after he ran a series of ads in a local newspaper. These offered to send via mail for $2 each "a guaranteed, radical, and successful way of curing greasy hair."

Readers who dispatched their $2 received a slip of paper advising them to "Shave your head bald."

The young man claimed he did it as a joke. Basle authorities missed the humor. Basle, indeed, is a city which takes itself seriously.

In Zurich, one government bureaucrat granted an interview to a visiting American for "first thing in the morning." Next morning that American arrived promptly at 9 A.M. to be greeted by a disgruntled bureaucrat who already had been on the job for an hour. An 8 A.M. start for a day which ends at 5 P.M. or 6 P.M. is common in Zurich. This city takes work, as well as itself, seriously.

Working foreigners require official work permits. Students at the University of Geneva need none, and there are no class attendance checks. So, when I.O.S. Ltd., the big American-managed mutual fund, experienced difficulties in obtaining work permits for personnel during its period of expansion, it quickly solved the problem. It enrolled newly hired non-Swiss as students at the university. They only had to appear at school the first day of each semester. Then, they went to work at I.O.S. Everybody seemed satisfied. Geneva is a tolerant, cosmopolitan city which somehow seems to find answers to most of its problems.

Basle, Zurich, and Geneva are key banking centers. They are all different, yet united in their welcome for the dollar, the French franc, the mark, the yen, or the escudo. Here are found the banks which give Switzerland its reputation as an international banking center.

Geneva was the first of the three cities to develop as a banking center. Then, for a time, it looked as if Basle might become the nation's financial heart. But, it is Zurich which grew into the unquestioned money capital of the country. There are those who insist that nearly everything of real import which happens in the country occurs in Zurich. They are apt to be Zurchers. They are apt to be right.

Zurich bustles and throbs with activity, a city of over a half million population. Banks are lined all along Bahnhofstrasse, the city's main shopping street. Smart stores display expensive goods which reflect the prosperity of this Germanic community which has become a truly international financial market.

Fitzgerald described Switzerland as a country "where very few things begin, but many things end." This is especially true if you are talking about money transfers. Switzerland, indeed, is a country built on a foundation of money, not all cash from outside either.

The Swiss have nine million bank accounts, which indicates that careful citizens don't like to leave all their savings in one place. One study made in the 1964–68 period showed that in those five years, inclusive, gross savings amounted to 28 percent of the gross national product, annually. Swiss not only save their equivalents of pennies and nickels, they save dime, quarter, and dollar equivalents, as well.

It was the Reverend Sidney Smith who said: "I look upon Switzerland as an inferior sort of Scotland." The Scots have a reputation for frugality, too. But, when calculating machines tabulate totals, the Scots are far behind the Swiss. One Swiss proverb says: "Don't buy what you need, but what you can't do without." Another says: "First eat the black bread, then the white." The Swiss don't just save for a rainy day, they save as if it were raining every day.

Including rural credit cooperatives, there are about 1,650 banking institutions in the country. They honeycomb the land with a network of 4,400 offices and branches. There is one savings outlet for every 1,400 people, or more banks than dentists.

Banks are classified into seven groups: big banks, cantonal banks, local banks, savings banks, loan associations, private banks, and other banks. A special category is that of the two mortgage bond banks, institutions which help raise funds for mortgage financing. In addition, there are Swiss National Bank and the Bank for International Settlements, which will be described later.

The twenty-eight cantonal banks operate mainly within their own cantons. Switzerland is composed of twenty-two cantons, three divided into half cantons, for twenty-five political units which conform in a small way to the states of America. In Switzerland, cantons rather than the centralized federal government retain most of the political clout.

Savings, local, cantonal, and cooperative institutions are local or regional in character. They confine themselves to agricultural or small business lending, mortgage transactions, and savings. Some of the cantonal banks are fairly large. These banks are seldom of any importance to the outside investor. Nobody in Switzerland ever confuses them with the Gnomes of Zurich.

The differentiation between banks is one of geography and degree. Swiss banks are universal. This means that a bank may operate in any sphere it pleases. There is no tough bank legislation which forces institutions to specialize, as is the case in the United States.

"In Switzerland, there is no longer a clear delineation between commercial banks, savings banks, and private banks," said Dr. Alfred Schaefer, chairman of Union Bank. "To traditional banking services have been added investment savings programs, installment lending, cash dispensers, leasing, factoring, handling of checks and credit cards, cashless salary payments, and other facilities."

Big banks are universal, indeed. They take deposits of all types, handle any type of credit or loan, operate as investment bankers to arrange mergers and other such transactions, and deal in foreign exchange.

Banks attract deposits by:

—acceptance of fixed term deposits, usually for three, six, and twelve months, either on account or in the form of certificates of deposit.

—savings accounts, usually with withdrawal restrictions (a limitation on monthly withdrawals, for instance).

—cash bonds with three- to eight-year maturities, with five years being the most common. These *Kassaobligationen* bear rates according to the market.

—issuance of bonds with maturities longer than eight years. The savings bonds are not listed on stock exchanges. Those with longer maturities are.

By Swiss law, bank capitalization must be at least 10 percent of the bank's assets. Banks retain earnings in good years to help meet this obligation. In recent years, with assets of banks soaring because of the heavy inflows of funds from abroad, most banks have been compelled to increase their equity capital with rights issues.

For the Americans and other non-Swiss, the banks which count are the big banks, the private banks, and the limited liability banks which often are American or non-Swiss controlled. Some of the private banks can be choosy indeed. They sometimes operate with a clublike atmosphere and if you don't look like a personable club member, you won't be invited into the inner sanctum.

Fear not. There are other Swiss banks which solicit business as avidly as does your local Fuller Brush man. The big banks seldom turn any legitimate business away. American banks located in Switzerland such as American Express Inc., Bank of America, First National Bank of Chicago, First National City Bank, and others will welcome your account.

Universality is more advantageous for many people than is that highly vaunted bank secrecy. You can keep money in a deposit account, shift it into stocks, switch into bonds, play commodity markets, deal in foreign exchange, and do it all from one account. Fortunes have been made in recent years through playing the foreign exchange market.

Still, there always is some allure in bank secrecy. The Swiss are great ones for proverb citing, and they have one of their own which goes: "Silence may often say enough."

Indeed, Swiss bankers are advised to listen for silence by their own trade association, though this is a bit like telling the cat to depart quietly. One directive of the Swiss Bankers' Association urges members to avoid anything "that might subsequently provoke criticism of the country and its asset-administering business."

Often a banker says nothing publicly unless it is couched in those awesomely trite platitudes which sometimes serve as the technical language of bankers.

There are exceptions. Alfred E. Sarasin, partner in A. Sarasin & Co., Basle, and president of the Swiss Bankers' Association, is an athletically built man of fifty with a strong personality which he projects into any discussion. Dr. Alfred Schaefer, chairman of Union Bank of Switzerland, the country's biggest bank, sounds like a university lecturer in a Great Books Course when he discourses about banking, with references to history, the philosophies of Aristotle or the Roman stoics. Dr. Samuel Schweizer, chairman of Swiss Bank Corp., until retirement June 30, 1972, sometimes speaks bluntly when deriding those who want to remove gold from the monetary system. Felix W. Schulthess, chairman of Swiss Credit Bank, Zurich, can stress the importance of old-fashioned virtues while making them sound fresh enough for application today.

Swiss banks do promote business in their own way, though

sometimes it seems as if they are trying to talk loudly in a quiet voice. They advertise in international editions of *Time* and *Newsweek*. Bank executives address business groups in foreign lands, and find time to answer questions about opening Swiss accounts. Personal calls on prospective clients are common.

Soliciting is done in low-key style in the U.S., too. Swiss banks maintain offices in New York and elsewhere. Polite clerks offer advice about Swiss bank accounts. Banks sometimes use finders who are rewarded in cash for every depositor they bring to a bank, though reputable bankers frown on this.

One enterprising finder opened accounts at a Swiss bank for many of his American friends in the States just before one Christmas. Each account had an initial $50 gift in it. Only on receiving the bank's Christmas cards did the friends learn of the existence of their accounts overseas.

What does one do in a case like that? Some closed the accounts, accepting the money as pennies, if not from heaven, at least from Santa Claus. Others inquired about the bank, discovered the simplicity of Swiss banking. They transferred substantial amounts to Switzerland, providing the finder with a commission worth much more than his Christmas spending.

Five banks sit atop the Swiss banking structure, with the top three in size known as the Big Three. These are Swiss Bank Corp., Basle, Union Bank of Switzerland, and Swiss Credit Bank, Zurich.

At start of 1972, the balance sheets of these three showed total assets as follows:

Union Bank of Switzerland	Sfr 38.2 billion ($9.9 billion)
Swiss Bank Corp.	Sfr 36.1 billion ($9.4 billion)
Swiss Credit Bank	Sfr 31.1 billion ($8.1 billion)

Each bank has one or more branches abroad, including offices in New York City, plus affiliated companies in Canada, the Bahamas, Panama, and Bermuda. Representative offices are maintained in international finance centers extending from Latin America through Beirut to Hong Kong, Tokyo, and Sydney.

The top five banks are rounded out with Bank Leu, Zurich,

and Swiss Volksbank, or Banque Populaire, Berne. These two run a poor fourth and fifth behind the Big Three when it comes to volume of business. At the end of 1971, Swiss Volksbank had assets of 7.5 billion Swiss francs ($2 billion), while Bank Leu's balance sheet showed total assets of 1.6 billion Swiss francs ($416 million).

The extraordinary growth trend of Swiss banks is indicated by the fact that total assets of the Big Five rose from 7.98 billion Swiss francs in 1950 (about $1.8 billion at rate then prevailing), to 17.54 billion Swiss francs ($10.7 billion) in 1960 and to 114.5 billion Swiss francs ($29.8 billion) at the end of 1971. That is more than a sixteenfold increase of assets from 1950 to the end of 1971, a remarkable growth record.

Often when compiling data, statisticians limit themselves to the top seventy-two banks in the country. These account for 80 percent of the assets and volume of business handled by Swiss banks.

The Big Five handle finance business of Switzerland's major corporations, of foreign corporations, of individual depositors and investors. Often when foreigners speak of Swiss banks they really mean the Big Five. These banks deal with more foreigners than do all other Swiss-owned banks combined.

Swiss Credit Bank's four-story, gray limestone headquarters fills a whole block on Paradeplatz in the heart of Zurich. The institution was founded in 1856, making it the oldest of the Big Three, though far from being the nation's oldest bank. A pseudo-Grecian front faces the square. The building looks imposing enough to house the municipal bureaucracy. Blue-painted streetcars clatter by at all hours on Bahnhofstrasse, which borders one side of the bank.

The lobby contains a huge revolving drum with ten sides. It operates like a slow-moving merry-go-round above the heads of clerks at an information desk. Six-foot-high boards on the drum provide latest stock quotations of Swiss, American, British, German, Dutch, and French companies. Sixteen clocks give the time at any particular moment in major cities around the globe. Flags of a score of nations intermingle in a colorful wall mural behind counters of tellers. "We are international, you know," one bank official offered, as he pointed to the wall.

It was Aphra Behn who said: "Money speaks sense in a language all nations understand." Swiss certainly have learned all of the dialects of money without any help from Berlitz.

Swiss Credit Bank's assets of 31.1 billion francs ($8.1 billion) at end of 1971 compared with 28 billion francs a year earlier and only 6.2 billion francs in 1962. That is a fourfold increase of assets in nine years.

It was in this particular bank that Mrs. Clifford Irving came to grief after she opened a bank account as H. R. Hughes in the Howard Hughes autobiography swindle. Bank officials hope the bank will be remembered for more than that. They can tell you that a new representative office opened in Tokyo in April, 1972, that the bank had 7,338 employees as of December 31, 1971, that it helped Corning Glass, Burlington Industries, and Texaco to raise money in 1971. Everyone would just as soon forget the Hughes affair.

Upstairs, F. W. Schulthess, bank chairman, occupied a spacious corner office above the muted noise of Bahnhofstrasse. A gilt gold wall clock ticked away above the wide mahogany table which served as his desk. A Persian carpet covered the floor.

He stood up, a silver-haired slender man in a well-tailored charcoal suit who could have passed for a venerable university professor. He is the first non-American to reach the presidency of the International Monetary Conference. This is a prestigious group composed of sixty American presidents and chairmen of banks, and the same number of top executives from European banks.

He, like other Swiss bankers, fears that Switzerland's banking system has been growing at too fast a rate during the monetary unease of the past few years. The assets on balance sheets of Switzerland's seventy-two largest banks jumped from Sfr 111.8 billion in 1968 to Sfr 133.8 billion in 1969 and to Sfr 159.6 billion in 1970. (Sfr 3.84 equal $1.)

Schulthess takes a dim view of those who evaluate a bank by the amount of assets it possesses. Said he, "The true stature of a bank can be ascertained as little by its total assets as that of a person by his chest measurements."

He painted an intriguing picture of what it takes to be a Swiss banker. "We are well advised not to forego the basic Swiss caution which has characterized our country in the past, in spite of all the smart slogans brought to bear on us in our daily conversations, in the press, on the radio, and on television."

Then, he said, "However different individual bankers are according to their place of origin and professional background, they ought, above all, to have three characteristics in common: integrity, sense of responsibility, and expert professional knowledge."

It takes long years on the job to acquire that expert professional knowledge which Swiss value so highly. This is why Switzerland doesn't have any young, go-go managers in positions of responsibility.

Swiss Credit Bank's management structure is akin to that at the other Big Three banks. Except for Chairman Schulthess, the board of twenty-four is composed of outsiders who form a cross-section of Swiss industry. As an example, the board in 1972 included Dr. Herbert Wolfer, vice chairman and managing director, Sulzer Bros. Ltd., Winterthur; Emanuel R. Meyer, chairman and managing director, Swiss Aluminium Ltd., Chippis; Dr. Theodor Waldesbühl, member of the board, Nestlé Alimentana S. A.; Dr. Samuel Koechlin, a member of the executive committee, Ciba-Geigy Ltd., Basle; plus other well-known Swiss businessmen.

The bank functions with six general managers, headed by Dr. E. Reinhardt, chief general manager, a position akin to president in an American bank. His general managers operate like executive vice presidents, though Swiss banks don't believe it is necessary to create an army of vice presidents in a bank. Each manager heads a wing of the bank's operations. The team under Dr. Reinhardt consists of Dr. R. Lang, Dr. H. Escher, R. H. Lutz, Dr. H. R. Wuffli, and Dr. O. Aeppli.

In the foreign exchange section, telex machines clatter. A dozen clerks punch calculating machines. Traders hang on to telephones tied to New York, London, Frankfurt, and other markets. Millions of dollars change hands so casually that a visitor doesn't even realize the volume until he is given several order slips to study.

On busy days, the foreign exchange turnover at the big Swiss banks exceeds $2 billion in one day. This doesn't mean, of course, that this much cash is changing hands. Foreign exchange cover is utilized to protect businessmen against risks of changes in currency values in about the way insurance is utilized. If you wanted to insure your house for $50,000 you would not pay $50,000 to do it. You would merely pay the premiums. In buying and selling foreign exchange, the customer pays only the commission and the difference between two buy-sell transactions, or the hedging costs.

Thus, suppose a Swiss investor wanted to invest $1 million worth of Swiss francs into American treasury bills in New York on a three-month basis. He would buy dollars first through his bank. But, then, he must worry about the future dollar rate. If the dollar loses value, he might lose more than he would gain on the interest.

To protect himself, he purchases $1 million of spot dollars on a three-month contract. In effect, one purchase balances the other. If the dollar loses value, he loses on one contract but gains on the other to come out even in foreign exchange terms.

For this protection, he pays a rate which at the end of February, 1972, would have been 4.78 percent on a per annum basis, or 1.195 percent over three months. Naturally, the three-month interest rate in New York would have to exceed European rates plus the cost of the foreign exchange, or it wouldn't be worth the deal. Unfortunately, in February, 1972, the interest rates in New York were too low for that, which explains why money was not moving back to the U.S. as the American government hoped would be the case after the December, 1971, currency realignment.

Most foreign exchange transactions in world money markets are completed by phone, telex, or cable. During normal trading days, buy-sell orders may cancel at an even level. When there isn't any equilibrium, financial reporters write about a movement of money from one country to another. What they mean is that the accounting figures on one side of the ledger are mounting faster than on the other. Of course, foreign exchange rates for the strong currencies will climb upward as the market seeks to adjust to equilibrium again.

At Swiss Credit Bank's bank note department, a queue waited. Lines are not normal in Swiss banks, except at windows of bank note changers. Tourists think of this business as "foreign exchange." It is. These transactions, however, are only a small part of the overall foreign exchange market.

Bank notes draw no interest when stuffed in a drawer waiting for a tourist to appear. Swiss bank rates are among the lowest in the world. So, Swiss banks lose less in undrawn interest than most banks elsewhere with bank notes. This is a key reason why Switzerland has become such an important bank note center. Money export-import freedom also counts.

Newspapers often quote foreign exchange rates which never seem to apply to you. There's a reason for that, too. Such rates are interbank foreign exchange rates, applicable for minimums of $250,000. If you happen to be changing $250,000 worth of travelers checks on a particular day, you can claim those interbank rates.

Individuals cashing less must be satisfied with a bank buy-rate a couple of percent less than the interbank rate, and a bank sell-rate a couple of percent higher. Whenever currency unrest develops, the money changer takes no risk at all. He immediately reduces his buy-rates and hikes his sell-rates, not only for the weak currency but for all currencies. If a money changer expects a 10 percent devaluation, he may discount that currency by 15 to 20 percent to be on the safe side—his safe side, not yours.

Travelers checks are easier for a bank to handle than is cash. So, banks give a slightly higher exchange rate for checks than for cash.

The annual turnover of the bank note business in Switzerland is over $500 million, enough to give the banks the world leadership. Almost any Swiss bank will sell you pounds, Italian lire, Portuguese escudos, South African rand, Yugoslav dinars, or almost any other currency you want. You might have a little delay if you asked for Russian rubles. However, there are a few banks which can produce rubles after a day or two's delay, at a rate less than a third of their value in Moscow. Don't stock up with them if you are going to the Soviet Union. Russians don't like it. If they catch you, look out.

Union Bank of Switzerland is a hundred yards up Bahnhofstrasse from Swiss Credit Bank. It is built like a citadel of stone. Gold coins and bars glitter in windows facing the street. It is

Switzerland's biggest bank, and the headquarters looks it. There is a brisk, businesslike air, the sort of no-nonsense approach which one likes when one's own money is involved. Levity is a virtue only when someone else pays the price, which is why little humor seems to be found in a bank.

Executive offices are guarded by porters who quickly separate the human chaff from the wheat. Long, soft-carpeted halls lead to executive suites. Walls are decorated with tasteful works of art. The atmosphere is as subdued as that of a cathedral on Good Friday. The key office is occupied by Dr. Alfred Schaefer, chairman.

He has been called Switzerland's number one banker, and he usually is at the center when anything is happening in Swiss banking. He is not a man for putting on airs or for evading hard questions. He entered banking in 1931, almost by chance, on what was to be a year's assignment. He is a history buff, and early in his life he wished to become a history professor. That interest shows in his speeches, which are apt to be well leavened with historical references. A large portrait of a mounted Napoleon hangs on a wall of his spacious but plain office.

When encountered in that office, he wore the charcoal suit which seems to be the uniform of the Swiss banker. A pearl pin centered his blue polka dot tie. Gold-rimmed pince-nez glasses sat on his thin nose. He is a trim, straight man who keeps fit at sixty-five by riding some of his thoroughbreds over his estate in Aarau, three dozen miles from Zurich. Like all able-bodied Swiss, he served in the Army Reserve, attaining the rank of colonel in a cavalry unit.

As he fielded a question about Swiss bank secrecy, he took off his glasses, wiped them, then reset them on his nose. "It isn't bank secrecy alone which prompts people to bank in Switzerland," he said. "It is our banking experience. We know languages. We are internationally minded. Our government and our economy are stable. We have a free enterprise system. Bank secrecy is merely our philosophy concerning the handling of that money."

Union Bank, generally, is regarded as among the most innovative of Swiss banks. It has taken the leadership in promoting mutual funds through Intrag, Ltd., a company founded in cooperation with three private banks. Combined assets of the funds with which Union Bank is associated totaled 4.35 billion Swiss francs ($1.1 billion) at the end of 1971. This represented a gain of 35.2 percent over the level of a year earlier.

In 1963, the total assets of the 107 mutual funds included in statistics of the Swiss National Bank amounted to 6.6 billion francs ($1.7 billion). On March 31, 1971, assets of funds totaled 9 billion francs ($2.3 billion), with the figure rising to 10 billion francs ($2.6 billion) by the end of 1971.

In the spring of 1972, UBS officials were busily engaged in a massive reorientation of operations to computerize the bank's activities. The bank had ordered a $60 million computer system from Control Data AG, Zurich, Swiss subsidiary of the American company.

An intrabank report said: "This order is the first step in the development of a computer network to which all of the UBS offices will be connected over the next eight years." The nucleus of the entire system—two Control Data Cyber 70s (Model 73)— were being installed in Zurich during the first half of 1973.

At close of 1971, UBS had 168 business offices in Switzerland, of which eighty-one were branch offices and eighty-seven were agencies.

In 1971, Union Bank, like other Swiss banks, experienced a massive inflow of capital. Demand and time balances due to other banks rose from 6.1 billion Swiss francs at the start of the year to 11.7 billion at the end of 1971.

The 1971 Union Bank report avers that: "These funds, which flowed into Switzerland as a consequence of the monetary crisis, were invested by us abroad or sterilized as minimum reserves at the Swiss National Bank."

All of the big banks float bond issues. Swiss banks have so much liquidity that they are prime customers for any money-short corporation. However, until recently, Swiss banks have been followers rather than managers and co-managers of foreign bond issues. They bought pieces of issues for their own account, or for the accounts of portfolio customers. Others did the managing.

But in recent years each of the Big Three established overseas subsidiaries to operate in this area. Now, big Swiss banks compete hard for foreign bond business.

Union Bank's 1970 annual report listed several score bond issues with UBS participation. Companies included: Corning Glass, Burroughs Corp., Dow Chemical, Du Pont de Nemours, Monsanto Chemical, International Nickel, International Telephone and Telegraph, and others.

When Swiss banks do organize foreign bond issues, it often is done through a permanent issuing syndicate headed by the Big Three banks. This syndicate undertakes the negotiations with the borrowers, handles dealings with the National Bank, signs agreements, and arranges for the bonds to be traded on the Swiss exchange.

For the purpose of participating in underwriting syndicates active on the American market as well as for security trading in America, UBS established a subsidiary in New York, American UBS Corp. The corporation is a member of the Philadelphia-Baltimore-Washington stock exchange. Such a corporation, of course, has no bank secrecy when operating in the United States. It must conform to American disclosure regulations and U.S. securities and banking laws. In 1971, Deutsche Bank, Frankfurt, bought a half share in this company and it was renamed UBS-DB Corp.

Union Bank's corporate structure at the top follows the pattern found among Swiss banks. There is a twenty-two-man board of directors headed by Dr. Schaefer, with a twenty-third member—honorary chairman Dr. Fritz Richner. All members of the board except Dr. Schaefer are from outside the bank, executives who are powers in their own right outside the banking field.

For instance, the Union Bank board in 1972 included Dr. Carl M. Jacottet, chairman and managing director of Sandoz Ltd., Basle; Dr. Adolf Jann, chairman and managing director of F. Hoffmann-La Roche & Co., Ltd., Basle; and Giuseppe Bertola, managing director of Brown, Boveri & Co., Baden; plus other prominent businessmen.

Checking the boards of directors of the Big Three banks, some interesting cross links are noted. For example, Mr. Bertola, managing director at Baden for Brown, Boveri is on Union Bank's board. Dr. Rudolf Sontheim, a Brown, Boveri director, is on the board of directors of Swiss Credit Bank. Franz Luter-

bacher, chairman of Brown, Boveri, is on the board of directors
of Swiss Bank Corp., Basle.

Suzler Bros. Ltd., also has directors on the boards of each
of the Big Three banks: Georg Sulzer, chairman, is on Union
Bank's board; Alfred Schaffner, managing director, is on Swiss
Bank Corp.'s board; while Dr. Herbert Wolfer, vice chairman
of Sulzer, is on Swiss Credit Bank's board. In early 1972, Swiss
Bank Corp.'s vice chairman (and subsequently its chairman) was
chairman of Ciba-Geigy Ltd., Basle; while Swiss Credit Bank's
board claimed Dr. Samuel Koechlin, a member of Ciba-Geigy's
executive committee.

There's nothing wrong with such cross-linkage in Switzerland. After all, Switzerland is a small country and it is necessary
to stretch executive talent as far as it will go. Still, the cozy
relationship between Swiss banks and industry leads to some
criticism.

Dr. Schaefer is impatient with such complaints. Said he,
"The reproaches leveled against the allegedly excessive power
of the big banks must be taken seriously, but they are not justified. In contrast to the situation in other countries, our industry is completely independent of the banks. Its collaboration
with the banks is based on a mutual interest in promoting exports, and in a fair distribution of capital flows."

Chairman Schaefer has tried particularly hard to develop a
sound management team under him. Philippe de Weck heads
the staff departments. Dr. Robert Holzach is in charge of administration. Dr. Niklaus Senn heads finance. Guido Hanselmann is in charge of the foreign division. Dr. J. M. Clerc is chief
of commercial lending for French- and Italian-speaking Switzerland. Dr. Gerhard Tobler supervises lending in German-
speaking Switzerland, the most important section of the country for the bank. The first four hold general manager titles,
while Clerc and Tobler are deputy general managers. B. Saager
is a general manager without portfolio.

Under the organizational setup, de Weck corresponds to
what would be the bank president in an American institution.
At the end of 1971, the total staff numbered 11,700. Included in
this figure were approximately 1,600 apprentices. These work
with the bank for limited periods.

"This high figure illustrates the Bank's objective to carry out the training of its staff members largely by its own efforts," reads one bank report. The bank now has a network of vocational schools in Zurich, Geneva, Bern, Basle, Aarau, St. Gallen, and Lugano. Trainees are put through a three-year program.

In 1969, the bank launched a university graduates recruiting program to develop an executive training cadre within the bank. Currently, there are fifty such grads who are being put through an on-the-job training program. Not long ago, UBS acquired an old castle at Wolfsburg on Lake Constance and this is being renovated to function as a management training center for the hierarchy.

Operational methods within the bank have been formalized with the help of McKinsey & Co., management consultants, and departments now operate on a basis of goals and long-range plans.

In developing its managers, UBS seeks to create well-rounded men with broad knowledge of cultural, social, economic, and political trends, rather than technicians who master a narrow operational field. Top management looks to Japan rather than to the U.S. in searching for incentives to inspire management and employees to top-class performance. It thinks that incentives of the spirit may be far more successful than the material rewards stressed by American industry.

Bank Leu, oldest of the Big Five banks, began in what some modern conservatives might term "a socialist manner." In the early 1750's, Zurich suffered from a surplus of liquidity. Thrifty burghers of Zurich had saved so much money that local interest rates dropped to ridiculously low levels. In 1755, Hans Jacob Leu, the treasurer for the city, talked the city council into establishing a bank with a capital of 50,000 guilders. The institution sold 3 percent bonds to the public to sop up the excess liquidity. Money was invested through the Bank of England in British government bonds. It was Switzerland's first venture into the international money market.

Bank Leu still is in business, its connection with the city of Zurich severed long ago. Today, it is the smallest of the Big Five, one of Switzerland's least talkative commercial banks, a force in the coin market and the occupant of a pseudo sixteenth-century building in Zurich which has been redone in stone instead of wood.

All banks are experiencing labor shortages in all categories. At the end of 1971, employment statistics showed that only two hundred and twenty-one people in this 6.3 million population country were registered as unemployed. The monthly average through the year was only one hundred. This was for all occupations, not merely banking. So banks must scrounge for people.

Banking still is very much a man's job, except in low ranks. Invariably, when one proceeds beyond the tellers' cages in a bank, one finds himself in a masculine atmosphere, except for secretaries and file clerks. Female militants might blame this situation for the declining efficiency noted in Swiss banks in recent years. But there are few female militants in Switzerland.

Basle, too, is a man's city, and Switzerland's physical gateway to the world. It straddles the Rhine at the point where Germany, France, and Switzerland meet. With its historic connections to Erasmus and the painter Holbein, it has maintained a lofty tradition of art and culture since the Renaissance.

Its Rhine river sailors make the city's waterfront a utilitarian barge port of pipes and coal piles and towering grain elevators. Its chemists discovered both DDT and LSD. Its bankers, in 1872, created Swiss Bank Corp., one of the country's Big Three.

Swiss Bank's headquarters are in the center of Basle, where five streets come together to form a busy intersection. Banks occupy all five corners. Bank Corp.'s four-story concrete-block building is a solid structure which looks like most people figured a bank should appear in those days before architectural license decided that buildings could be art, too. Stock and bond prices are posted in one window at street level. Gold coins glitter in another window display. A sign in French and in German declares: "You will find a wide choice of gold and silver numismatic coins in our gold and silver departments."

In its advertising, the bank stresses its *Unsere 57 Dienste*, its fifty-seven services. Savings bank, brokerage house, coin retailer, gold seller, investment advisor, bond dealer—Swiss Bank is all of these and more.

"We could even open a department store or a textile shop

if we wanted to," one official of the bank said. One suspects that the bank would do just that if returns were greater in the retailing field than in banking.

But Swiss Bank Corp. is not hurting. It achieved a net profit of 141.6 million Swiss francs ($36.8 million) in 1971, a substantial improvement from the 126.1 million francs ($32.7 million) of 1970. While Union Bank has been the biggest bank in Switzerland for some years, Swiss Bank Corp. has been the most profitable. In 1971, Union bank finally passed Swiss Bank Corp. in profits as well as in the overall volume of business. Union Bank netted 143.1 million francs ($37.2 million) in 1971 versus 124.5 million francs ($32.4 million) in 1970.

Dr. Samuel Schweizer, chairman until his recent retirement, was very much its top man. He ran a tight ship. The bank's 8,846 employees (at end 1971) compare with 11,700 at Union Bank. Still, Union Bank won the profit leadership by only a narrow margin.

Schweizer, who remains a director, joined the bank in 1929 after graduating from law school. He is a short, thin-haired man with a high-bridged nose who is ultra-conservative, a trait evident at the bank, too. He is a firm believer in a sound currency backed by gold. He also is a cultural leader in Basle. When he relaxes, he tucks his violin under his chin and plays melodies of Kreisler or Strauss. He started with nothing and climbed to the top by sheer ability.

Swiss Bank's new chairman, Dr. Max Staehelin, is the son of a former chairman. He worked for a few years at the bank, then went on to carve a career as a chemical executive. He was vice chairman of Ciba-Geigy, Ltd. when appointed to the top job at Swiss Bank, with Dr. F. Emmanuel Iselin as his first deputy.

It is the self-made man who is most apt to believe in those old slogans about early to bed, early to rise, etc., or about the devil finding use for idle hands. Schweizer ran the bank on those lines, operating with six general managers. Four are located in Basle, Dr. E. F. Paltzer, H. Strasser, Dr. H. Grob, and L. Mottet. Two are in Zurich: P. Feurer and Dr. F. Schmitz.

Dr. Paltzer is a reticent, dour man with long features and a blunt jaw who gives little away in any conversation. But he leaves no doubt that he believes the time-tested laws of supply and demand should be given free play in banking.

Bank Corp. noted a 28 percent increase in assets on its balance sheets in 1971, biggest gain of all the banks. It ended the year with 3 billion francs ($780 million) in cash, again the highest total of all the banks. Normally, it might be a black mark on a bank to end the year with a big wad of cash, but 1971 was not a normal year. This was a year of monetary unease, when caution undoubtedly was the best policy.

Yet, it certainly was a record year for Swiss Bank Corp. Figures show: balances with other banks, up 47 percent in the year; loan volume up 18 percent; mortgage volume, up 37 percent; securities volume, up 22 percent; deposit and savings accounts, up 48 percent; and medium term lending, up 40 percent.

Though headquartered in Basle, Swiss Bank divides its operations between this city and Zurich. The bank's building on Paradeplatz in Zurich probably does a larger volume of business than the parent. But, Zurich is only an hour away by train or car, and twenty-five minutes by air. So, the inconveniences of the split arrangement are slight.

In all, the bank has one hundred and thirty-one branches, agencies, and offices in Switzerland. Overseas, it has two branches in London, two in New York, one in San Francisco, and one in Tokyo. Affiliates includes Basle Securities Corp., New York City, Swiss Bank Corp. (Overseas) Ltd., Nassau, Bahamas, and Swiss Corp. for Canadian Investments Ltd., Montreal and Toronto, Canada.

Basle also contains a unique institution which is in Switzerland geographically, but which really is international. This is the Bank for International Settlements. It is a central bankers' central bank. The majority of the institution's voting rights have always been held by founder central banks of Belgium, France, Germany, Italy, and the United Kingdom.

The seven founder countries also included the United States and Japan. Shares of the American issue were distributed to the public. Japan's membership ceased after World War II. The Netherlands, Sweden, and Switzerland now also have representatives on the board. Shares held by American citizens are voted by the Federal Reserve Bank of New York. The latter is represented at all meetings, sometimes accompanied by officials of the Federal Reserve Board in Washington.

All central banks in Europe except for the Soviet Union are affiliated with BIS. This includes central banks of Albania, Bulgaria, Czechoslovakia, Hungary, Poland, Rumania, and Yugoslavia. Japan regularly sends observers to meetings.

The bank was founded in 1930 to settle financial questions stemming from World War I. It has moved far beyond its long-finished task of collecting reparations from Germany, and currently is more powerful than ever.

Functions are: to promote cooperation among central banks, to serve as a "central bankers' club," to act as agent for international financial settlements entrusted to it, and finally to serve as an economic and monetary research center.

It is a bank in every sense. It collects deposits from member central banks. It deals in gold. (The Soviet Union often sells its gold to the West through BIS.) It extends loans to nations. And it turns a profit. The bank's 1971 annual report showed a net profit of 99.4 million gold francs in the year ended March 31, a figure which rose to 148.8 million gold francs in the year ended March 31, 1972. The gold franc is a quaint, but very sound unit worth 2.82 to the dollar in 1972, or about 35.4 U.S. cents each.

The club atmosphere is evident ten times a year when directors meet in Basle on the second Monday of each month (except for two summer months). Usually, bankers arrive on Sunday. Immediately, they gather at the bank's headquarters opposite the railroad depot in Basle. Meetings are informal. Information is traded concerning economic and monetary conditions in individual countries.

Proceedings are secret. However, in recent years, monetary crises have focused so much attention on BIS meets that gatherings attracted dozens of journalists. Some important monetary news has come from Basle.

The bank can be an effective agent when financial arrangements are being concluded among nations. It has assembled packages of cash and credit for Britain when that nation fought to prevent a devaluation. It arranges swap deals when currency runs develop between countries. In such a deal, a central bank agrees to swap its own currency, on request, for that of a partner country up to a prearranged amount. Provisions call for a reverse swap at some future date. Such swaps help absorb the surplus currency after a currency run, sometimes preventing speculators from forcing the devaluation of a weak currency.

It is generally admitted in Europe that BIS economic and monetary data produced by its research is among the best available. Sometimes BIS makes information public, as it does with its studies of the eurodollar market.

"The difficult phase through which the Western world is at present passing brings out even more clearly the usefulness of the functions carried out by the Bank for International Settlements in the monetary field," says Dr. Antonio d'Aroma, secretary general of the BIS.

In addition to BIS and Swiss Bank Corp., Basle is home to several private banks. Such banks in Switzerland are primarily portfolio managers, handling investments for Swiss citizens and for foreigners from Hong Kong to Santiago and from Abu Dhabi on the Persian Gulf to Rio de Janeiro.

How Swiss banks handle their investments for bank customers is worth a book in itself.

CHAPTER III

SECURITIES MANAGEMENT, THE SWISS FINANCIAL SUPERMARKET

Lombard, Odier & Co., one of Geneva's oldest and biggest private banks, warned its customers in August, 1970, that the Swiss franc was becoming a candidate for revaluation. Gold and foreign exchange reserves behind that currency were expanding steadily. Many customers reduced dollar holdings, shifted into Swiss francs. They benefited handsomely in 1971 when the franc appreciated by 13.9 percent against the dollar.

Clients of Switzerland's private banks expect such advice from their banker. They have been getting it from Switzerland's private bankers for generations. Lombard, Odier has been in business since 1798. Rahn & Bodmer in Zurich opened doors in 1750. La Roche & Co., Basle, started in 1787.

Today, there are forty-seven private banks operating in Switzerland, thirty of them belonging to the Swiss Private Bankers' Association. They form an exclusive club which has left an indelible mark on Swiss banking. It is marked in black ink rather than red. Customers of private banks seldom die broke.

Some of these banks don't even accept accounts of less than $100,000. Few of them advertise. All are essentially portfolio managers. Most are conservative. They are unlikely to make any rash promises about how rich you might become by letting them manage your money. If you press them hard, they are apt to say that their prime role is to defend your assets. Appreciation is secondary, but important.

They feel they must appreciate your holdings enough to defeat inflation. They know, too, you must do better than the 6 to 8 percent return on bonds, or there wouldn't be any reason for you to contact a private banker. This means they shoot for at least a 10 percent annual return to justify their existence. Often they exceed that level.

Private bankers have plenty of company in Switzerland in handling portfolios. Union Bank, for instance, has a third of its 11,700 people in its trust department. Still, anyone analyzing Swiss investing should start with private banks. They are the specialists.

The private banker's task is uncomplicated in aims, complex in strategic application. He is the financial physician for his clients, a monetary psychiatrist who analyzes financial problems and suggests remedies. Wealth has its problems, too. They are apt to be bigger than average because more zeros may follow the figures in an individual's tabulation.

The world may grow more permissive. Egalitarianism attracts more adherents. But holders of wealth are not easily persuaded that the world would improve if they parted from their assets. They aren't convinced that egalitarianism is best attained by taking from the haves to give to the have-nots. So the moderately well off and the wealthy undoubtedly will always search for expert asset management in order to protect holdings. The search may end in the discreet offices of a private banker. One of their bastions is Geneva, home of Lombard, Odier.

Perhaps it is symbolic that Voltaire, the liberal French philosopher, lived in exile in Geneva for many years. It was Voltaire who stated: "Those who say that all men are equal speak the greatest truth if they mean that all men have an equal right to liberty, to the possession of their goods, and to the protection of the laws." Then, the great Voltaire added a postscript: "But, equality is at once the most natural and most chimerical thing in the world, natural when it is limited to rights, unnatural when it attempts to level goods and power."

This the Swiss private banker believes. He seeks to make the rich richer, the moderately wealthy wealthier. He deals hardly at all with the little man who might measure his savings in the $5,000 to $50,000 range.

"There are savings banks for such savers," one Geneva private banker testily said.

In Berne, Dr. Edgar H. Brunner, partner, Armand von Ernst & Co., a private bank founded in 1812, said: "Clients with limited funds don't look for a private bank. It is mostly the wealthy who patronize us."

Max Zaugg, manager, J. Vontobel & Co., a big private bank located in Zurich, said: "We get a lot of letters from people in the United States who want to put a few thousand dollars with us. This is peanuts. We let them know that we are not interested."

It was Ogden Nash who said: "Bankers are just like anybody else, except richer." This holds true of the Swiss private banker. A man needs a fortune to start or to operate a private bank in this country. Under Swiss law, a private bank is unincorporated. It operates as an unlimited partnership. Partners are responsible to the last franc of their private fortunes for affairs of the bank.

Private banks file audits with the Swiss Banking Commission and the Swiss National Bank. They are not compelled to publicize balance sheets unless they advertise for business. Balance sheets provide only slender clues to operations anyway. Since the primary function is portfolio management, a bank may show assets of only a few million dollars. Yet, it may manage several hundred million dollars for customers.

Because a Swiss bank charter is universal, a private bank may engage in all of the activities of big commercial banks. Big private banks such as Julius Bär & Co., Zurich, not only manage portfolios but also make commercial loans, deal in letters of credit, provide guarantees, undertake collections, and perform other financial duties handled by commercial banks. A distinguishing feature is that the commercial bank is a corporation. The private bank is an unlimited partnership.

Roots of Switzerland's private banks go back to the seventeenth century. Most started as merchandising and trading companies. Successful trading houses attracted customers across Europe. Business generated credit. Merchants found themselves discounting drafts on foreign deals. They learned how to handle foreign currencies. By the nineteenth century, some of these trading houses had thriving bank operations.

Trading houses of Zurich discovered more profit could be made from money than from goods. Among archives of the city of Zurich is its first commercial register dated in 1792. It lists such banking houses as Pestalozzi, and Casper Schulthess & Co. Zurich's two oldest private banks, Orelli im Thalhof (1759) and Rahn & Bodmer (1750), were more traders than bankers at that particular time.

Today, Zurich's private banking business still includes some of the old names. New banks have emerged, too, such as Julius Bär (1890) and J. Vontobel (1924).

In 1962, when it appeared that big banks might crowd little banks from the bond market, these two banks joined Rahn & Bodmer and Wegelin & Co. of St. Gall to form the *Groupement de Banquiers Privés Zurichois*. This group underwrites bond issues and helps give the private banks a toehold in the underwriting business.

Geneva's banks have a different history. While Zurchers were traders, Geneva was a city of refuge, for French Huguenots and others. Refugees arrived with money. They helped establish the city's early banks, though first banks had a difficult time. Geneva was the home of Protestant reformer John Calvin. He was a stern moralist who established anti-usury rules along with his moral precepts. Interest rates were limited to 6 percent. This forced subterfuges. Banks have always developed scales of charges with fine precision when prevented from setting profitable interest rates. It wasn't until the eighteenth century that bankers here managed to launch real banks.

Geneva looked to France for its political, intellectual, and cultural inspiration. It didn't become part of Switzerland until after the Napoleonic Wars. It looked to France, too, for an investment idea which stimulated a unique financial business in Geneva.

At that time, the French Crown sold life annuities to its citizens, calculating life expectancy of a purchaser at fifteen years. After fifteen years, if alive, a man could start collecting at the prescribed rate.

One Geneva financial wizard, Michel Audéoud, had an idea. Why not buy some of these annuities in the names of healthy, young females with life expectancies far beyond fifteen years? Girls would cooperate for nominal sums. Owners might have sound investments.

"*Bonne idée!*" exclaimed many Geneva burghers. They rushed to invest in the syndicate which Audéoud launched. The syndicate had no trouble finding thirty young females with constitutions of oxen. The French Crown, always far removed from the scheming of ordinary citizens, sold annuities without question.

Audéoud, who probably would have been a slicker on Wall Street if living today, developed a secondary market in those annuities. An investor could offer them for sale to another investor without waiting fifteen years for the payoff. Banks offered loans on the paper.

Then came the French Revolution. Overnight all crown annuities were cancelled. The life annuity paper became worthless. And as for Audéoud? There wasn't any Securities and Exchange Commission to reprimand him. But citizens had their own brand of rough justice. Audéoud was summarily hauled before a local court, asked to say his prayers, and beheaded.

Geneva recovered quickly from the disaster. The influx of capital brought by French refugees of the Revolution stimulated the local economy. New banks emerged, some of which still are in existence. Names among Geneva's private banking houses include Ferrier, Lullin & Co. (1795), Hentsch & Co. (1796), Lombard, Odier & Co. (1798), Pictet & Co. (1805), and Darier & Co. (1837). These, plus three other private banks, De L'Harpe, Leclerc & Co., Bordier & Co. (1844) and Mirabaud & Co. (1819), formed the *Groupement des Banquiers Privés Genevois* to engage in underwriting and syndicating bond issues.

Basle, the third banking center in Switzerland, has three private banks which are over a hundred years old. They are La Roche & Co. (1787), Ehinger & Co. (1810), and A. Sarasin & Co. (1841). Dreyfus Söhne & Co. (1823) started as a private bank but was incorporated as a commercial bank after World War II. Still, it is often regarded as a private bank by people having contact with it.

Bern, Switzerland's capital, lists Armand von Ernst & Co. (1812) as its oldest and most notable private bank. Lucerne has Falck & Co. Chollet, Roguin & Co. is in Lausanne.

Though Swiss private bankers are notably discreet about the amount of business they handle, it is generally admitted that Julius Bär, Lombard, Odier, and Pictet & Co. are the three largest of the private banks.

"We like to think we are the biggest," said Edouard Pictet, a partner in Pictet & Co., and a Harvard Business School trained executive who occupies a small office in the old part of Geneva. Indications are that this bank has close to $2 billion of assets in its portfolios. It has more clients outside Switzerland than in. While there is no minimum on the size of an account which may be opened, Pictet admitted that an investment account of $50,000 is considered small at his bank.

He shrugged when asked to describe the average account among those of his clients.

"We don't deal in averages," said he. "Every account is handled on an individual basis. This is why people come to a private bank. They want individual service, and we provide it."

This individuality and attention to service are characteristic of all the successful private banks. Is the investor interested only in appreciation? Has he a speculative bent? Does he seek the highest possible income? Is he concerned about building an estate? These questions, and many more, are asked by the private banker.

"We analyze the portfolios of each client once a month. Large banks are apt to do that once a year," said partner Brunner of Armand von Ernst.

In Zurich, Dr. Nicolas Bär, a partner in Julius Bär & Co., said, "With one of the Big Banks, an investment advisor must handle 800 to 1,200 accounts. With us, each investment advisor handles 150 to 200 accounts."

The house of Bär launched operations in 1890 when Ludwig Hirschhorn and Theodor Grob founded a money-changing business. A few years later, Julius Bär (1857–1922) became a partner, and subsequently the firm evolved into a Bär family enterprise. In the fifties, the eldest grandsons of Julius Bär, Dr. Nicolas J. Bär, Hans J. Bär, and Peter J. Bär, assumed managerial responsibilities.

Today, the bank has about eight thousand portfolio accounts, three-fourths of them belonging to people outside Switzerland. It manages about $1 billion. It operates subsidiaries in London and New York City, and has a representative office in Mexico City. The staff numbers over three hundred, a staff which is outgrowing its headquarters at Bahnhofstrasse 36.

Nicolas Bär, at forty-eight, is a tall, graying man with angular features who obtained his Ph.D. from Zurich University with a dissertation on the monetary policies of the Roosevelt Administration from 1933 to 1941. He has an admiration for things American which is not unusual among Swiss bankers. When he has any spare time, he golfs, or swings his lanky frame aboard a horse to canter across the countryside. Currently, he is secretary general of the Swiss Equestrian Federation.

He is extremely articulate, with a flair for public relations which is unusual among Swiss bankers. His bank issues a weekly news letter which not only contains résumés of market trends in major equity markets of the world, it also frequently contains philosophical discussions and political comment in a conservative vein.

The first letter for 1972 examines the international political scene in a few tightly written paragraphs. Then it adds: "The revolutionary groups within the Western camp have lost initiative, especially in those cases where they proved to be merely a new edition of totalitarian and fascist methods. The authorities and the courts in Switzerland are also resorting to somewhat more severe methods in order to preserve constitutional order and control."

The March 3, 1972, issue engaged in a philosophical discussion concerning the conflict between Utopian dreams, and the "art of the possible." Conflicts between these social forces are deep, the letter said, referring to the present clash between growth and progress on the one hand, and environmental pollution on the other. It then said: "Unquestionably, the present decade will be characterized by the search for far-reaching new value systems."

Only after this discourse does that March letter report the status of shares on various markets. So, this is an investment advisory letter? Of course it is, when one takes a broad view of financial markets around the globe. Social and economic changes over the next decade will play a very important role in the direction of all investments made. Anyone who ignores the implications of the social forces now at work does so at his own monetary peril.

The Julius Bär bank sign displayed on Bahnhofstrasse in Zurich is visible for about three blocks on the street. But entrance is via a side door just off the thoroughfare, with a porter on guard to cull out unwanted visitors. Swiss private banks do not like to have curious souls wandering into their places of business to ask foolish questions. Usually they don't have offices on the ground floors of buildings where street traffic may spill passers-by into lobbies.

Nicolas Bär occupied an average-sized office which seemed to be a place for working, not for overwhelming visitors. A painting of a village shrouded in flowers, by Swiss painter Ernst Morgenthaler, hung on the wall behind his desk.

A vase of tulips adorned that desk and a small breadfruit tree thrived in a corner. Plants and flowers are found in most offices, along with tasteful works of art, and perhaps a painting or two of the bank's founders. If the Swiss banker has a green thumb, flowers may come from his own garden, which probably will be in a suburb. Some banks allow floral expense accounts for their executives, along with other perks of office.

Bär towered above his desk as he arose to shake hands, blue eyes staring straight at his visitor. A carnation decorated his lapel. White handkerchief peeked from his breast pocket. With his bow tie and neatly tailored suit, he looked a bit like a Madison Avenue executive handling a health farm account which requires him to keep in trim.

"We are a private bank, but we also are a universal bank," he explained, as he slumped into a black leather chair. "We trade every day in the free world's currencies." He went on to explain how the bank deals in certificates of deposit. It places medium-term money in high-yield bills of selected state-controlled, semi-state-controlled, or private business organizations outside Switzerland. The bank has been represented on the Zurich Stock Exchange almost since its start. It deals in unlisted and listed securities; cash, forward and premium; and through puts and calls.

While the Bär bank likes to have at least $125,000 in a discretionary account, it does not scorn the little fellow. For him, it offers investments in internal (house) mutual funds. There's a three-year-old bond fund which has noted an appreciation of nearly 14 percent since being established, while paying a return of 8.5 percent a year. There's a year-old convertible bond fund which noted a 10 percent appreciation since launching, while paying a 5 percent return. Then, there's a recently established equity fund which the firm hopes will be good for a 10 percent a year appreciation.

In Basle, Alfred Sarasin emphasized that private bankers thrive on their ability to give personal service to customers. Sarasin is a big, wavy-haired man who is a civic leader, and a hunter and fisherman in his spare time. He spent six years in parliament. He is president of the Basle Stock Exchange and of the Swiss Bankers' Association, a guiding figure at the Basle Museum of Natural History, and a get-things-done person where civil enterprises are concerned.

"A man must do something beside merely working for money," said he. It is a philosophy which one often finds among bankers in Switzerland. Union Bank's top man, Schaefer, oversees the Zurich Art Museum as well as the bank, and he is on the board of directors of the Schauspielhaus, the city dramatic theatre. Geneva's cultural life is sparked by bankers who understand Verdi or Beethoven as well as interest rate trends and the latest quotation for the forward dollar. Dr. Nicolas Bär collects modern art.

Offices of the Sarasin Bank are on Freiestrasse, adjacent to a cluster of sixteenth- and seventeenth-century houses. The imposing sixteenth-century red sandstone Rathaus or City Hall is just down the street, its façade decorated with frescoes.

The Sarasin Bank has the quiet elegance of another century. Cashiers' windows are beyond a marble foyer. The ground floor looks more like the tasteful headquarters of a successful industrial concern than a bank. A life-sized statue of a winged Mercury stands on the landing leading to the second floor. Here are found the offices of the partners, and the investment advisors who welcome customers of the bank.

The bank has over 5,000 clients. A little more than half are Swiss, the rest from foreign lands.

It is not uncommon among many long-established banks to have accounts passed from father to son through succeeding generations. "We have three generations of some families among our clients," explained Sarasin.

In prosperous Switzerland almost every citizen inherits something in his lifetime. Stability over decades can do that for a nation. A man inherits something, adds to it, leaves it to his heirs, and so on. It is considered profligate for a Swiss to inherit money, then to quit work to live on it. The mark of the sixteenth-century reformer Ulrich Zwingli still lies on the Swiss soul, at least in the Protestant areas which predominate. Work and thrift are cardinal virtues. If you have money, there's no reason for purchasing a new Cadillac if the three-year-old Chevrolet still functions.

When one Zurich banking official in a responsible position suggested a visit to a bank subsidiary recently, he first asked the visiting American if he minded walking. "It's only about a mile and a half," said the official. Then he glanced at the clock on the wall of his office, frowned, and added: "No. Better we drive."

The American expected that the automobile might be a, well, a German Ford or General Motors Opel at the very least. The car proved to be a Volkswagen.

"I hope you don't mind," the banker said, airily. It was a friendly remark, but it was evident that he felt no embarrassment at all at being caught with his Volkswagen exposed.

This country does not believe in keeping up with the Joneses, for the Joneses were put on a rail and run out of the country years ago. Generally, neighbors keep to themselves. One Swiss proverb goes: "Love your neighbor, but don't pull down the hedge." This doesn't mean, though, that you can't peek over it to note his scale of living, for he will be peeking in your direction, too.

Any sign of extravagance is cause for head shaking. The spendthrift might be accused of a mortal sin, living off his capital.

One bankers' joke heard in Basle and Zurich goes like this: a Zurcher meets a friend whom he hasn't seen for a long time. The friend notes the dejected appearance of the Zurcher. "What's the matter?" asks the friend.

"My house burned down last week," says the Zurcher.

"How terrible," says the friend.

"A few days ago a truck backed into my car, demolished it, and my insurance had lapsed, as it had on the house."

"Awful," says the friend. "But, it is fortunate that your wife has a job, too."

"She had, up to the day before yesterday," says the Zurcher. "She fell and broke her leg."

"Well, if I were you," says the friend, "I would live off my capital in the bank. Surely, your neighbors won't be able to criticize you for that, now."

An apocryphal story. But it does illustrate the Swiss character as does a proverb sometimes heard in the country: "Where there is money there is the devil. Where there is no money, there are two devils."

The Swiss private banker isn't allowed to be a mere safe-keeper for the funds entrusted to him. As the years pass, he finds himself privy to financial secrets of his customers. Where the American or the Englishman might seek advice from the local pastor when troubled, the Swiss is apt to turn to his banker.

"Our relationship with our customers is on a personal friendship basis," said Sarasin. Sitting at the head of a table in the bank's conference room, he outlined some of the things that his bank does for customers. "Of course," said he, "the management of funds and brokerage services are the most important activities of our bank."

On every trading day, Sarasin & Co. is represented on the floor of the Basle Stock Exchange. Orders to buy and to sell securities may be transmitted through the bank to other Swiss and foreign exchanges. The bank also deals in over-the-counter securities.

"For our services we charge commissions at the minimum rates applied in Switzerland," said Sarasin. "In most new bond issues we either participate as members of the underwriting syndicate or we accept subscriptions at the same conditions as the underwriters. We may also obtain, at the prevailing best conditions, shorter term bonds issued by the state banks of the Swiss cantons, or by the most important Swiss mortgage banks."

Safety deposit vault rentals are obtainable. A property management service is offered. A custodial security service includes the collection of principal, interests, and dividends, and the supervision of drawings and calls for redemption, conversions, and subscription rights.

"In short, we are prepared to handle all the investment problems of the client," said Sarasin.

Swiss and foreign customers include not only individuals but foundations, pension funds, trustees of security accounts, and industrial, financial, and insurance companies. Major private banks in Switzerland are involved in pension fund management, certainly one of the fastest growing segments of the world's financial business. Lombard, Odier reports it is deep in this field. Pictet and Julius Bär run what they call the Investment Institute for Pension Funds, acting as the custodian bank for collective investments by pension funds. Many pension funds, of course, are so small that fund managers find it difficult to diversify, when investing alone.

La Roche; Lombard, Odier; Chollet, Roguin; and Union Bank of Switzerland bid for pension fund business through Helvetinvest, a mutual fund established in mid-1971 with Intrag Ltd., Zurich fund managers.

Headquarters of La Roche & Co. are not far away from Sarasin Bank on Rittergasse 25, a street of medieval mansions on a high bluff parallel to the Rhine river. The bank is housed in a yellow stucco, one-time lordly residence. Iron grillwork bars first-floor windows. Shutters frame upper-floor casements. Only a small doorplate indicates that the building is a company domicile. Architectural reticence seems to be a feature of most of Switzerland's private banks. Legally a private bank cannot advertise for funds without making itself eligible for rules requiring the publication of accounts. Private banks go to extremes to make themselves inconspicuous. Banks garner clients by word-of-mouth advertising. Sometimes, too, bank officials publicize banks at investment seminars.

At La Roche, Dieter R. Gloor and Dietrich J. J. Forcart, two of the firm's four partners, greeted their visitor in the conference room. A huge porcelain stove of eighteenth-century vintage reposed in a corner. Nineteenth-century prints adorned walls.

Both gentlemen admitted that the firm is conservative with other people's money. "We have been in business since 1787," said Gloor. "We don't try to break any records when the market is going up, and usually we are in position to see that customers are not caught in down markets, either."

Forcart explained that banks charge fees of $1 to $1.50 per $1,000 in annual custodian fees. Brokerage fees are among the lowest in the world when shares are bought through local exchanges. When shares aren't listed in Switzerland, however, the purchaser will be paying the foreign brokerage fees plus the Swiss commission on a trade.

The long-term investor may not be too concerned. But thrifty Swiss pay close attention to fees and charges. Sometimes they confine themselves to American shares listed in Switzerland simply to save brokerage fees. An unlisted share selling at $35 a share, for instance, has commissions equivalent to about 6 percent, whereas the charges on a like listed share are half that figure.

In 1972 there were forty-four American companies which had their shares listed on the Zurich Stock Exchange, Switzerland's chief securities trading center. These were mainly blue chip companies such as General Motors Corp., CPC International, Minnesota Mining, Du Pont, and International Telephone and Telegraph.

Zurich's private banks were trading shares two centuries

ago. But the idea of developing stock exchanges to introduce order into trade came rather late in Switzerland's bank history. Geneva's stock exchange opened in 1850. Basle established its exchange in 1876. Zurich came last in 1877. Today, Zurich handles more business than all other exchanges in Lausanne, Bern, Neuchatel, St. Gallen, and Chur put together.

Turnover on the Zurich exchange is about $10 billion a year. There are one hundred and thirty-one shares of Swiss companies which are listed, many of them converted from the original bearer shares into registered shares. This is to prevent nonresident foreigners from acquiring a controlling interest in any Swiss company. Nearly one hundred foreign securities are also traded, just under half of them American and Canadian.

There is a thriving bond market in Zurich, with 1,200 fixed-interest issues traded. The bulk of these are Swiss. At present, there are twenty-six banks which are members of the Stock Exchange Association. A hundred other firms, about two dozen of which are foreign, also have licenses for trading off the floor.

A visit to the Zurich Stock Exchange can be an enlightening experience, akin to a cross between attending a revival meeting and a public auction. Just before 10 A.M. the hall on the fourth floor of the Exchange on the corner of Talstrasse and Bleicherweg fills with people. The dealers, known here as *Stellvertreter* or representatives, take their places at two circular counters known as rings.

All are in shirtsleeves. Each man carries a sheaf of papers which he spreads on the waist-high counter. There's no sitting down in a market such as this, except for the exchange commissioner and clerk.

Here and there are groups of men conversing. Are they talking about the market? One heavy-set trader smiles embarrassedly at the question, shakes his head.

"We were talking football," says he. Then, as if to excuse this lapse, he adds: "There is a time for business, and a time for —ah, no business."

Three men take positions at a table in the center of the ring. One is the Stock Exchange Commissioner of the Canton of Zurich. Another is the Exchange clerk. The third man feeds stock data to a closed television network.

Precisely at 10 A.M. a hush falls over the exchange. The Swiss exchanges, like others in Europe, use the *à la criée* system, which is a simple auction. Operations are very much like commodity exchanges, with dealers bidding against each other, after the clerk calls out a share.

That moment of silence lasts only a few seconds. At the first call, a dozen voices shout bids. Television screens flash bid and offered prices, with small sets conveniently located around the building. Noise intensifies as the clerk moves to another share and another. Still, despite the chaos, an orderly market is being established.

"It is a quiet day," says an official of the exchange when a block of Aluminium Suisse shares changes hands at the same price as on the preceding day.

Starting an account with a Swiss bank may be conditioned for foreigners by the current monetary situation. In a crisis, money pours into the country in such volume that banks are almost overwhelmed. The Swiss National Bank may ask banks to restrict opening of new accounts, or to suspend interest payments. At times, Switzerland even introduces a negative interest rate on new foreign deposits. This means that you pay a tax through the bank to hold your money.

Generally, though, there shouldn't be any trouble about opening a portfolio account, especially if this is for the purpose of investing in equity markets outside Switzerland. In 1972, purchase of Swiss shares or bonds designated in Swiss francs and of Swiss real estate was temporarily prohibited. Foreigners who held such property were allowed to hold it.

J. Vontobel & Co., Zurich private bank, has a twenty-page handbook, *What You Want to Know About Investments Through Swiss Banks*. Vontobel starts by telling readers: "A bank account may be opened either by letter or at the teller's desk. In both cases, the basic formalities are exactly the same. However, the banks do like to know their clients personally. Therefore, if an account has been opened by way of correspondence, a personal call is recommended as soon as feasible."

Americans must remember, though, that United States taxes probably are due on any dividends, interest, or equity appreciation.

A portfolio account may be handled in either of two ways, as a discretionary account, with purchases and sales left to the judgment of the bank, or as a straight nondiscretionary account where the bank merely holds securities and executes client orders.

What is it like dealing with a Swiss bank?

If Swiss bankers are described in one compound word, it probably would be business-like. It was Calvin Coolidge who dryly said: "The business of America is business." This might be said of the Swiss banker, too, though Alexandre Dumas may have been closer to the mark when he said: "Business? That's very simple. It's other people's money."

Here is a scene in one of Switzerland's private banks, a scene repeated thousands of times a day in different institutions around the country.

A well-dressed Lebanese businessman walks into the private bank carrying an attaché's briefcase. He is ushered into a small, mahogany-panelled office which contains a table, several chairs, and a stack of magazines in French and German. It could be an empty doctor's anteroom, for, though tastefully furnished, there is a sterility about it. A painting of one of the bank's founders stares from the wall, as if still keeping an eye on business.

The visitor is joined by an executive of the bank, a youngish fellow who has been well briefed about the state of a dozen stock markets at a morning session of the bank's portfolio managers. Like most Swiss bankers, he is conservatively dressed in a dark suit, with a neat press. His tie is a color which won't remain long in anybody's memory. He has a thin dossier in his hand.

"Charles! It is good seeing you again," the banker says in French to the long-established client.

Charles, who speaks four languages, answers in English. This is the language he had been using at lunch when discussing a fruit exporting deal with several British importers. He learned his English at the American University in Beirut and there is a trace of an American accent when he says: "Hello, Mark. I'm back to see how you have been doing with my account."

A few pleasantries are exchanged. The banker knows that

Charles is interested in music and he mentions that the Suisse Romande Orchestra is playing at the Casino that evening. The bank has some tickets.

Then, the banker seats himself at the table, opens the dossier. A sheet looks like this:

100	Lonza	Sfr	212,000	Sfr	212,000.00
100	Nestlé (bearer)	Sfr	388,500		388,500.00
250	Commerzbank	DM	58,250		68,989.82
3,000	Thorn	£	13,680		125,856.00
100	l'Oreal	FF	228,000		172,824.00
50	IBM	$	20,200		76,558.00
100	Syntex	$	8,300		31,457.00
160,000	FL 8% Nederlands	Fl	201,140		243,379.40
	Uninvested balance	Sfr	52,350		52,350.00

Total Market Value Sfr 1,371,914.22

"It comes up to a little over $360,000," the banker explains.

Charles looks up quickly. "Dollars? I thought the account had been switched to Swiss francs?"

"It has," the banker says, without changing expression. "We have had it in Swiss francs for the last year and a half, as you know. But I thought you might like the comparison."

Charles relaxes. It is obvious that he likes the look of the account.

"Who is l'Oreal?" he asks.

"It is a French cosmetics company, and it is dominant in its field," says the banker.

"I note you've added a couple of American stocks."

The banker nods. "We think the American market will be very favorable over the next twelve months. We will be switching funds from some of those Netherlands bonds into more American stocks when we see opportunities."

Charles nods. This is a discretionary account, with the bank handling the investments. Now he reaches for an envelope in his briefcase, takes out a batch of large bank notes. "I have another $25,000 I want to put into that account," says he.

"To be invested in the usual way," the banker says.

"Yes," Charles says. He studies the list of shares in his portfolio, fixing the figures in his head. The banker makes out a receipt for the money, passes it across the table. Charles rises. The meeting has lasted less than a half hour. The banker is already studying the notice of another caller as Charles departs.

The typical Swiss bank portfolio will be international, though at any particular time American shares may predominate. Swiss say that the only wise way to invest, today, is internationally, with money moving back and forth across borders as investment opportunities arise.

In recent years, monetary problems have added to investors' risks and opportunities. In November, 1967, the British pound sterling was devalued from $2.80 to $2.40. In March, 1968, the international gold pool collapsed and a two-tier market was created. In August, 1969, France devalued its franc by 11.1 percent. The German mark, the Swiss franc, and the Japanese yen became strong. The dollar weakened.

Speculators played each development skillfully. Perhaps the term speculator is a misnomer. To some, it has a connotation akin to that of a river gambler, if not quite that of a crook. A speculator is more apt to be a big international company like Standard Oil Co. of California or International Telephone and Telegraph, than some shyster money-changer. The treasurers and comptrollers of multinational companies deal in dozens of currencies daily. They are paid to safeguard capital of stockholders. They do that by hedging their dealings in foreign currencies and by trying to keep as much of their money as possible in strong currencies.

But these speculators may fire massive currency runs between nations. A flood of money into any country may stimulate inflation, pushing prices upward on stock markets as well as on consumer markets. An investor may play price shifts to his advantage.

"Monetary matters will have an ever more important bearing on investments in the future, either directly or through their influence upon domestic policies" said Dr. Nicolas Krul, research director of Lombard, Odier. He and Armand Lombard, another official of this long-established firm, had been asked to amplify how the bank determined where an investor's money should go.

The bank's headquarters are at 11 rue Corraterie, near the base of the hill on which are clustered many of Geneva's remaining old medieval buildings. Lombard occupied a small, modern office decorated in orange and white, with abstract paintings on walls. He is a young, swinging executive, with sideburns and a gay-blade manner, who doesn't conform at all to the Swiss banker pattern. Krul is a shrewd, broadly-based forty-year-old economist who skis to keep fit and who might look younger than his years were it not for the heavy mustache under his nose.

"We like to think of ourselves as an international rather than a Swiss bank," explained Lombard.

The Bank's eighty-page *1971 Review and 1972 Outlook*, prepared for customers, discussed developments in nine stock markets in detail.

Companies in Canada, France, Germany, Italy, Japan, the Netherlands, Switzerland, the United Kingdom, and the United States were analyzed. Charts and graphs presented some aspects visually. A vast amount of research material is now available in the international investment field for those who know where to look.

Both Lombard and Krul emphasized that markets are dynamic. A market which looks favorable in January may look less so in February. This means that research must be revised constantly. Lombard, Odier has twenty people in research who are constantly evaluating economic and financial information received from about the world. Officials visit companies in Switzerland, Germany, France, Holland, Britain, and elsewhere. Research and investment committee meetings are held daily to review trends. The firm also has a seat on the Boston Exchange and a local research representative in New York City.

Importance of money parity changes on equities is emphasized by Pictet & Co. in its *L'Evolution Boursière en 1971*. This is a thirty-two-page research work which also analyzed trends in major international markets.

To see how prices are affected by currency changes note the Pictet table below. It shows variations in the stock indexes of various markets in 1971 compared with 1970, and in 1967 compared with 1971. Figures show index gains in local currencies. In parentheses are the percentage gains of an investor who had his portfolio denominated in Swiss francs before moving into the particular market.

VARIATIONS IN STOCK MARKET INDEXES

	1971		1967–71	
Great Britain	+40%	(+35%)	+54%	(+27%)
Japan	+37%	(+41%)	+87%	(+93%)
Sweden	+23%	(+19%)	+36%	(+31%)
Switzerland	+13%	(+13%)	+102%	(+102%)
Germany	+7%	(+8%)	+42%	(+57%)
United States	+6%	(−4%)	+13%	(+3%)
Canada	+5%	(−5%)	+23%	(+13%)
Australia	−2%	(−6%)	+51%	(+46%)
Netherlands	−5%	(−4%)	+35%	(+35%)
France	−7%	(−10%)	+20%	(+3%)
Italy	−14%	(−19%)	−27%	(−30%)

Figures show clearly that the Swiss investor would have benefited most by investing in Japanese stock index shares in 1971. The actual gain in share values on the market would have been 37 percent versus a 40 percent rise in Britain. But the Japanese yen appreciated too, so the real return when the Swiss investor cashed in his Japanese stocks for Swiss francs represented a 41 percent gain versus the 35 percent rise in asset values from the British stocks.

The statistics for the United States indicates why few foreigners were purchasing American shares in 1971. Even though the Dow Jones average increased by 6 percent, the decline in the dollar's value, coupled with the rise in the Swiss franc's value, meant that the Swiss investor actually lost money if he bought Dow Jones average shares in 1971.

Even more interesting are the statistics which show what happened in the 1967–71 period. Had the Swiss investor left his money in Zurich Stock Exchange Swiss index shares, he would have had a 102 percent rise in the value of his assets. Since he started with Swiss francs and finished with Swiss francs, his real gain would have been the same 102 percent. Had he purchased American shares in 1967 and kept them, he would have noted a 13 percent rise in their values in the stock market. But he would have received only 3 percent more in Swiss francs, because of the devaluation of the dollar coupled with the appreciation of the Swiss franc. Monetary conditions can, indeed, have an important bearing on an investor's returns.

Generally, the Swiss portfolio manager plays markets long. He invests rather than trades. He believes in diversification, rather than in putting all eggs into a good basket. This is contrary to preachments of some Wall Street seers who advise plunging heavily when an investment opportunity arises.

Swiss bankers probably won't make you the richest man in town if they manage your account. But, then, they are unlikely to leave you a pauper, either. Moderation. That's the Swiss way. That viewpoint might be difficult for the speculative American to accept.

Economic growth in particular countries helps determine how stock markets may go. Statistics prepared with help of Swiss bankers, for instance, show that the compounded annual growth rate from 1955 through 1970 was as follows in various nations:

Japan	10.5%
Germany	5.4%
France	5.1%
Italy	5.1%
Netherlands	4.6%
Canada	4.0%
United States	3.5%
United Kingdom	2.7%

But early in 1972, when the research director of one major Swiss bank was asked to estimate growth trends through 1972, he produced the following for seven of the above countries:

Japan	8–10%
United States	5–6%
France	4–5%
United Kingdom	4%
Switzerland	3–4%
Germany	2.5%
Netherlands	2%

Thus, in the spring of 1972, most Swiss portfolio managers were bullish about prospects for the American stock market. The Japanese market looked good, too. But equity prices in Japan had discounted much of the anticipated advance for the next year or two. So portfolio managers kept returning to the U.S. market as they scanned prospects.

Still, managers also had the 1971 currency parity realignment negotiated in December in Washington to consider. That parity change had produced the following results:

	CHANGE IN GOLD PARITY	NEW PARITY (TO DOLLAR)	DEPRECIATION OF DOLLAR
U.S. dollar	−7.89%	—	—
Japanese yen	+7.66	308.0	16.88%
German mark	+4.61	3.223	13.56
Dutch guilder	+2.76	3.245	11.36
Belgian franc	+2.76	44.81	11.60
French franc	—	5.116	8.60
Swiss franc	+7.01	3.84	13.9
Italian lira	−1.00	581.5	7.48
British pound	—	2.606*	8.60

*dollars to the British pound

An investor can't make much money if his shares are in a weak currency country where the value of the money is dropping faster than the stock market gain. Sometimes, of course, the local market doesn't have to rise at all for a profit to be made should a currency strengthen.

It isn't enough, of course, for a portfolio manager to select the particular market for his investing. He must select a particular company or companies. When switching into a country in anticipation of a market rise, the typical Swiss money manager invests in market leaders. In the United Kingdom this is likely to be a company like Imperial Chemical Industries. In Germany, it would be Siemens, one of the big chemical companies or similar trend setters. In Japan, it might be Sony. But, market leaders are not sought so avidly in the United States, for each market upturn seems to be led by different companies. Moreover, money managers are becoming much more se-

lective in foreign lands, too, insofar as market leaders are concerned.

"The market leaders are typically chosen in Europe, but no
longer exclusively, and certainly not in the United States," said
Krul of Lombard, Odier. "Our U.S. list was mostly composed
of IBM, Avon, IFF, Three M, Baxter, Black and Decker, Com-
sat, Western Union, Johnson and Johnson, Marley, Upjohn,
American Hospital Supply, and Sears, Roebuck. In Holland, we
preferred Heineken and Bols, plus some of the banks, over the
internationals. I know that we are far from alone in being more
and more afraid of market leaders."

The typical money manager enters a market cautiously,
until the trend becomes apparent. Then, further purchases are
made, following company research data. Here, comparisons
with companies in other countries may be made.

For instance, suppose that research indicates that the
American market should be due for a rise, and with the food
industry expected to surge. The researcher may look for an
industry leader like CPC International. But the typical interna-
tional investor doesn't plunge directly into that investment.
Comparisons are likely to be made between CPC International,
Nestlé in Switzerland, Calpis Food in Japan and Unilever in the
Netherlands.

One Swiss money manager who made just this comparison
noted that these companies had share price changes of -7, $+15$,
$+81.3$, and $+34.5$ percent in 1971, respectively. He concluded that
Calpis would be the best buy, despite the improved American
market and the already strong rise in Japan.

IBM, the computer market leader, has no competition to
speak of, abroad. So, if the American market and the computer
business seem destined for a rise, Swiss money managers don't
ponder long. IBM wins every time, unless the price of the stock
already is considered inordinately high. Then, the manager may
wait for a market reaction.

Analyzing purchases of Swiss money managers, it is clear
that they like blue-chip companies. They seldom venture into
the over-the-counter market. They like to keep a minimum of
about 10 percent of a portfolio in bonds, with that percentage

rising during recessions to 40 or even 50 percent. In recessions, too, they like a good portion of a portfolio to be in time deposits of strong currencies.

Swiss bankers are neutral internationally. Each country's market is judged on the basis of political stability, economic possibilities, and monetary factors, not on subjective emotional factors. You will never hear a Swiss money manager say that he won't invest in Spain because he doesn't like General Franco, or that he will not invest in South Africa because he hates apartheid.

The Romans had a proverb, *Pecunia non olet*, (Money has no smell). William James said, "The art of being wise is the art of knowing what to overlook."

Swiss bankers may not like Communism, but they can overlook their dislikes when financial business is available. That was the case not long ago when this author visited Zurich. In one particular bank, an executive indicated a departing client who had been negotiating a eurodollar loan. "That," said the banker, "was the head of the Hungarian Foreign Trade Bank."

When the Soviet Union has gold to sell, it sometimes does it in Switzerland. Russians like to deal with the Swiss, for the men of Moscow know that emotional factors will not interfere to dampen any business deals.

Swiss banks have operated mutual funds for years. But it was only in recent years, when faced with stiff competition from such companies as I.O.S. Ltd., that Swiss banks have actively promoted this part of their business. As of January 1, 1972, there was about $2.6 billion of investment trust assets under Swiss management.

Biggest of the Swiss fund groups is Intrag, Ltd. It was founded in 1938 by Union Bank, Lombard, Odier, La Roche, and Chollet, Roguin & Co., Lausanne. At the end of 1971, fifteen Intrag mutual funds held 4.3 billion Swiss francs ($1.1 billion) in assets. This represented a 35.2 percent gain over the total held at the end of 1970.

The 1971 Union Bank annual report listed the asset values of the specific funds. Figures follow, with the investment area of each fund listed in parenthesis:

	End 1971	End 1970
	million Swiss francs	
Amca (America-Canada)	630.5	607.6
Safit (South Africa)	180.8	208.8
Fonsa (Swiss equities)	460.0	388.0
Sima (Swiss real estate)	805.1	650.9
Canac (Canada)	137.6	131.4
Itac (Italy)	14.1	18.4
Eurit (Europe)	117.2	123.2
Francit (France)	31.3	34.2
Espac (Spain)	29.1	29.8
Denac (retail trade and foods shares)	42.6	42.6
Germac (Germany)	30.3	20.9
Globinvest (international)	528.0	505.2
Pacific-Invest (Pacific area)	165.5	139.3
Bond-Invest (international bonds)	1,086.2	314.0
Helvetinvest (Swiss fixed-interest)	88.4	–
Total	4,346.7	3,214.3

In 1939, Swiss Bank Corp. and Swiss Credit Bank jointly acquired another big fund group, *Société Internationale de Placements*, Basle, which is often referred to as SIP in Swiss banking circles. This group has nine stock and bond funds and nine real estate funds. These include: Intercontinental Trust, for global investing; Canasec for Canadian shares; Europa-Valor, for European shares; Ussec, for American stocks and bonds; Actions Suisses, for the Swiss market; and Energic-Valor, for investing in stocks and bonds of energy companies around the world.

Early in 1970 Swiss Bank Corp. formed a new division within the bank to promote investment savings. The division also develops new mutual funds tailored for customers' needs. In the spring of 1970 Swiss Bank acquired a majority share holding in International Investment Trust Co., Basle, also known as INTERFONDS, a fund manager. Universal Bond Selection, a fund for bond investments, was launched with INTERFONDS as manager. Newest fund of these two is the Japan Portfolio.

Swiss like diversification. At the end of 1971, Europa-Valor had just under $18 million in assets. Holdings included equity shares of eighty-three companies, ranging from Pechiney in

France to Slater Walker Securities in Britain and from Cockerill-Ougree in Belgium to AEG-Telefunken in Germany.

In addition, there were bonds of forty-six companies and organizations in the portfolio. Largest investment was in Royal Dutch Shell, a holding which accounted for 5.12 percent of total assets.

How have some of these funds fared? Well, if you had invested $575 in Actions Suisses in 1950, it would have increased to $1,875 in 1960, to $2,425 in 1970, and to $2,825 at end of fiscal 1971. That's a threefold gain since 1960, and a fivefold gain since 1950.

Ussec, a SIP fund which invests in the American market, has done less well. If an investor had put $458 in this fund in 1951, the money would have appreciated to $916 in 1961, and to $1,091 at the end of the 1971 fiscal year.

At the end of its fiscal year, August 31, 1971, this fund had 72.68 percent of its $28 million in assets invested in equities, 13.58 percent in convertible bond issues, 6.97 percent in straight bonds, and 6.77 percent in cash or liquid assets. Among its largest holdings in percentages of assets were: Eli Lilly (3.92 percent); Merck & Co. (2.72 percent); IBM (5.41 percent); R.J. Reynolds (2.31 percent); American Telephone & Telegraph (1.28 percent); Sears, Roebuck (1.73 percent); General Motors Corp. (1.23 percent); and Minnesota Mining (1.15 percent).

Truly, Swiss money managers like blue chips, and they like to spread risks.

Though Swiss bankers are retailers of gold bricks to the people who want to collect them, Swiss portfolio managers don't recommend gold in portfolios.

"Gold is a dead asset which pays no interest," said Edouard Pictet in Geneva. "It does give some people a feeling of safety, but it is a poor investment. We don't recommend it to our clients."

Swiss bankers realize that they are not going to convince gold lovers that the yellow metal may be a wasteful asset. So, they have developed the most efficient gold market in the world to serve the gold trade, not only in Switzerland but around the globe. You find agents of major Swiss banks in Beirut, in such Persian Gulf ports as Dubai, in Hong Kong, and anywhere else where gold buyers congregate. It's a lucrative trade for the Swiss banks, too, even though the Swiss may look with faint disapproval at buyers. And nowhere is that trade more lucrative than in Dubai, where sleek dhows lie in the muddy harbor ready to smuggle precious bars of gold into India.

CHAPTER IV

A SWISS FETISH

Two and a half million dollars in ten tola gold bars rested in the hold of British Overseas Airways' Flight 774 as the VC-10 jetted across Saudi Arabia at a six-mile altitude. Captain N. L. E. Dupee held the controls.

Stars glittered brightly in the desert sky. The plane's tail jets droned steadily in the night. Four gold bullion dealers from London occupied first-class seats. Two Arabs in *abas,* those ankle-length robes edged with gold braid, talked in low tones at the magazine rack.

One had identified himself as a merchant from Bahrain. The second claimed to be a landowner from Buraimi Oasis on the edge of Saudi Arabia's Empty Quarter. A steward said both were smugglers returning to Dubai on the Persian Gulf. The gold bullion dealers were on their way to Dubai, too, to do business with some of their best customers, other smugglers like the two on the plane.

"The gold ends somewhere in India after being smuggled from Dubai," said one official of Samuel Montagu & Co., Ltd., a reputable London bullion dealer. His presence confirmed the legitimacy of this gold trade, which has one leg in London, another in Switzerland, and a third in the little sheikhdom of Dubai in the Union of Arab Emirates.

Swiss banks are refiners, retailers, bankers, dispatchers, and storekeepers in the gold trade. Switzerland allows its citizens to buy gold in bar or coin form as easily as they may purchase eggs at a supermarket. No questions are asked. There are no taxes. Purchases may be stored with the selling bank, carried away, or consigned. Distant buyers may purchase by telex or cable. Most Dubai smugglers not only have Swiss bank accounts, they also have enviable repayment records.

"We do not inquire if the gold is being reshipped somewhere else when we get an order from Dubai," admitted one Zurich banker. He merely shrugged when asked how tiny Dubai could support a gold trade which accounted for one-fifth of the nonsocialist world's annual gold supply in 1968–70.

In Dubai, authorities don't inquire about destinations either when gold departs in holds of teak dhows. It is a convenient arrangement which provides some lucrative cargo traffic to B.O.A.C., steady gold-sales commissions to banks, huge profits to smugglers, and a hedonistic life style to Persian Gulf merchants who might otherwise be living in camel-hair tents in the desert.

Swiss banks have no direct interest in any of the smuggling. They are familiar with so many legal ways of making money that they do not have to seek shares in questionable Persian Gulf ventures.

Swiss banks *do* have the faciltes and the discreetness which are valued by anyone who smuggles gold. Big Three Swiss banks each have their own gold-refining subsidiaries which are ready to pour gold bars in any size. It isn't for a bank to moralize should a certain size just fit pockets of a smuggling jacket.

Swiss Bank Corp. has its subsidiary, Metaux Précieux S.A., at Neuchâtel. Union Bank of Switzerland and Swiss Credit Bank have their subsidiaries, Argor S.A. and Valcambi S.A. respectively, in Chiasso. The town almost straddles the Swiss-Italian border amid the soft, green mountains of Switzerland's Ticino.

The location is fortuitous. Italy is the largest producer of gold jewelry in the world. Moreover, Italians are notoriously lax in paying taxes. Official sales of gold are easy for tax men to track in their tax computations. So Italian jewelers make frequent trips to Chiasso to admire the scenery. Sometimes they return with a few bars of gold hidden in innards of the family automobile.

Valcambi occupies a modern three-story plant fronted by a four-story tower, on Chiasso's fringes. In the background, Swiss Alps blend into Italian Alps. Vineyards form terraces on slopes.

In a smoky foundry, workmen in white coveralls poured molten gold into open molds, the size of building bricks. In a display case on velvet, various sizes of gold bars were on view. Prominently exhibited was a small, ten-tolas bar. An egg-shaped stamp on its face bore the Credit Suisse designation, with an inset of the figures 999,0 (the comma is used for a period in Europe). The figure meant that the gold was 999 parts per 1,000 pure.

"People in the Middle East like this size," explained a Valcambi official. He fondled the glistening yellow bar, which had a warm, inner glow. Gold obviously fascinated him, as it does many people who come into contact with it.

A tola is a Mideast weight equivalent to .375 fine ounces. So, a ten-tolas bar weighs 3.75 ounces and is about the size of a three-eighth-inch-thick calling card.

Gold is one of the heaviest of metals, 19.32 times its own volume of water. It is rated in purity in parts per 1,000. Purity also is measured in carats. One hundred percent gold is 24 carats. Twenty-two carat gold is 22/24 pure. Copper or silver often are the alloys.

"Did you know," asked the Valcambi official, "that if you poured all the gold in the world into one block, it would form a cube fifteen and a half meters long?"

"About fifty feet by fifty feet by fifty feet," the visitor translated the metric figure.

"Yes. And it would weigh about 80,000 metric tons."

Such a cube would fit easily onto the stage at Radio City Music Hall in New York. No stage built, however, could hold such a massive weight.

The ten-tolas bar went back to its case, probably for future inspection by some Mideasterner. The gold in the hold of B.O.A.C.'s Flight 774 was in ten-tolas form, too, packed like sample bars of soap in small boxes. Flight 774 landed just before midnight on an asphalt strip laid on desert sand near the Persian Gulf. Unloading of the gold was casual, only minimum security visible.

"We have no crime here," explained W. R. Duff, the lanky Englishman who was the sheikhdom's general inspector of ports and customs.

Indeed Dubai has little crime, though it is one of the world's major smuggling centers. But smuggling is not a crime here. Dubai is the capital of a 1,250-square-mile principality of about 65,000 people. Gold pours into it as if it were a mint, only to disappear into the iniquitous quicksands of international smuggling. There's not a silver mine around, yet only the United States and the Union of Soviet Socialist Republics export more silver annually.

Dubai is a barnacle on the Indian bottom. Every year about $200 million worth of gold is illegally smuggled into India, and much of it comes from Dubai along with cases of watches, cameras, and such. On the back haul silver is smuggled from that almost limitless Indian hoard which has provided so many headaches for American and European speculators in silver. Precious cargoes cross the 1,200 miles of water in specially built, sleek dhows which look like simple fishing boats until an Indian Coast Guard patrol boat approaches. Then, the 325-horsepower diesel engines of the endangered dhow roar into resonant life. The dhow departs hastily, leaving the befuddled Coast Guard skipper far behind.

Or so smugglers hope the scenario will develop. It doesn't always, for the Indians introduce faster and faster patrol boats. But the game goes on, as it has for decades along India's palm-fringed shores. And the villas of the Dubai gold smugglers rise in marbled magnificence along the beach west of Dubai town, swimming pools set in ornate patios. Houses are staffed with obsequious Pakistani servants, and decorated with attractive females airfreighted in first class from the bawdy houses of Beirut.

Dubai in the hot daylight bustled with the colorful life of a busy port. Gulls circled above a clump of mudbrick buildings thrown together haphazardly along a creek as if sited by one of the area's frequent sandstorms. New glass and steel buildings of six to eight stories rose at intervals.

Buildings advertised the prosperity of alley stall merchants who had graduated to the ranks of real estate magnates. Often they had done it through smuggling profits. Date palms grew in empty sand lots, fronds sagging in the heat. A minaret of a mosque lifted above a row of mud huts, each with its wind tower to collect any passing breeze.

A fleet of sleek dhows lay at anchor in the quarter-mile-wide estuary, like yachts waiting for a race. Indian crewmen lounged on teak decks. Coffee boiled on the charcoal brazier of one of the vessels. This aroma added fragrance to the smell of cardamom, nutmeg, cloves, and other spices in the open-air market.

Dubai's gold fleet consisted of about fifty dhows. Each was a trim craft of fifty to sixty feet in length, equipped with a mast to carry not the customary sail but a radio antenna. Bows advertised speed and trim grace.

The First National City Bank of New York City building hugged the waterfront. It was a concrete block of airy, lacework design, looking like some pavilion constructed for an international fair. First National City opened a branch here without intending to enter the gold traffic. It found that a Persian Gulf bank had to be in gold. Reluctantly, it obtained U.S. Treasury permission to deal in the metal, one of the few U.S. corporations so authorized. First National City, like everybody else, disclaims any foreknowledge of cargo destinations.

"Gold is imported legally and departs legally," said Customs Inspector Duff. "What happens to it after it leaves here isn't our affair."

That backhaul of smuggled silver coming from India is one

of the ways India's gold receivers pay for smuggled gold. Every year, Dubai exports at least 10 million fine ounces of silver, with the figure hitting 16.5 million fine ounces in 1971.

Mr. Duff smiled wryly when asked about the silver's origin. Said he: "It just appears here from the silver mines at the end of the creek." He pointed in the vague direction of the Persian Gulf.

Ahmad Osman, a clean-shaven native of Bahrain and owner of a freight forwarding company, outlined the rudiments of the business while sipping coffee in the lounge of the Carlton Hotel. This is the class establishment in Dubai, a six-story mini-Hilton with Arab trimmings.

Some of Mr. Osman's gold had arrived on the B.O.A.C. flight the previous night. A few days earlier, he had telexed a Zurich bank to ship four hundred and fifty bars of ten tolas each to the National Bank of Dubai. The gold's cost, about $72,000, had been debited to Mr. Osman's account in Zurich. The bank placed the order with Johnson, Matthey (Bankers) Ltd., a London bullion dealer in order to catch B.O.A.C. Flight 774. Mr. Osman had not yet claimed the shipment from the National Bank of Dubai.

"They have a vault. I don't," he explained.

An agent in India had already contracted for the shipment at an agreed price of $100,000. The Indian, who also had a Swiss bank account, had agreed to pay for half of the shipment with a $50,000 transfer to Mr. Osman's bank. The other half was to be paid in bullion silver which would be smuggled from India on a dhow's backhaul. Mr. Osman already had negotiated sale of this silver to a London bullion dealer.

India is one of the world's great storehouses of silver, a fact that silver speculators in Europe and America discovered rather late in the game. Nearly every family has collected its share of silver bracelets, necklaces, rings, spoons, and various other items. As the price of silver climbed in world markets when America demonetized silver, enterprising silver dealers in India offered higher and higher prices for items brought to them. The silver was melted down and shipped through the smuggling route to Dubai, and thence to world markets.

Gold is prized even more highly in India, as a store of

wealth. Indians have almost a mystical veneration for gold, the metal of Lakshmi, Hindu goddess of wealth. Since 1947, import of gold has been illegal. Smugglers disregard that law. Today, there are six major and several minor Dubai syndicates in the traffic.

It is easy to obtain a share in a smuggling venture in Dubai, Mr. Osman, for instance, did not have a dhow of his own. He held a piece of a $35,000 craft in conjunction with a dozen other citizens of the town.

Syndicates spread risks by selling shares for a season to anybody with cash. A season starts in September. Summer monsoons in the Indian Ocean are a hazard to the dhows, so the season usually ends in June. A minimum of about $800 is required as an investment from an individual investor.

"I like to gamble a few thousand bucks every season," said one husky American oil drill rigger who worked on a Continental Oil Company offshore rig. "I average a 30 percent return, which isn't so bad . . . better than I've been doing in the American stock market."

There are no stock shares or written commitments of any kind for an investor in this business. Still, most Dubai smugglers not only have bank accounts in Switzerland or Beirut, they are honest . . . well, relatively. Their accounting is within reasonable distance of truth. So shares are sold as casually as a broker sells shares of General Motors. There are some differences. Instead of a fancy certificate, an investor receives a handshake and perhaps a cup of heavily sugared cardamom coffee. The transaction is filed in the head of the syndicate chief.

Settlements are made in cash at the end of the season. Quarterly reports are given verbally. There may be an interim report sadly detailing that the Syndicate's dhow has been confiscated by Indian Customs. Risks certainly exceed any of the economic dangers faced by an investor on Wall Street.

Dubai operators load their gold into smugglers' jackets for ease of handling. Such a jacket looks much like the hunting vest of a hunter who carries much ammunition. Dozens of pockets snugly take ten-tolas bars. A husky smuggler may carry as much as $50,000 worth of gold hidden in a jacket. And a jacket may be used like a mail sack when not being worn.

Once the gold is loaded aboard, the dhow's seven-man crew takes stations. The anchor is hoisted. The vessel slips past Dubai's Customs Shed toward the open Persian Gulf and a 1,200-mile journey to India.

Dhows cruise at about ten knots to avoid attracting the attention of passing ships. By prearrangement, the vessel meets a fishing boat from a village along India's western shore. Messenger couriers travel back and forth on B.O.A.C. flights between Dubai and India, providing the communications links.

Seamen lash the boats together. The heavy, gold-laden jackets are quickly passed from dhow to fishing craft. Any backhaul traffic, such as silver bars, is transferred to the dhow. Then, vessels separate. The dhow departs quickly, perhaps with the crew getting nothing more than the rich humus smell of that Indian coastline.

If the rendezvous is disturbed by a sudden visit of a Coast Guard vessel, the gold goes over the side in the jackets. Since gold is 70 percent heavier than lead, jackets disappear as soon as plunked into the water. Boats separate and skippers hope to out-talk Customs investigators. And the fishing boat's captain will carefully note the position. At a later date, divers will descend to pick up the gold.

With the gold safely aboard, either through an undisturbed rendezvous, or through a salvaging operation, the Indian fishing boat swings leisurely toward that lush, humid coast where green vegetation and swaying palms crowd the shore. Shortly, the gold disappears into populous India.

In distant Switzerland, telex machines click. Telephones ring in gold dealing rooms. Fresh orders arrive. And gold profits mount for Swiss banks.

The typical Swiss banker is apt to smile tolerantly when talking to an American about gold. The banker knows that the average American has little understanding of it. Ever since March, 1933, the U.S. has been off the gold standard, its citizens forbidden to hoard the metal. Today, most Americans are easily persuaded that gold is a useless metal of little consequence in the economic sphere.

Yet all attempts to downgrade gold have foundered on the metaphysical altar that gold hoarders have erected in their minds. Swiss bankers have unquestionably helped to keep alive the religion of gold.

"If you want a ton, or two tons or three tons, we can deliver it to you," said G. Pelli, a director of Swiss Bank Corp., who headed this bank's gold operations for twenty years from his Paradeplatz office in central Zurich. Sitting at a desk where a poinsettia plant bloomed beside an intercom set, he emphasized that Swiss Bank Corp. is the leading gold seller.

In Zurich, Basle, Geneva, or any other Swiss city, gold glitters in prominent window displays of banks. In the lobby of Union Bank of Switzerland in Zurich, eight sizes of gold bars were exhibited in a case. Smallest was the size of a postage stamp. The largest, weighing 2.2 pounds, was the size of a bar of laundry soap.

At a counter, a clerk tabulated the amount due on a travelers check. Noting the visitor's interest in gold, he asked: "Do you want to buy some coins or bars?"

He asked the question in English, having already noted the American passport. Before the visitor could respond, the clerk said: "Of course, you know Americans aren't allowed by their government to hold gold."

"Oh," said the visitor, as if disappointed.

"Do you want to buy some gold?" the clerk asked again.

"But you said you couldn't sell me any."

"No." The clerk shook his head. "It is bank policy to warn every American about America's regulations. If you then want to buy gold, we will sell you all you want."

"Not today," the visitor said. "But suppose I wanted to buy some bars and store them in the bank?"

"Very simple," said the clerk. "You pay only the free market price of the gold, no commission, and then you will have a storage charge, a dollar and a quarter a year for every thousand dollars of gold stored. But since you are an American, you will have to store your gold in a safe deposit box yourself."

"Oh," said the American. "So officially the bank will not be holding any gold for an American."

"Something like that," the clerk said. He picked up a one-hundred-gram bar priced at 780 Swiss francs or $206.35 that day. "This size is popular for Christmas presents. It makes a nice toy."

An expensive toy, perhaps. But, then, Switzerland is a prosperous country, like where you might receive a gold bar in your
Christmas stocking. Still, the average Swiss citizen values an
interest return too much to invest in gold. Gold in bar form is
a plaything to be collected as conversation pieces, or as paper-
weights on desks.

In one economic study for Charter Consolidated Ltd., London-based mining house, chief economist Luc Smets wrote:
"Gold is really the most romantic of research topics and de-
serves better than to be considered purely in statistical terms."

Gold can kindle the imaginations of many people besides
certain economists. There is a mystique about gold which is
difficult for the rational mind to grasp, for the rational mind
usually is incapable of lavishing affection on mere metal.

Because of its durability and high value in small size, gold
makes a convenient monetary metal. Over the centuries, more
than one hundred and fifty substances, animal, mineral, and
vegetable, have been used for money. None performed the function as well as gold.

Gold remains in monetary use to this day, though many
nations, including the United States, no longer mint coins or
allow citizens to hold gold, except in coin collections. Gold's
role in coinage is being steadily reduced because there isn't
enough gold in the world to meet all demands.

But gold remains as the standard of value against which
most currencies are measured. Until August 15, 1971, the U.S.
dollar was equivalent to 1/35 of an ounce of gold, and it was
common to claim that "the dollar is as good as gold." That claim
is no longer true.

Gold's value is the price that men put on it. The free market
rates its value well above the monetary price.

"The idea that gold's monetary role can be abolished by
gentlemen sitting in Basle or Washington would therefore be
liable to be treated by the peasant gold hoarder with a certain
skepticism," says Charter Consolidated's Luc Smets.

It is not only the peasant who hoards gold. In banks in
Switzerland, one encounters well-dressed businessmen buying
gold, usually for deposit in the bank, though they may occasionally depart with gold bars tucked into briefcases.

The rationale of the hoarder is difficult for most Americans to understand. But, then, as violent as America sometimes seems, it is an oasis of peace compared to most of the world. During political upheavals overseas, often paper money has become worthless. Only gold, in coin or bar form, was acceptable for food, for transportation, or for the bribes which saved lives.

When White Russians fled from Russia in 1917, those with gold coins or bars hidden in luggage had capital for fresh starts. Those with Czarist paper money had nothing. Two world wars left Germans destitute, except for holders of gold. France, too, has had upheavals which weakened faith in paper money.

In a small sidewalk café in Paris near the Grecian-styled Bourse, one French stockbroker recently expounded his theories about gold during a trading break on the exchange. Paris traffic flowed by on the rue Notre Dame des Victoires with the angry hum of an ill-tempered city on the move. Patrons of the café sat like spectators at a circus, idly watching human conflicts developing from the vehicular plot.

The broker lifted his glass of Beaujolais, studied its ruby color for a moment, then said: "There is a fascination about gold. . . . " He paused, noticed that his companion had commenced scrawling notes on a pad. He grinned, tolerantly, then added: "*Oui.* A gold hoarder am I. I have a few bars. It is my insurance for that time when francs again may be only paper."

This gentleman has a lot of company. Citizens of no other nation in Europe hoard gold as avidly as do Frenchmen. Nearly everybody has a few gold coins hidden behind picture frames, in wall partitions, or in other nooks. France has had sixteen devaluations of its currency since 1914. In that time, the franc's value has been slashed and slashed again until the modern franc is worth only 1/300 of its 1914 value. No wonder that Frenchmen have around $6 billion in their gold hoards.

As for that interest which might be lost when hoarding gold? One Frenchman answers: "What matter the interest if that interest comes back in worthless paper?"

Germans are more hardheaded than the French, yet Germans have over $1.5 billion in safe deposit boxes, much of it in gold coins.

Many an American may look derisively at those hidden hoards. Why not invest in stocks, or something else which pays a return, he may ask? To which the hoarder asks: How valuable would that stock be if bombs leveled all the plants represented in that equity?

Even some Americans have been hoarding gold lately, despite regulations against it.

Sometimes it is difficult to separate the gold speculator from the gold hoarder. Generally, a hoarder is one who buys gold as a defensive measure against wars and currency upheavals. A speculator is a short-term operator who buys gold in anticipation of a profit from a price rise.

Speculation reached a peak in late 1967 and early 1968 after the British pound sterling had been devalued. Speculators broke the London Gold Pool.

Collapse of that gold pool neatly shifted the gold trade focus from London to Zurich, directly into the hands of Swiss banks. For years, the London Gold Market had controlled the release of the non-Communist world's annual 1,000 to 1,300 metric tons of newly mined gold. The United States, Britain, and other major industrial nations operated a gold pool through the Bank of England to hold the price of gold at $35 an ounce, plus insurance and handling charges.

The price fluctuated in a narrow range, between $35.08 and $35.20 an ounce. As the price would climb, the Bank of England would release more gold onto the market to drive the price down. When the price fell toward $35 an ounce, gold would be withheld from the market to push the price up.

It was a clever, well-managed system which seemed to guarantee a perpetual price of just over $35 an ounce, with commissions. Then came the pound devaluation in November, 1967. Worried speculators rushed to buy gold. Nations in the gold pool fed their gold to the London market to hold down the price. Demand soared to twenty tons a day from a normal one or two tons. From the fall of 1967 to the spring of 1968, speculators bought almost $3 billion worth of gold. That included all of the world's new production plus about $2 billion which was siphoned from treasuries of major nations, including the U.S.

In March, 1968, representatives of major nations voted in Washington to end the gold pool. Henceforth, the free gold price was to be allowed to float in the market, with market forces establishing its level. The monetary price was to remain at $35 an ounce.

Up to this time, London gold traders dominated the market. Swiss saw the collapse of the gold pool as a chance to seize that domination. Big Three banks organized their own pool, tapped South Africa for a supply of gold, and kept a gold market going while the London market was suspended.

On the Monday following establishment of the two-tier gold market, Swiss fixed the free price at $43 to $45 an ounce. Under the pool arrangement, South African gold was purchased as a bloc, but each bank handled its sales individually.

Swiss banks wildly misjudged the market with that price. Full details of this misjudgment are shrouded under that Swiss bank secrecy which conceals bank operations when the truth might be embarrassing. But sources in Johannesburg report that Swiss banks contracted to purchase substantial quantities of gold at $40 to $41 an ounce.

In subsequent weeks, the Zurich free market price fell to as low as $37 an ounce. There were some sad bankers in Switzerland for awhile. But if the initial attempt to seize the world's gold leadership proved disappointing, and expensive, today there are few regrets.

"Now, about 60 to 70 percent of the world's gold trade is handled in Zurich," Swiss Bank Corp.'s Mr. Pelli categorically claimed in one interview.

If a gold buyer worries about putting his money into an investment which returns no income, Swiss bankers have a suggestion: buy the gold, get a loan on it, and invest the money in an asset which does pay a return. "There's no better collateral for a loan than gold," admitted one Basle banker. While the client's credit rating determines the margin, some banks will loan a customer up to 70 percent of the value of the gold.

Then there are futures contracts, a favored speculative route for the man who has a hunch that the gold price may be higher in a month, three months, or six months. The price of a futures contract is the spot price of the gold plus the going interest for the length of the contract. The buyer puts up a percentage of that total price as his margin. Often this is 30 percent. Thus, a man purchasing $1,200 worth of gold at $60 an ounce would receive twenty ounces to his credit and would pay $360, plus interest, for the term of his contract. He would not take physical possession, receiving only a receipt.

If the gold's price rises, the speculator collects the gain. If the price drops by 30 percent, the investor loses his money. In this case, if the price jumped to $70, the speculator could sell for $1,400, receiving a profit of $200 minus interest.

If the speculator or hoarder tires of gold bars, there's always the gold coin market to consider, another area where Swiss bankers are experts. But whether speculating or hoarding, or merely buying a coin for a numismatics collection, the buyer had better beware of counterfeits.

CHAPTER V

COINS

In an alley shop in Milan, Italy, a worker placed a glistening flan, or flat disk of gold, onto the die of a hydraulic press. He touched a lever. The machine emitted a wheeze, slammed hard, and a United States $10 gold piece appeared beneath the hammer.

The United States hasn't minted any gold pieces since 1933, and is unlikely to do so ever again. But unscrupulous forgers mint fake gold coins of their own to sell to collectors. The $10 coins are of the same 900 parts gold and 15.04 grams weight as the real thing. However, they lack that patina of age and authenticity which gives a numismatic coin a value many times its metal content. Passed as the real thing, this particular coin would sell for about $70, triple its gold value.

"A counterfeiter would be a fool to reduce the gold content in a fake, for it then would be too easy for a buyer to detect the fraud," said Otto Breithaupt, manager of Swiss Credit Bank's Monetarium, or money shop, in Zurich. Breithaupt is a forty-year veteran with the bank who can still sound youthfully enthusiastic when discussing coins. But he was serious when he talked of counterfeiting. The problem is especially bothersome to Swiss bankers. Zurich claims to be the center of the world's coin market.

The coin business is much more than a matter of small change. This is especially true when coins happen to be rare Roman denarii, or something equally scarce. Zurich not only deals in numismatic coins, it also caters to hoarders who treasure gold coins as a financial hedge.

"Coins always have been an important part of banking in Switzerland," said Ernst Bigler, manager of gold and foreign exchange at Swiss Credit Bank. "Zurich is by far the world leader in this field."

"And," added another Zurich banker, "nobody is bigger than Bank Leu in the coin field."

Swiss Credit's business is large enough to sustain a separate Monetarium on a side street behind the bank's headquarters. Ancient coins of the Roman Empire are displayed behind thick glass windows facing the street. Inside, buyers may browse through case after case of rare coins under the watchful eyes of clerks.

"Anyone who collects coins should patronize only those banks and dealers who are known to be reputable," said Breithaupt. He wiped his hornrimmed glasses, then lovingly picked up a Swiss Vreneli, carefully holding it by the edges.

"We always have a big demand for Swiss coins," he said. He pointed to an 1888 Helvetia, a coin about the size of an American quarter which had a price tag of 13,000 Sfr, or $3,380.

"In 1968, this was worth 16,000 francs ($4,116)," he explained. "Prices dropped sharply from that peak, but are coming back."

Coin prices are based on supply and demand. So there are price rises and slumps. In the long run, coin prices in general are likely to go up. But it was John Maynard Keynes who said that "in the long run, we will all be dead." There are reports in the coin field, for instance, that the Soviet Union may unload some of its museum coin hoards. If so, this could drive down prices of some coins.

In 1972, however, the price trend was up. Breithaupt explained: "Dealers and collectors are holding on to their coins. It is becoming increasingly hard to get merchandise."

Bank Leu is equally enthusiastic about the business, though in a quieter voice. The bank prides itself on discreetness.

"We don't believe in talking about ourselves to outsiders," H. Moeschinger, a manager of the bank, said by way of greeting. He had grown gray in the service of the bank, and now he had that cautious air of a man who deals all day in requests for money. Information is something that is given away heavily at Bank Leu. He did say, after some prodding, that "coins are a very important part of our business."

Endorsement came from Silvia Hurter, a slender, attractive brunette who hides behind a pair of hornrimmed glasses. She is an exception in Swiss banks, a female who holds a management position, deputy manager of the coin department.

Miss Hurter's enthusiasm overcame that bank secrecy which shrouded operations. She majored in history in school, and that interest drew her to coins. After seventeen years at the bank, she is one of Switzerland's experts in the field.

"Demand for first-class coins keeps growing on average at about 10 percent a year rate," said she. The bank's coin business is evenly divided between numismatics and serving gold hoarders. Buyers are worldwide, with West Germany and France among major buying countries.

What is the most valuable coin she has encountered? She mentioned a Syracuse 400 B.C. tetradrachma which sold for $15,-000. She said: "Old Greek coins in good condition are rare, and always bring good prices."

Swiss coin experts differentiate between coin collectors and hoarders. There are purists, too, who insist that medallion collecting is not part of numismatics. The purist also claims that any coin minted for collectors is not worth saving. To them, numismatics consists of collecting coins which were minted for circulation. Most valuable are those which never circulated, even though minted for that purpose. This would seem to outlaw those attractive gold coins sometimes minted by emerging nations.

Such distinctions may not appeal to some coin collectors. Still, a collector should be aware of the strictures suggested by purists.

The average Swiss is a pragmatist who seldoms gives play to imagination. Yet, the true coin collector is a romanticist at heart, and one finds Swiss coin experts to be historians, literary scholars, archaeologists, and dilettante poets.

"It is all right to be romantic about money, when the romanticism is confined to the viewing rather than to the investing of money," one Swiss coin expert said.

He then provided a capsule history of the Greek drachma as he displayed a case of them.

He could become rapturous about an authentic coin. When he showed a badly worn denarius from the Roman Republic of 100 B.C., he explained that the coin was in use in the time of Lucius Accius. A dim phrase of Accius' in a long forgotten Latin exercise came to mind: *"Oderint, dum metuant."* (Let them hate, so long as they fear.) This was the motto of the Roman legionnaires as they conquered and held most of the known world of their day.

That particular denarius had a price tag of Sfr 130 or about $33.80. Another denarius minted in the 54–51 B.C. period under Julius Caesar sold for Sfr 220 or about $57.20.

Numismatics was a popular hobby among nobles of the Renaissance. Their collections preserved many coins of earlier epochs. Some of the popes cherished coins. Italian noblemen in the city-states of the thirteenth, fourteenth, and fifteenth centuries coupled coin collecting with accumulating archaeological artifacts. Wealthy citizens of Florence, Venice, Sienna, and other cities assembled statues and art works of Greece and Rome; they also treasured the denarii, the dupondii, and other coins of ancient days.

Indeed, numismatics started as a branch of archaeology, with emphasis on the collecting of coins of an earlier era. Little attention was paid to current coins during most of the history of numismatics.

"Coins in circulation aren't of much use to serious collectors," one Zurich coin dealer said. He illustrated with an anecdote from a coin buying trip to New York a few years ago.

One day, an elderly American arrived at the dealer's hotel

with a coffee can full of Indian-head pennies dating back to the nineteenth century. The American had been collecting them for years.

"The fellow rattled those coins in the can as if he had something of value," the dealer said. "He didn't even realize that rubbing one coin against another reduces their value. Keeping them in a can is about like storing fresh eggs in the sun."

Collecting pennies may be a satisfying hobby for some people. Collecting low-value coins seldom will make anyone rich. Most of the American coins contained in catalogues of Swiss bank coin departments are 1-, 2 1/2-, 5-, 10-, and 20-dollar gold pieces. An 1839 Liberty-head $10 gold piece, for instance, in only ordinary condition, had a price tag of $1,725.

Swiss have a penchant for categorizing men and things, placing them in neat pigeonholes. They do this when talking about coin collectors, too. They not only divide collectors into hoarders and numismatists, they separate the latter into technicians and scholars. The technician becomes an expert on mint marks, years of issue, and peculiarities of design. The scholar views a coin as an archaeological relic, a tiny piece of metal which probably bears the image of the ruler at a particular period.

Some Swiss banks encourage historical study to stimulate the collecting of coins. Swiss Credit Bank, in one coin report, says: "With a mastery of the ancient Greek alphabet, which can be achieved quite quickly with practice, it becomes simple to determine the origin and value of an antique Greek coin."

But what makes a coin valuable? Why is a Roman aureus of A.D. 177 worth Sfr 8,000, while an older aureus minted in A.D. 134 is worth Sfr 4,100?

Design is important. Some coins simply are more attractive than others. Certain coins develop personalities, too. The U.S. Kennedy silver half-dollar is an example. In 1972, these sold in Switzerland for 75 cents to $1.25 each.

"This reflects the charisma which your president John Kennedy exerted over people," said one Swiss dealer. "When John F. Kennedy's memory fades, will this adversely affect demand for the half-dollars?" The silver content also adds to value.

The rarer a coin, the better the price, all other factors being equal. A British Edward VIII three-pence piece is worth $3,000 or more. These coins were minted in 1936. But Edward Windsor abdicated the throne "for the woman I love" before coins were released. A few did escape from the mint and these have become collectors' items.

Numerous coin catalogues are available to describe various coins, giving collectors some ideas of their worth. Record books show the number of coins minted in specific years. There were only 10,000 Swiss one-rappen pieces minted in 1939, for instance, whereas 5.3 million were minted in 1938. Rarity means the 1939 rappens have price tags twenty to forty times those of the heavy mint year.

The condition of a coin is important. Amateurs may conclude that any old coin is worth a small fortune merely because it is old. This is not necessarily so. An old, worn coin may have to be rare, indeed, to be worth much.

Coin collectors and dealers have a euphemistic system of designating the condition of coins in their catalogues. They start with superlatives for the poorest condition, then continue in six or more stages in about the way the French rate their hotels (i.e. first class is a dump; deluxe means passable; super deluxe is comfortable).

The six classes usually found in coin books are:

Proof	Proof
Fleur de coin, or Brilliant Uncirculated	FDC or BU
Uncirculated	Unc.
Extra Fine	EF
Very Fine	VF
Fine	F

Proof means these are specially minted coins struck from dies with a highly polished surface. These are very rare, and hence rate the highest prices. *Fleur de coin*, or Brilliant Uncirculated, is the top condition for a coin which has been minted to circulate.

Uncirculated coins are just that, coins which have been taken up by collectors before being allowed to slip into the coinage stream. Extra Fine signifies that the coin has a slight blemish or sign of wear. Very Fine isn't as good as it sounds.

Such a coin betrays wear, and serious numismatists seldom like to drop to this level when purchasing coins for their collections. Fine signifies a well-worn coin. Sometimes classifications continue down to Very Good (VG) and Good (G). Really these should be classed as bad and very bad.

Numismatists obtain coins through established dealers, coin auctions, antique dealers, banks, and other collectors. Bank Leu, for instance, holds coin auctions twice a year.

While banks may give guarantees with numismatic pieces, this no longer is so with gold coins. Banks are afraid that an unscrupulous buyer may take a guarantee with the bona fide coin, depart, then return shortly with a fake, claiming he has been gypped. There is no way to differentiate between gold coins, for coins are unnumbered.

Dr. H. R. Wuffli, a general manager of Swiss Credit Bank, suggested that gold coins be purchased, then left with the bank as are most stock certificates. "Coins would never leave the bank's possession," he explained. "So when the client wanted to resell them, the bank would have to pay the market price for the genuine coin. There would be no question of fakes."

This system answers the problem for the coin investor or hoarder. It does not serve for a coin collector who wants to add a gold piece to his collection. Most of the joy of a collection lies in studying the various coins in it.

For the numismatist, it is *buyer beware* when dealing in gold coins. As long ago as the mid-seventeenth century, Thomas Fuller said: "Men have a touchstone whereby to try gold, but gold is the touchstone whereby to try men."

Human nature hasn't changed much since he said that.

But even as Swiss banks worry about the vexing matter of coin counterfeiting, they have another problem on their hands, a foreign invasion which brings competition to their front doors.

THE FOREIGN INVASION

When John Van Stirum, a twenty-year veteran of Dow Chemical Co.'s financial department, first proposed in 1965 that the
company enter the banking business in Switzerland, there were
gasps of amazement. Dow, a long-established $2 billion sales
chemical company, go into banking? And in Switzerland, the
home of the Gnomes of Zurich? It didn't seem to make sense.
As the banking project materialized, skeptics waggishly named
it Van Stirum's Folly.

Today Dow Banking Corporation is a thriving operation
located in a modern glass and steel building at Bahnhofstrasse
24 in Zurich. Assets totaled nearly $300 million at end of 1971, a
21 percent increase over the year earlier level. Depositors include

so many other banks that Van Stirum terms the facility a bankers' bank. Customers include numerous multinational American companies.

If Dow Bank were geared to the needs of the parent, there would not be anything extraordinary about it. But it isn't a house bank at all. It is a full-fledged bank geared to service other corporations.

Van Stirum's office is in a corner of the bank, half-shielded by a row of artificial rubber plants which provide a garden touch. Proudly he said, "Other American companies have seen our success and are trying to emulate us with banks of their own."

He is a tall man, with thin, rather saturnine features who greets visitors with a hearty manner, as if they might be potential depositors. Even when he finds they are not, the friendliness remains. You realize immediately that this is not a Swiss bank, though it is located on Bahnhofstrasse. It is as American as Sinclair Lewis's Main Street.

It isn't surprising that big American banks like Chase Manhattan or Bank of America have branches in Switzerland. They are in the overseas wave of multinational American companies. At the start of 1972, American corporations had over $85 billion invested in plants, refineries, warehouses, and other production facilities abroad, about $27 billion in Western Europe.

Corporations have a continual need for funds to expand and for working capital. They need bank assistance overseas, the same as they do in America. So, today, American banks, branches and subsidiaries, are found in Japan, Brazil, England, and over two score other countries. On January 1, 1972, there were thirteen American banks operating in Switzerland. In addition, there were several small banks unconnected with any America-based institutions, which were predominantly American owned.

Banks with branches in Switzerland were: First National City Bank, New York; Bank of America, San Francisco; Chemical Bank, New York; Morgan Guaranty Trust Co., New York; First National Bank, Chicago; and American Express, New York. Seattle–First National Bank, Seattle; and Bankers Trust and Chase Manhattan, New York, have subsidiaries. All told, at the start of 1972, there were one hundred foreign-owned banks in Switzerland, eighty-six of them subsidiaries and fourteen branches of foreign banks.

Dow Bank is of a special breed among those one hundred. It is a multinational industrial company which has ventured successfully into European merchant banking. Others of this breed are Bank Firestone Ltd., Zurich, which is 100 percent owned by Firestone Tire and Rubber Co., Akron, Ohio; Trans-interbank, Geneva, which is owned by Cummins Engine Co., Columbus, Indiana; and the Bank for Investment and Credit Ltd., or BANKINVEST, Zurich.

Shareholders of the latter are: Boeing Co., Seattle, Wash.; C. T. Bowring & Co., Ltd., and Brown & Root Overseas Ltd., London; Capital National Corp., and Gray Tool Company, Houston, Texas; Cooper-Bessemer of Canada, Ltd., Stratford, Canada; the Royal Trust Co., and Distillers Corporation-Seagrams Ltd., Montreal; N. V. Maastrust, Rotterdam, Holland; and Minute Maid S. A., Zurich, subsidiary of Coca-Cola Corp.

Switzerland's juiciest bank scandals over the last decade have involved foreign banks, which is one reason why Swiss dislike the foreign invasion. Some years ago, two banks controlled by the Spanish financier Julio Muñoz folded with a particularly loud crash. Strands reached into the Swiss Banking Commission. After the banks collapsed, it was learned that Max Hommel, the president of the Swiss Banking Commission, had been financial adviser to Señor Muñoz. This wasn't illegal, but Hommel tried to conceal the connection.

This wasn't considered quite proper, and Hommel was forced to resign.

"Four-fifths of the irregularities which the Federal Banking Commission had to deal with in recent years concerned foreign banks," said Heinz Portmann, economic editor of the *Neue Zürcher Zeitung*, in an article contributed to *The Banker*, a London-based magazine.

Obviously, foreigners may bank with any Swiss bank. But many people outside Switzerland like to bank with someone of their own nationality, for language and other reasons. Arabs may like to bank with an Arab bank in Switzerland. Latin Americans may like to bank with Latin Americans. So, you have the foreign bank in Switzerland. Most have high standards. Still, there have been scandals, and the aggressiveness of these banks irks Swiss.

Chairman F. W. Schulthess of the Swiss Credit Bank, told the 1971 stockholders' meeting: "It would be reasonable on the part of foreign banks to show a measure of restraint. It seems to me that these bounds have been overstepped, since what has happened in the course of years looks almost like an invasion."

He added: "It is desirable that these foreign banks should adapt themselves to the Swiss environment, and that, as regards competition, they should keep within those limits that are well befitting a foreign guest."

Swiss banks aren't afraid of competition. They just don't like it to be too sharp. Swiss banks have gentlemen's agreements among themselves limiting competition. If businessmen must cut each other's throats, they should do it like gentlemen. But foreigners come to Switzerland as bankers and they insist on behaving like foreigners. This the Swiss find difficult to accept.

Dow started operations in July, 1965, in a two-room office with a $23 million investment. Van Stirum was the general manager, backed strongly by Carl A. Gerstacker, Dow Chemical's chairman. A bank charter in Switzerland, of course, is universal. So Dow could go into all branches of banking. There's one thing American banks can't do, though, without permission from the U.S. Treasury. That is deal in gold. This is no inconvenience at all for Dow Bank.

Van Stirum was well fitted to launch a bank from scratch even in this citadel of banking. A native of Cambridge, Massachusetts, he started his business career with Chase Manhattan Bank in New York. He served five years in the U.S. Army in Europe in World War II. Then came service in the state department, as deputy financial adviser to John J. McCloy, U.S. High Commissioner for Germany, and as senior economic adviser to General Maxwell D. Taylor in Berlin. He joined Dow Chemical in 1953.

Dow moved abroad in the 1950's and 1960's. Its chemical complexes sprouted on flat fields of Holland, near the heel of Italy at Livorno, in Chile, Germany, France, Mexico, Australia, and elsewhere. Dow plastics and chemicals found ready markets. Foreign business boomed to the point where sales volume outside the U.S. about equaled that in the U.S.

"Overseas expansion has become a way of life for American business," said Robert B. Bennett, treasurer of the company. "But European finance is relatively new to all of us. We now have to make decisions in European money markets with different currencies, interest rates, exchange controls, credit ceilings, tax problems, and lending practices."

Dow gained experience in the field. As it did so, it found other corporations, many of them Dow customers, trekking to Midland, Michigan, to analyze why Dow was doing so well abroad. Van Stirum thought that a Swiss-based bank would better enable Dow to serve some of these customers.

"It became evident that American companies new to the European scene needed assistance," explained Van Stirum. "We identified an emerging need and thought we had the competence to satisfy it. Off we went to Switzerland to build a new kind of international merchant bank based on the ever growing eurodollar market."

Initial reaction of Swiss bankers and authorities was cool. What did this chemical company know about banking? Was this the gimmick of a big company to assure a stream of low cost funds for itself? Wouldn't it be competing directly with established Swiss banks which had been in business for decades?

In Switzerland, wags used to say that it was easier to open a bank than a barber shop. It's not true anymore. But, there already are those one hundred foreign banks solidly entrenched in Switzerland. The number might have been larger were it not for the spectacular crashes of a couple of those foreign banks. These, plus the shenanigans of certain other foreign banks, have prompted Swiss to become decidedly selective in the granting of charters to open new banks, where outsiders are concerned. And it isn't only legislation which affects operations of a foreign bank in Switzerland.

Swiss bankers do have a clubmen's camaraderie. They can express their hostility in various ways if a nonmember of the club seems to be dirtying the carpet, moving the furniture about in an unwanted manner, or making too much noise.

"We patiently explained that we did not intend to establish

a house bank." said Van Stirum. "Then, the hostility changed to puzzlement. They couldn't figure out what sort of animal we intended to be."

The "animal" is an American-managed eurobank, which tries to offer service: on a European or even worldwide basis.

Treasurer Bennett of Dow Chemical spotlights the frustration sometimes encountered by American multinational companies. Said he: "In France, we get a French answer to a French problem, in Italy an Italian answer to an Italian problem, and so on in a dozen countries. To an international treasurer, a still-fragmented Europe can be frustrating. We at Dow Bank give an answer to a total European problem because, from our own experience at Dow, we understand the complexities of operating throughout Europe."

Dow tried to fill the banking gap which existed. It sought other banks and corporations as depositors. It focused on euro-dollars. It stressed three-to-five-year financing.

"We knew the eurodollar market was growing. We had no idea that it would grow as fast as it did," said Van Stirum. He picked up a graph from his desk showing a steeply ascending curve, then added: "Our bank has grown right along with the expansion of the eurodollar market."

The bank added a branch in Amsterdam, then another in London. Representative offices are in New York City and San Francisco. A joint subsidiary, Eurocapital S.A., was established in Luxembourg to underwrite euro securities. Partner is Eurofinance, Paris.

Dow Bank's report to directors in March, 1972, said of the preceding year: "Amid dramatic events on the international monetary scene, culminating with the suspension of dollar convertibility in August and the realignment of currency values in December, Dow Banking Corporation continued to expand profitably in 1971."

Deposits reached Sfr 951 million (nearly $250 million). Total assets amounted to $300 million. Loans and discounts outstanding on December 31, 1971, stood at Sfr 621 million ($161.4 million), a 12 percent increase in the year.

Customers ranged across a broad spectrum. A British firm sought guidance on financing a Continental expansion despite

United Kingdom exchange restrictions. A Dutch exporter financed sales in Yugoslavia. An American corporation, facing financial troubles because of U.S. foreign direct investment regulations, obtained off-shore financing at Dow Bank. A Japanese bank was helped to swing a loan in Swiss francs for one of their corporate clients.

Dr. Baard R. Stokke, a slender, zestful economist in his early thirties, outlined bank services. Among them:

—Planning for and developing European sales and investment opportunities.

—Legal and fiscal structuring for multinational operations.

—Identification, evaluation, and negotiation for acquisitions, joint ventures, and disposition of companies or major capital items.

—Euromarket financing.

Firestone followed Dow. Bank Firestone, Ltd. started in a modern building in Zurich in April, 1971. Kishore M. Premchand, chairman, admitted that Dow's success stimulated the move. Bank Firestone's assets soared from $1.8 million at the start to $25 million at the end of 1971. In that truncated first year, profit was $540,000.

The facility is 100 percent owned by Firestone Tire & Rubber Co., the Akron, Ohio, giant. Firestone has been an international company for decades. Its worldwide operations provide a wealth of informational data which can be used in banking, said Premchand. With Firestone knowledge, and sometimes the suggestions of overseas people, the bank is in position to advise customers in many ways. Recently, it helped a European specialized instrument maker to close a barter deal for the sale of company products in India. In another transaction, the bank helped a company to launch a manufacturing operation in Southeast Asia, an area where Firestone has had long business connections.

Premchand emphasized: "Our business is not limited to serving the parent company, but in providing a wide range of banking services to individuals and to corporate clients."

H. J. Keller, managing director of BANKINVEST, admitted that it is odd to find a bank in Switzerland which has such diverse owners as a subsidiary of Coca Cola Corp., Boeing Aircraft, and others. Still, all of these companies have far-flung international interests, either through subsidiaries or through sales abroad.

Explained Keller, "We conceived this bank as a vehicle which shareholders could use, but not exclusively."

Originally the bank was opened in Berne, then transferred to Zurich in May, 1971. In January, 1972, it was licensed to buy and sell securities. Operations are geared to helping corporations locate in the European market, to analyzing their markets, to investigating joint ventures for them, and to engaging in similar activities.

In recent years another approach to corporate servicing has been taken by banks in Europe. Some banks have joined with American institutions to form consortia and joint ventures which aim at providing customers with multinational as well as domestic services. In London, there is the Orion Banking Group, which includes Chase Manhattan Bank, Credito Italiano, National Westminster Bank, Royal Bank of Canada, Mitsubishi Bank. and Westdeutsche Landesbank Girozentrale. The Midland and International Banks, Ltd., also London based, joins Midland Bank Ltd., Standard Bank Ltd., the Toronto-Dominion Bank, and the Commercial Bank of Australia Ltd. The World Banking Corp., Ltd., Nassau, is owned by Bank of America, Banque Lambert, Commerzbank, Toronto-Dominion Bank, Banque Nationale de Paris, F. van Lanschot Bankers, and Skandinaviska Enskilda Banken.

Several dozen more examples might be cited. Some focus attention on the quick assembly of eurodollar or eurocurrency credit packages. Others provide a broad line of financial services to multinational customers, offering one-shop facilities to a client who might otherwise require two or more transactions in different countries.

Big Swiss banks have held aloof from such consortia. In his report to stockholders in March, 1972, Union Bank's Schaefer noted the trend. Then he cautioned against believing that it offered some universal panacea. Said he: "Lasting solutions in this somewhat turbulent period characterized by the formation of numerous new groups have not yet surfaced, and owing to their *sui generis* position, Switzerland's big banks would be well advised not to follow any fixed pattern of group formation. Swiss bankers are both international managers of capital as well as credit merchants. Clients want to deal directly with them, and to make use of their expertise as well as their freely operating money and capital markets."

He added: "Such clients are not interested in doing business with mere components of international conglomerates, which in many cases overlap and have led to overbanked situations as well as to disappointment in the wake of high-flown expectations, especially on the euromarket."

Dr. E. Reinhardt, chief general manager of Swiss Credit Bank, said: "We have chosen in recent years not to opt for the founding of foreign branches." He added that "We do not in principle function as a bank of deposit in other countries. The collection of savings flowing from thousands of small channels and the redistribution of these savings to thousands of small users is carried out by the large Swiss banks only on their home territory."

Abroad, Swiss Credit uses correspondents, said Dr. Reinhardt, thus avoiding "a direct competitive struggle with the banks of these other countries and maintaining with them friendly relations which often lead to mutually profitable business."

This doesn't apply to those banks which open operations in Switzerland to compete with Swiss Credit at home. Said Dr. Reinhardt, "We naturally exercise a certain restraint toward those banking houses which compete with us for traditional kinds of business on Swiss soil."

Meanwhile, the foreign invasion of Switzerland in the banking field continues almost without interruption. And banks have been joined by American brokerage firms. Some of the latter, it is true, have been here for years. Others have opened offices recently. Those around awhile include Merrill Lynch, Bache & Co., Shearson Hammill, Dean Witter, White Weld, Smith Barney, First Boston, and others.

Chase Manhattan Bank (Switzerland) is found at 118 rue du Rhône in Geneva, in a section where banks are almost side by side for several blocks. Wander inside and a piece of literature on a counter attracts attention. One page says: "Chase has teams of bankers in offices throughout Europe, linked together in a multinational banking system called Chase Network Europe. This system can help you get the competitive edge you need in this prosperous, rapidly-expanding area. When you want to finance on a multinational scale throughout Europe, Chase Network Europe can tell you where to finance to meet your needs. How to finance. And when."

First National City Bank, Chase's competitor, has four branches in Switzerland. They are at 16–18 Quai Général Guisan, Geneva; at 43 rue de Bourg, Lausanne; at St.-Peter Str. 16/Bahnhofstrasse, Zurich; and at 9 Corso Pestalozzi, Lugano.

"We have more coins in more fountains than any other bank in the world," First National City proudly boasts.

Not only are American banks carrying cash to Newcastle by coming to Switzerland, they're also dumping coins in the fountains. If you don't find any of those coins on your next trip to Europe, at least you can find Bank of America's man-on-the-spot at Börsenstrasse 16 in Zurich. This fellow sure gets around with that black briefcase, which undoubtedly is stuffed with money.

At the Zurich Bank of America facility, officials emphasize that they "can provide you with everything from U.S. dollar travellers checks to import-export financing."

In addition to the banks which are allied to American parents, there are other banks in Switzerland that are owned and controlled by Americans. For example, there's the Banque Indiana Suisse in Lausanne, which is owned by Gary, Indiana, interests. It's a long way from Gary to Lausanne. The distance emphasizes the interest which Americans have been displaying in Swiss banking since about the mid-1960's when it became apparent that the U.S. dollar was slipping in world monetary society.

At Biasca, Switzerland, not far from Lugano, for instance, there's a small bank which has been allied to Tulsa, Oklahoma, interests. One source from that part of Switzerland, reported: "A lot of people in Tulsa have accounts at that bank."

There's nothing wrong with having a Swiss bank account. In fact, two would be better than one. The American citizen need only remember that any taxes due from profits of an account should be paid to Uncle Sam. For a good many decades, a lot of the world's citizens have believed that even better than just having money, is to have it in Switzerland.

What about Swiss banking secrecy for the American banks operating in Switzerland? Dow Bank reported that the Zurich head office does not accept accounts from individuals of any nationality, only from corporations and banks, and all of these are registered taxpayers. However, other banks do accept deposits from individuals.

In any case, every bank registered in Switzerland must conform to Swiss banking laws, just as any foreign bank registered in the United States must conform to American laws. The Swiss are very sensitive about their bank secrecy. Still, you can't expect to hide behind that secrecy if you attempt to defraud the U.S. government, or individuals and corporations elsewhere.

American banks have company in this foreign invasion. Over a dozen British banks have set up shop in the country. Many serve as links between the eurodollar business in London and the Continent.

Geneva is popular with British banks. The British seem to get along better with French-speaking Swiss than with German Swiss. So there is a long tradition of British banking in Geneva. Lloyds' Bank, for instance, has had a full branch in this city since 1920. It obtained the account of the League of Nations when that organization was established. Subsequently, the bank captured the account of the United Nations in Geneva, and it still services most of the U.N. people there.

Kleinwort Benson came to Geneva in 1968, buying into Banque Intra, the Swiss affiliate of a Lebanese bank which went broke in spectacular fashion. Kleinwort Benson has added its own brand of stolid English banking know-how to an operation which had been much more successful than its luckless Beirut parent. The London bank owns the British bullion firm of Sharps Pixley. So the Swiss operation provides a link for it between the London gold market and the retail gold business in Switzerland. Hill, Samuel & Co., British Bank of the Middle East, and National and Grindlays are other British banks with branches in Geneva.

Zurich has long been the Swiss home for a Swiss private

bank controlled by Samuel Montagu & Co., which is a big operator in the gold and foreign exchange fields in London. The bank
is Guyerzeller Zurmont Bank AG.

Rothschild Bank AG is affiliated with both the Paris and the
London Rothschilds. Schroders, the London merchant bank,
has a Zurich outlet. Other British banks likewise enjoy the climate and the financial advantages of doing business in Switzerland.

The coterie of foreign banks runs the gamut, including
French, Italian, Israeli, German, Scandinavian, Dutch, and
other nationalities. Geneva, for instance, always has been a favored banking location for oil-rich Mideastern sheikhs, and
there are Arab-owned banks which cater to this lucrative trade.
Arabs like the congenial atmosphere of Geneva, the gay nightlife which can be reminiscent of Beirut, and the attractive hos-
tesses who are found in such spots as the Moulin Rouge, the
Pussy Cat Saloon, the Piccadilly Club, and other of the city's
night clubs. Zurich dims its lights and rolls up its sidewalks
every night at midnight, while Basle has the night life of a
provincial town of puritan roots, which it is. Geneva's clubs are
open until 4 A.M. Years of catering to the diplomatic set has
generated a tolerant attitude toward nighttime pleasures. The
city is magnetic for young women who feel an irresistible pull
toward money, especially when it is in the hands of free-spending gentlemen.

Geneva's bankers, however, don't join in the nighttime festivities, nor do the good burghers of the city. The night life is
almost exclusively for the expatriates who work for one of the
international agencies, for a diplomatic mission, or for one of
the multinational companies headquartered in the city, or for
nonworking visitors.

No matter where the visitor comes from, he is sure to find
some bank where officials will speak his language if he has
money to deposit. Foreign banks bid as aggressively for the
business as do any of the Swiss-owned institutions.

The balance sheet totals of all foreign banks in the country
added up to about $6.7 billion at the end of 1971, according to the
Swiss Bankers' Association. That doesn't look like much when
compared with the assets held by some of the big American
banks. Those figures tell only part of the story.

Foreign banks hold portfolio accounts for customers, too. These would not appear on their balance sheets as assets of the banks. Thus, the apparently small foreign-owned bank which sits on a sidestreet in a Swiss city may have only $1 million of assets on its balance sheets, yet it may manage assets of many times that figure for its clients.

Moreover, foreign banks concentrate activities in foreign transactions. It is estimated that approximately a third of the foreign transactions of Swiss banks now are being made through foreign banks.

The Swiss Bankers' Association has watched unhappily in recent years as the foreign invasion has swept the country. Swiss bankers have cozy arrangements which restrict competition. They make voluntary agreements among themselves to set interest rates, define limits of competition and to control credit limits. Foreign banks don't always adhere to these agreements.

American banks, of course, have a reason for avoiding any rate fixing cartels in Switzerland. They have U.S. anti-trust laws to worry about.

Swiss bankers claim, too, that foreign banks aggravate the country's monetary and inflation problems. They bring unwanted money into the country in times of monetary unease, and they assist foreigners in utilizing the Swiss franc in place of their own currency.

"Our franc thus faces the danger of acquiring the status of an international currency, a role which never was intended for it," said Alfred E. Sarasin, association president, when addressing the 1971 annual meeting of the group.

In 1972, foreign banks operating in the country banded together to form the Association of Foreign Banks in Switzerland. It was established as a wing of SBA to ensure closer cooperation with Swiss.

"The foreign banks are quite aware that they are guests in Switzerland. In the majority, they try not only to act in accordance with the Swiss laws and regulations, but also to pay attention to the rules of the game that are used in Swiss banking," said Erik Gasser, manager of J. Henry Schroder Bank AG, Zurich affiliate of the London bank, and first chairman of the new group. He added: "The foreign banks know that not only as far as the other banks, but also as far as the Swiss public is concerned, a lot of public relations work has to be done to remove prejudices and to transmit the correct picture of the activity and role of the foreign banks in Switzerland."

Dr. E. Stopper, president of the Swiss National Bank, has been highly critical of the way some foreign banks advertise abroad as "Swiss banks" and sometimes transact business "in a way that is not exactly apt to enhance Switzerland's reputation."

The Swiss Banking Commission has introduced new regulations requiring foreign-controlled banks to obtain permits for new subsidiaries or branches. Provisions are reciprocal. Switzerland permits a bank to open a branch only if the home country or state of the new bank permits a Swiss bank to do likewise. Moreover, the title of the new branch in Switzerland must clearly indicate that it is foreign owned.

The spectacular failure of the United California Bank in Basle with over $50 million in losses didn't help the cause of foreign banks very much. This case will be discussed in detail in later chapters. Suffice it to say here that, today, every time the question of foreign banks arises among Swiss nationals, the UCB case is apt to be cited as a horrible example of how not to run a bank.

In the present atmosphere in Switzerland any foreign bank doing business in the country must be above suspicion. Certainly, such a bank will not bid for any domestic industrial business, for that would be regarded as the height of rudeness by the host country. Bank-to-bank transactions are acceptable.

To understand what makes a Swiss banker act and react to certain stimuli, it may be well to examine the Swiss psyche. If the Swiss banker is somewhat suspicious of foreigners, he is merely being Swiss. Bankers aren't a race apart which has been superimposed upon little Switzerland. They emerged from the same society which produced William Tell, Zwingli, cheese fondue, the *landsgemeinde* (town meeting), and the mountain railway.

CHAPTER VII

THE SWISS PSYCHE

In April, 1970, Ufitec, Zurich, a well-known international financial institution engaged in short- and medium-term financing, undertook placement of a loan issue which was to cause much handwringing among Swiss money men. The amount was for "something in the order of 250 million Swiss francs," admitted one Ufitec official. That would be about $59 million at the rate pertaining.

The issue involved Penn Central Railroad, then an ostensibly going concern which nobody in Switzerland believed was going into the ground. The deal seemed a bargain. There was no interest rate. But the privately placed notes had a price of around 91, with the railroad to pay off at 100 in eleven and a half months. (Not all the notes were placed on the same day, and the rate was geared to meet the applicable high eurodollar rates.) This apparently guaranteed a return of 9 3/4 to 10 1/4 percent.

Many Swiss banks grabbed notes, taking them for their own account or for accounts of portfolio customers. Swiss have always had a weakness for American railroad shares, and especially for the Penn Central. This was one of the first American companies to be listed on the Zurich Stock Exchange. For decades, conservative Swiss investors had been purchasing shares of American railroads with abiding loyalty.

On June 21, two months after placement of notes, the Penn Central Co. filed a bankruptcy petition for its railroad subsidiary.

In Zurich, as one banker detailed this story, he shook his head. "Everybody makes mistakes," said he. "Everybody." Then, he quoted a Swiss proverb: "Even the careful man has also tumbled downstairs."

"But why this one?" he was asked. In retrospect, it should have been apparent that Penn Central had troubles. The railroad had one of the worst winters in its history in 1969–70. Snow blocked lines. There was much overtime for snowplow crews. Maintenance costs soared. The railroad reported a 95 percent profit drop for the year 1969 from 1968. Moreover, that report came February 5, two months before the note issue.

Lamely, the banker mentioned something about the huge real estate holdings which Penn Central allegedly possessed, holdings which reportedly gave the company a book value of anywhere from $200 to $500 a share, depending upon whose glowing tale was accepted.

"You see—" the banker kept shaking his head all the while—" we Swiss have weaknesses, and one is . . . well call it investment loyalty, or tradition. Buying Penn Central seemed natural, even though the issue manager cautioned us that this was a high risk situation. We went into it with our eyes open. Nobody could even dream that the Penn Central would go bankrupt. The Penn Central, mind you!"

Swiss do have their idiosyncrasies, and they are not confined to Penn Central. They have their strengths, too, and both weaknesses and strengths are rooted in the mountains, forests, and way of life of this scenic land. To understand Swiss money men, one must know something about the Swiss character and the conditions which shape it. It is a land which cherishes its traditions, which honors experience rather than youth, which believes that good is rewarded and evil punished, which values intellectual accomplishments, which conserves everything from money to clothing purchased a decade ago, which is fascinated by things mechanical, and which is precise, hardworking, and frugal. All of these characteristics are found in varying degrees among Swiss money men.

There are paradoxes, too. Switzerland is a neutral country which hasn't been involved in war since the time of Napoleon. Nevertheless, in 1972, the cost of national defense was budgeted at 2.3 billion francs, equivalent to 24 percent of the total budget. Teenagers are encouraged to enter rifle shooting matches. These are held as casually as softball meets all over the country. A boy learns how to shoot before he learns how to dance. Gunners compete for gold medals which are prized as highly as athletic letters in an American high school.

Every able-bodied man serves in the Army reserves from twenty to fifty, joining a 650,000-man force which is one of the best militia armies in the world. Every year for years, a man spends a couple of weeks drilling with his particular unit.

Preparedness has helped keep Switzerland neutral. Swiss learned long ago that the best way to win a war is to make certain that it doesn't start. They do that by playing so hard at being soldiers, that they deter potential invaders. Swiss are convinced that "the peace of God, which passeth all understanding" is based on possessing a strong defense force. Every family in the country has a gun in the house.

"Switzerland definitely proves that it isn't guns, but people behind those guns, which determines whether or not guns are a bad thing," said one Swiss bank manager, a fellow who also happens to be a captain in the reserves.

It is a modern army in most respects. But the Swiss still cherish some anachronisms.

In the spring of 1972 Swiss Defense Minister Rudolf Ghaegi raised a storm in a Swiss cocoa cup when he proposed to disband the last remaining units of the Swiss horse-mounted Dragoons.

There still were 3,000 of these soldiers in eighteen squadrons. The Defense Minister ordered that these men be transferred to mechanized units.

Indignant horse lovers wrote bitter letters to newspapers. Some citizens said it would be a shame to disband units which had four centuries of tradition behind them. Three members of parliament petitioned for a national referendum on the subject. But newspapers supported the Defense Ministry's position. "The army is not the place to maintain and look after museum pieces at considerable cost," said the influential *Neue Zürcher Zeitung*. Nevertheless, in 1972, horse lovers gathered 432,000 signatures on a petition requesting retention of the mounted Dragoons. Faced with this response, the Swiss lower house of parliament voted to retain the cavalry, but then decided to phase out the dragoons for economy reasons.

In Switzerland a fellow who shows ability to command in the Army also rises to executive position in industry, commerce, and banking. The Swiss Army doesn't have any generals, except in war. But if you find yourself a colonel, chances are he will be in the hierarchy of the company that employs him. Dr. Alfred Schaefer, head of Union Bank, for instance, was a colonel in the reserves.

He spent six years in the Army during World War II when Switzerland maintained vigilance along borders, and in subsequent training periods. He doesn't regret a bit of it. Said he: "It was a valuable experience. Military virtues are excellent for anyone who heads a large firm. The Army teaches you how to command and how to obey. It teaches punctuality and precision."

In Zurich, one naturalized Swiss (a rarity) who is an executive with a finance company, said: "This love of the military life is a Germanic trait you find among the German-speaking Swiss. If you don't succeed in the Army, it is a black mark against you in this part of the country. Conversely, if you do well, you probably will have no trouble obtaining an executive position somewhere."

Still, Switzerland is a neutral nation which studiously avoids foreign entanglements. It doesn't even belong to the International Monetary Fund, though it provides statistics regularly to that organization. Switzerland's National Bank is a member of the Bank for International Settlements, the central bankers' club headquartered in Basle. Yet the Swiss National Bank avoids taking any positions which might sound even faintly political. Switzerland cooperates with the Group of Ten, an international money group formed by the ten leading countries of the nonsocialist world, actually making this a Group of Eleven. Still, Switzerland won't publicly admit to being Number Eleven.

Switzerland contributes to maintenance costs of the United Nations force on the island of Cyprus. It cooperates with all of the U.N. foreign aid agencies. It works closely with the Council of Europe and with international research agencies. And, of course, the European headquarters for the U.N. are housed in the Palais des Nations in Geneva. World headquarters of the International Red Cross Committee, which was founded by Swiss, are not far from that Palais, overlooking the broad sweep of Lake Geneva (Lac Leman to the French).

Swiss portray themselves as a tolerant people who have blended four nationalities together to form a homogeneous whole. Peace-loving German, French, Italian, and Romansh nationalities are pictured in happy harmony, as if they might be striding down the same road together, arm in arm, men and women in peasant costume. It really isn't like that at all. In the first place, Switzerland is basically a German country with an Italian and a French minority.

Seventy percent of the people speak German, 19 percent speak French, 10 percent speak Italian, and as for Romansh? Well, only 1 percent of the people speak that, and you must hunt in the high mountain valleys to locate them.

To complicate matters, Swiss speak various dialects of German, French, and Italian. A German from Schwyz may have trouble understanding a German from Basle. The French in Lausanne contend that they speak a purer French than you hear in Geneva. A Swiss from Lugano laughs at the accent of an Italian Swiss from Ascona. One linguist reports that seventy different dialects are found in the country.

Far from being a homogeneous people, Swiss have learned to live in diversity. Germans, French, and Italians don't mix freely, if they can help it. The Swiss seldom even seem to think of themselves as a people, at least among themselves. A person will be a Baseler, a Genevois, a Ticinese, or a Zurcher first, then a Swiss. The later designation probably will only be mentioned if foreigners are present.

In a world which grows steadily more egalitarian, the Swiss believe that true democracy consists in defending the right of people to be different. Swiss think that a government should provide an environment in which people are free to develop their own sense of identity, either alone, or working together. If the Baseler doesn't like the Zurcher, or vice versa, neither sees why they should be forced into the same mold, as long as each is not harming the other. Mutual dislike is considered to be a right, along with mutual respect.

Swiss don't practice any racism that is evident. But, then, the country has never had any but white citizens, except perhaps for the odd naturalization here and there. Swiss know whom they like and whom they don't. It's none of the federal government's business if the Zurcher believes that the Ticino would be a wonderful place if only there weren't so many Italians in it, or if they think that Geneva's fine, except for the French Swiss who live there.

It would be unthinkable in Switzerland for the federal government to dictate to citizens concerning civil rights. In the first place, the federal government doesn't have the power. In the second, somebody would call for a referendum, and the vote usually is against more federal control whenever this is a ballot box issue.

Feeling that way, Swiss have no moral qualms against campaigning to "kick-the-foreigners-out." They've even coined a derogatory word for it, *Ueberfremdung*. It means "over-foreignization," which is just another way of saying "Switzerland-for-the-Swiss."

Swiss work hard. But they are forming a dislike for the dirty jobs. Construction laborers, street sweepers, foundry workers, and such are usually foreigners, perhaps Italian. Sixteen percent of Switzerland's 6.3 million population is now foreign.

Industry would halt without them. Yet resentment exists

against the outsiders. Nearly a third of the three million labor force consists of outsiders, enough to make some Swiss feel that their country is being occupied by a new form of invasion. This sentiment resulted in a referendum in June, 1970, which aimed to limit the inflow of foreign workers. The proposal was defeated, but supporters have formed a political party and are fighting to keep Switzerland for the Swiss.

"Fine, if we can do it," says one Zurich industrialist. "But who will do the dirty jobs if we don't give work permits to outsiders?"

A Swiss is never far from the land from whence he came, no matter how long it has been since he departed. Encounter a thirty-year-veteran bank employee in Zurich and he shakes his head when asked if he is from Zurich. He still claims to be from Zug, about twenty miles south. One Lucerne mother lamented that she had lost a daughter by marriage, talking as if her son-in-law might have been a Tibetan living beyond the high Himalayas. Her son-in-law lived in Basle, a two-hour train ride away.

There is a clannishness about the inhabitants of each city or mountain valley. In their togetherness, they concoct fictions concerning inhabitants of other areas. Stereotypes become part of Swiss ethnological lore. The Bernese, for instance, are supposed to be thickheaded.

So, outside of Berne you hear: "Don't ever tell a joke to a Bernese on Saturday. He will get the point the next day, and may burst out laughing in church on Sunday morning."

As for the Genevois? "On the whole, they are lazy," says one Baseler, "and they have the morals of the French." This intriguing last sentence is left unexplained.

Switzerland is very much a man's country, where women know their place and accept it. They didn't get the right to vote until February, 1971. A national referendum gave them that right by a comfortable margin, 621,403 to 323,596. A lot of women were against it though, and, of course, none of them were voting in that particular election.

The referendum disappointed the Association of Women Against Female Suffrage. The president of this group, a Bernese housewife named Mrs. G. Haldimann-Weiss, declared: "We are still convinced that political equality for women is the first step in a dubious trend toward total equality for women."

In the United States women account for nearly 60 percent of the staffs employed by banks. In Switzerland the percentage ranges between 32 and 40 percent.

When women moved into mail clerks' jobs at the Zurich post office in the fall of 1971, the development was worth a story in the *Neue Zürcher Zeitung*. This is a 92,000 circulation daily which is considered to be the best newspaper in Switzerland. *La Tribune de Genève*, a French-language daily with a circulation of 63,000, is another respected paper. *Blick*, a Zurich-published paper, however, has the largest circulation, 210,000.

Swiss are avid readers of newspapers, books, and magazines. The illiteracy rate is only 2 percent, and an eager audience supports nearly three hundred fifty newspapers. English is a second language for the educated Swiss. So, Shakespeare is as popular in Switzerland as in Britain, though the more somber lines of Goethe are closer to the Swiss spirit.

On average, Swiss attend school until the age of seventeen, the oldest average of any country in Europe, except for Sweden. Swiss believe in education taught with a firm hand, with no nonsense from the back rows, and permissiveness left for more distant lands. "The Swiss are rich because their educational level is well above that of Europe in general," said Harald Meyer-Smith, economics editor, Schweizerische Depeschenagentur, a Basle news agency.

The authoritarian schools reflect the Aristotelian virtues which are cultivated by cultured Swiss. Rule youth well, for age will rule itself. Or to quote Aristotle directly: "It has been well said that he who has never learned to obey cannot be a good commander."

In June, 1971, a proposal to give parents a greater voice in the management of Zurich's elementary schools, through establishment of a Parent Advisory Council, was rejected by Zurich's cantonal parliament. In the debate members on the majority side argued that parent supervisory commissions would only complicate school management problems. Educational authorities knew best how to handle jobs, without any second-guessing from parents.

As might be expected in a nation with an educated popu-
lace, Swiss have a strong interest in art. A banker can converse
about Pissarro or van Gogh as easily as he might contribute
views concerning interest rates. One might expect Swiss to be
conservative in art. Indeed, you may encounter a Holbein or a
Dutch master in private homes in Switzerland. Yet Picasso is a
favorite, too. Zurich still talks about the Picasso exhibitions
organized in 1954 and repeated in 1967.

In 1967, Basle bought two Picassos for 8 million francs, or
a little more than $2 million after a public collection drive of
only a few weeks. One painting, the Seated Harlequin, now is
one of the stars of Basle's Fine Arts Museum. It is a representative work painted in 1923 during Picasso's neoclassical period.
The acquisition had an odd postscript. Since part of the money
collected came from the city government, a referendum had to
be held to certify the spending. Citizens voted overwhelmingly
to acquire the art works, certainly one of the few times when a
public ballot decided purchase of a painting.

Swiss are not innovators in the banking field, where anything as important as money is the center of focus. They *are*
originators in the mechanical and chemical fields, areas where
precision and orderly thinking are valued.

About the only time that the Swiss are willing to waste a
few minutes is when they're watching some mechanical contriv-
ance at work. In the terminal building at Geneva's Airport,
there is a Rube Goldberg contraption of gears, wheels, chains,
and connecting rods which stands about fifteen feet high near
the Duty Free Shop.

Innards whirl, spin, and revolve through the day, like some
perpetual motion machine doing nothing but exercise itself.
Swiss never seem to tire of watching that collection of nuts and
bolts. Close inspection reveals that the contraption really is a
giant water clock, and that reveals something of Swiss character,
too. Even when they create a mechanical gadget on Rube Goldberg principles, they want it to be doing some work.

Unemployment is almost unknown in the country. The
monthly average of unemployed in 1971 was one hundred, the
Federal Bureau for Industry reported in Berne. Meanwhile, the
monthly average for positions vacant was 3,964. Anyone with-

out a job was probably taking a rest before transferring to a new one, for there were enough positions vacant to provide jobs for everybody, including the lame and the sick.

With such a shortage of labor, it might appear that trade unions can dictate their own terms. Not so. Managements in Switzerland are paternalistic. Workers accept this as natural. Strikes are almost unknown, as are demarcation disputes. The closed shop is a foreign development which has no place in Switzerland. Managements convince labor that they must cooperate to progress.

Job hopping is discouraged. A man takes a position with a bank or company for life. Work is viewed seriously, with a puritan ethic which relates idleness to pursuits of the devil. Switzerland, indeed, is the land where time is measured, cut to appropriate sizes, then fitted to the work in hand. It is not for nothing that Switzerland has become the center of the world's watch industry.

In one Zurich office, the words of Jerome K. Jerome were quoted to a Swiss banker: "I like work: It fascinates me. I can sit and look at it for hours. I love to keep it by me. The idea of getting rid of it nearly breaks my heart." This banker didn't even show a smile. He merely shook his head and said: "You don't get much done with that attitude, do you?"

He had a small card on his desk, one side in German, the other in French, quoting a remark by Voltaire: "Work banishes those three great evils, boredom, vice, and poverty."

Swiss are seldom bored. They don't have much time for vice. And they certainly are not poor.

Along with work, Swiss revere frugality. They live to save, not because they love money so well, but because they see no reason for throwing money around. They dress well, eat well, and drink their occasional schnapps, but don't believe in spending merely because they have it. One Swiss proverb says: "He who would buy what he sees must soon sell what he has." A man leading a middle-class life who falls into some money will continue to lead a middle-class life, perhaps in the same house, in the same style.

Swiss frugality means that banks attract savings easily. So interest rates are among the lowest in the world. So is the interest margin (the difference between the loan rate and the deposit rate). One ten-year study of interest rates by Union Bank showed this margin averaged 1.80 percent.

At the end of 1971, the following interest rates prevailed in key money markets:

EUROMARKET
U.S. $ (3 months)	5.88%
£ (3 months)	5.00%
DM (3 months)	4.00%
Eurodollar bonds (yield)	7.70%

USA
| Treasury bills (3 months) | 3.73% |
| Federal bonds (yield) | 5.72% |

GREAT BRITAIN
| Treasury bills (3 months) | 4.48% |
| Government bonds (yield) | 8.46% |

GERMANY
| Private discount rate | 4.09% |
| Government bonds (yield) | 7.56% |

SWITZERLAND
Private discount rate	5.00%
Time deposits (3 months)	1.50%
Medium-term notes (average rate)	5.13%
Mortgage credits (12 cantonal banks)	5.56%
Federal bonds (yield)	4.99%

Bankers who operate with low interest rates are compelled to be conservative. They are selective in lending and may be satisfied with lower returns than are bankers who must offer high deposit rates to generate funds. The Penn Central 10 percent notes would seem to indicate the reverse of this. But this is the exception to prove the rule.

"If we had many Penn Centrals, we wouldn't be in business very long," admitted one Zurich banker.

Swiss have old-fashioned ideas about debt. When Swiss Credit Bank conducted a poll to determine what people think of their banks, it found installment credit to be one of the least utilized bank services. Only 6 percent of people queried used it. Only 9 percent had credit cards.

Every Swiss queried could name at least six different banks, and 87 percent could name the four biggest banks in the country. "Banking is obviously an institution which has deep roots in the country," Swiss Credit Bank said in commenting on the poll.

Bank secrecy has deep roots, too. That poll showed that 74 percent of the people queried believe that secrecy is a good thing. And most people view their banks as collection points for savings. Almost 90 percent of those interviewed utilized bank services in connection with their personal savings. Among the smaller savers interviewed, 87 percent said savings accounts were the best way to keep their money, only 9 percent viewed mutual funds as the best savings medium.

Among people who admitted to having larger fortunes, 75 percent listed bonds as their number one savings medium. Of these wealthy folk, 35 percent considered gold and precious metals to be a good method of savings.

Swiss Credit Bank reported: "The investigation shows up very clearly the solid-based ideas about investment policy held by the Swiss. Only after a Swiss investor has provided himself with savings he can draw on at any time, and adequate insurance protection as a basis, does he start to think about buying securities; and when he does, he starts with first-class bonds, only going in for purchase of shares and real estate at a later stage."

Safety first, and second, and third, with the Swiss.

Swiss conservatism is well illustrated by the respect which is paid to the country's history and heritage. Lucerne has a Clock Tower which has housed the same clock since 1535. For many years, this was the only public clock in the city.

When additional clocks of this type were built, the Zeiturm clock of 1535 was accorded a special honor. Citizens granted it the privilege of proclaiming the time first. It is always kept one minute ahead of the correct time. Thus, the Zeiturm clock is the first in town to strike the hour.

Folk festivals seem to be underway all the time in some part of the country. Roots of many reach to dim and distant pagan times. Neuchâtel has its wine harvest festival every October. Lotschental has its annual church festival. The Appenzell cattle show is a regular September event. Geneva's Fêtes de Genève occurs every August. Basle's spring fairs are a tradition.

Appenzell also has its *Aplabfahrt*, the descent of livestock from high mountain pastures every September. Men dress in their yellow breeches, white socks, and red vests. Heads are topped by black felt hats decorated with flowers. Colorful yokes are slung on cows. Animals amble slowly along in a parade, their big bells clanking, an occasional moo providing the right bucolic note. It is a time for merry-making and mirth, when the wine flows freely and the quiet reserve of the typical Swiss disappears.

Swiss like to don costumes and stage parades. Even staid bankers of Zurich and Basle sometimes will become participants, hiding behind masks of medieval knights or of folklore characters for a pageant which may have hundreds of years of tradition behind it.

Zurich's high point is the *Sechseläuten*, which is celebrated on the third Monday in April as a welcome to spring. At 6 P.M. on that day, Zurich's church bells toll the hour. A huge bonfire flares on the green field near the shores of Lake Zurich.

Members of Zurich's ancient guilds, garbed in colorful costumes of the Middle Ages, gallop on horseback around the rising bonfire. Perched atop the crackling pile of wood is the Böögg, a life-sized snowman filled with firecrackers. The flames take hold. As the snowman begans to melt, the firecrackers start exploding. Round and round, the horsemen ride, while thousands of spectators cheer the departure of winter.

This festival comes from some pagan ritual held first so long ago that nobody understands its significance. A thousand years from now, Zurich undoubtedly will be celebrating the same festival in about the same way. Swiss are like that.

Swiss share the view Thomas Paine had about government. "Government, even in its best state, is but a necessary evil; in its worst state, an intolerable one." Switzerland's federation government is so weak at the center that sometimes it seems to be in permanent recess. The cantons have most of the power, and even they don't have much. Switzerland has a government by participation, which means that citizens vote directly upon any question deemed important. Any question which involves taking money or some rights away from citizens and transferring same to the government is considered important enough for a referendum. It only takes 30,000 signatures on a petition to book the referendum.

So legislators always have citizens watching them closely. Sometimes the federal parliament will labor for half a year over a measure which members feel is necessary for the good of the country. The opposition will collect necessary signatures, and a referendum will be called. In one day, the people will veto the proposal, and that will be that.

It is town hall government practiced on a national scale. The first question a Swiss asks with new legislation will be: Is this proposal necessary? It had better be vital for an affirmative vote.

Switzerland has ten political parties. No single one has had a majority since 1919 in federal elections. So every government is a coalition. Everything is decided by compromise—until the people vote. Then, each man votes as he pleases.

The Swiss are by nature law abiding. They don't even have conductors on the streetcars in Basle and Zurich. You climb aboard, wait for somebody to sell you a ticket, and nobody does. Only after you arrive at your destination do you discover that there are ticket machines scattered at streetcar stops around town. You're supposed to buy a ticket to your destination on the honor system. Everybody does, except for the stranger who doesn't understand the system. He rides free.

The term "law and order" probably was coined by some Swiss. He meant it as something desirable, like one might talk about "health and happiness."

Swiss think you don't have to enact a law in order to behave. They believe in living by that gold rule with its steel edge: "Love thy neighbor as thyself, but count your change."

Voluntary agreements are preferred to legislation. Industries draw their own codes of conduct on a gentlemanly basis, like poker players setting rules before cards are dealt. Banks are governed by the same sort of informal rules, with only a minimum of government interference. The Swiss Banking Commission doesn't even audit books of banks. That's done by auditing companies which may be subsidiaries of banks under audit.

Since the commission doesn't have much more power than a little old lady at the old folks' home, banks are seldom bothered by its activities. And the Swiss National Bank has only minimal powers when it comes to controlling money movements. Recent money crises, however, are prompting it to add to its powers.

One Zurich banker explained: "Switzerland is a small country where everybody in the banking industry knows everybody else. There is enough of a club-like atmosphere among our banks to make these voluntary agreements work."

Union Bank's Schaefer defends voluntary agreements as examples of bank conduct which deserve high marks. Said he: "Such agreements are more effective than legislative intervention, mainly because they function more smoothly and can be adapted to changing conditions."

Switzerland is the land of *laissez faire*. There are few financial fetters, and bank secrecy protects bankers as well as customers. This is something which is not publicized when Swiss defend such secrecy. There is no Securities and Exchange Commission here to serve as a watchdog protecting public interests.

Laissez faire, laissez passer. Swiss bankers have little interference from government and almost complete freedom of movement in their jobs.

The whole structure of the Swiss banking system is based on the integrity, the sense of responsibility, and the professional knowledge of the banking people in the industry. The latter point comes from experience. The first two stem from the puritan moral code of Switzerland. Fortunately for those who bank in Switzerland, most Swiss bankers do adhere to a moral code which is based on old-fashioned virtues such as honesty, company loyalty, prudence, devotion to duty, and a liking for hard work.

F. W. Schulthess, chairman, Swiss Credit Bank, says: "The proof of integrity has to be established over and over again. As trustee of large portions of the national wealth, the banker does not deal in money alone, he deals above all in the capital of confidence. Once squandered, this would be very difficult to regain."

Swiss know that if foreigners ever lose their trust in Swiss banks because of the troubles of UCB Basle, I.O.S., and others, nothing will restore it.

So, dubious or suspect activity can provoke a ferocious reaction when exposed. Anyone suspected of violating those Swiss bank laws which do exist can expect little help from habeas corpus and sundry other Latin-designated legal devices aimed at guaranteeing the freedom and liberty of suspects in criminal cases. When the UCB Basle Bank scandal broke in September, 1970, seven officials of that bank were jailed immediately, without charge, initially without benefit of legal counsel and, for months, without bail. Over two years later, Bernard Kummerli, a key figure in the case, still languished in the seventeenth-century Basle jail waiting for court charges to be presented.

Mere suspicion in a case may put you in jail. The Swiss sometimes do seem overly suspicious, and they are suspicious of youth. This is a country which honors experience, expects a youth to prove himself before according him any privileges. Promotions usually are along military lines. Everyone is expected to start as a buck private, then rise through the ranks. Seniority is prized.

There are exceptions. Union Bank's Schaefer rose to the top at the bank in 1940 at thirty-three years of age. Today, you do see men in their forties holding vital managerial jobs at some banks whereas a few years ago those jobs would be held by fifty year olds, and older. But you will search hard to find anyone in his twenties doing much more than applying paper clips to collections of papers.

Schaefer of Union Bank, a deep student of history, takes a tolerant view of the generation gap but, like most Swiss bankers, he opposes change merely for the sake of change. "The conflict between the generations," he says, "is as old as the history of mankind. Hesiod, Socrates, Plato, and Plutarch had some heated words to say on the subject several centuries ago. On a three-thousand-year-old Babylonian clay tablet are inscribed the comments: 'The young people are completely debauched. They are impious and slothful. They will never be equal to the youth who went before, nor will they be able to preserve our culture.'"

In his 1972 address to stockholders on March 15 at the bank's headquarters in Zurich, he said: "A change for the better wins approval from us all. It is in fact necessary to challenge existing values. The demand for change solely for the sake of change is, however, nothing but a subjective and emotional negation of the present."

Subsequently, when this particular speech was included in one of those shiny, red-fringe booklets which Union Bank likes to distribute, a collection of quotes on youth was included in an appendix in case anybody missed the point in the printed address.

Swiss bankers do listen to the young all right. They just don't pay much attention to what is said. This may be one reason why the Swiss are so conservative, "square" some might term it. Still, it is a satisfying feeling to most people with money to realize that they will encounter no male longhairs when they enter the lobby of a Swiss bank, at least not on the house sides of counters.

The suspicion of youth extends to adoption of the new and untried. When the eurodollar, that Russian invention, first appeared in Europe, the Swiss didn't adopt it readily either, and not because they don't like Russians. But the eurodollar came to stay a while and the Swiss learned to love that currency as if it were related to their beloved franc. This only goes to prove that love is an acquired trait.

CHAPTER VIII

EURODOLLARS

Bankers, journalists, professors, and sundry other characters often like to explain the mysteries of eurodollars when demonstrating their multinational financial expertise (or lack of it). Usually what's said or written is wrong, though the explanation may be so complex that it lulls people into accepting misinformation.

So, what is a eurodollar?

Like all forms of modern money, a eurodollar is likely to be an abstraction when it flows in money markets, as invisible as the good will claimed by company raiders in merger deals. In a credit card economy, for instance, you may seldom see a dollar. Even when charges are settled, it may be via check. So if you don't see a eurodollar flying past on your next trip to Europe, don't be disillusioned.

Most American currency never leaves the United States. If you send money through your local national bank to Wilbur Jr., in Paris, the dollar bills won't leave the U.S. Your transfer may consist only of a transatlantic telex message notifying a bank on the other side to pay dollars to Wilbur. Wilbur may prefer French francs, since he probably will be broke, so he won't see any dollars. But that Paris bank makes an accounting notation on its books and it adds those dollars to its deposits, not physically, but as a claim against your local domestic bank. That deposit money can be loaned to a European borrower just as if it were cash.

And those dollars are eurodollars.

Still confusing? Not to the Swiss bankers who have one of the biggest stakes in the vital eurodollar market. They describe a eurodollar as an American dollar on deposit at an offshore bank.

Should you close a eurodollar account and ask for cash, you will find those dollars to be green, made of paper about six and a quarter inches long, and with a picture of George Washington on the one dollar denominations. In short, the eurodollar is the same dollar you have always known *but at work in a foreign setting.*

So, why all the noise and confusion? Well, when all this started in the late 1950's, it wasn't normal for a dollar to be a foreign currency. Banks accepted deposits and made loans in the domestic currency. British banks usually restricted their borrowing and lending to the pound sterling. German banks dealt only in mark deposits and advances. So it went, with the home currency having more allure than U.S. dollars which drifted into hands of financial people. Central banks accepted those dollars and returned them to the United States through normal monetary channels.

Enter the Russians, and this time as financial heroes. For years, the Soviet Union financed its nonsocialist foreign trade through dollars. Nobody wants the ruble, except the Russians. Nearly everybody understands the dollar.

Communists have no dogmatic scruples against accepting

and holding capitalistic dollars. In fact, it is rather amusing to wander into the foreign currency shop of the Russiya Hotel in Moscow, Russia's proletariat answer to Conrad Hilton. The cameras, phonograph records, fur jackets, bottles of vodka, and tins of caviar all have price tags in U.S. dollars. Clerks haughtily refuse to deal in rubles at all.

To handle the mechanics of their trade, the Russians established a bank in London, the Moscow Narodny Bank. It is a venerable institution which is operated strictly for profit, with no nonsense about Hegel's dialectical positions, or of the class distinctions of Karl Marx. As is the case in any bank, unused balances do accumulate. Since Russians dealt in dollars, that balance was in dollars.

Banks invest unused cash wherever a safe return is assured. With dollars abroad, it used to be the New York money market. But this was in the 1950's. The Cold War was active. Dollars invested by the Russians in New York could be frozen at the whim of the American government. Moreover, even though the Russians were using dollars for their trade, it didn't seem quite in tune with the doctrines of Marx and Lenin for them to invest in America's Wall Street.

So, what to do?

One banker at Moscow Narodny had a brilliant idea: why not keep any excess dollars and lend them to borrowers in Europe? Loans pay interest.

The good old American dollar in its new surroundings became the eurodollar. The dollar hadn't changed at all. It merely had found a new market, with interest rates conforming to that market rather than to the rates in the United States.

Ironically, the first borrowers of these dollars were U.S. corporations which were expanding their manufacturing facilities in Europe. Those companies worked daily with dollars. They preferred them to other currencies.

The infant eurodollar business drew support from the return of full currency convertibility in 1958. Through World War II and the postwar period, nation after nation had introduced foreign exchange controls to hoard vital foreign money needed for trade. Then, as prosperity returned to Europe, controls were lifted. The 1958 devaluation of the French franc opened the way for full convertibility among major countries. Money could flow freely back and forth across borders without restrictions.

This made it possible for the eurodollar to go international, and so it did. Other banks in Europe jumped into the market. They offered rates on deposits attractive enough to draw dollars, then reloaned the money at a profit. Dollar holders in Europe, the Middle East, Africa, and Latin America transferred dollars to Europe, often through Swiss accounts. Dollars streamed from the U.S. because of America's balance of payments deficits.

A country's balance of payments is the difference between its earnings and outgo in international markets. When a nation has a deficit, it is spending more than it is earning abroad, a chronic condition for free-spending America. The deficit reached its peak in 1971 when the U.S. was $29.8 billion in the red on an official settlements basis.

U.S. attempts to aid its balance of payments through controls and interest measures helped expand the eurodollar market. One assist came from a populist regulation of 1933, the Federal Reserve Board Regulation Q which restricted levels of interest on deposits. Usually, American interest rates have been lower than those in Europe. So, when the post–World War II network of American banks began to develop abroad along with expansion of corporations to foreign lands, more and more Americans found it convenient to deposit funds abroad rather than at home.

In 1963 the U.S. interest equalization tax was introduced, taxing dollars going abroad into foreign investments. This effectively destroyed international fund-raising junkets in the U.S. Foreigners and American companies abroad turned to the eurodollar market for their bond and long-term loan financing.

Then the U.S. restricted the corporate export of capital to overseas subsidiaries while limiting the foreign loan volume of American banks. More borrowers turned to the eurodollar market. Meanwhile, American multinational corporations found lucrative sales markets abroad.

It used to be fashionable to blame the American balance of payments deficit for most of the growth noted in eurodollars. This isn't quite true. There also is a growing market in other currencies, such as the euroyen and the euromark. Neither Japan nor Germany has experienced balance of payments deficits in recent years. So it is evident that the euromarkets have developed a velocity of their own.

The term *eurodollar* may be a misnomer for this burgeoning market. Dollars deposited in a Canadian, Japanese, or Lebanese bank are eurodollars just as much as are those banked in Europe. Moreover, not only dollars flow into this market; pounds sterling, German marks, French francs, Japanese yen, and Dutch guilders may also be part of it. In fact, any currency for which there is a demand may be utilized as a euro-currency.

But the euro prefix is now so firmly fixed to the dollar that the eurodollar term is likely to continue as a description for the entire market.

Charts showing growth of the eurodollar market form such steep curves that they look like cliffs in a mountain valley. The market grew from $1 billion in 1959 to about $80 billion in early 1973. Today the eurodollar market is a vast business which has become the world's only truly international capital market.

"The euro-money market is the only one on which interest rates are determined exclusively by the law of supply and demand," said Dr. Alfred Schaefer, chairman, Union Bank of Switzerland. "This market developed into a rather well-functioning international clearing house for short-term funds, directing capital to where it was most needed."

It is a market which has helped Pepsi Cola to raise $75 million in Europe for its worldwide operations. The Republic of Zaïre (Congo, Kinshasa) floated a $25 million issue to build and improve a road network to get production of palm oil, coffee, tea, and cotton from the interior to ports for shipping to world markets. When Italy wanted to expand its electrical energy capacity to more than 82 million kilowatts, it depended on the euromarket for a $425 million finance package. This was the biggest such package ever to be floated on that market. The list of big Americn companies which have used eurodollar financing reads like a list of firms on the New York Stock Exchange, plus many from the American Stock Exchange and the over-the-counter market.

Multinational corporations need the euromarket. As long as such corporations are around—and many people believe we are entering a period when these MNC's may dominate whole industries internationally—there will be a demand for a money market which corresponds to the euromarket.

A company with operations perhaps in every country in Western Europe plus many elsewhere finds it convenient to shift money back and forth between subsidiaries in the form of dollars, rather than attempt to change money each time a transfer crosses a national border. Moreover, by using eurodollars, the multinational company can play one loan market against another. If borrowing rates are better in Britain than in Germany, a company may borrow in the former, even though it wants to spend money in the latter. The eurodollar provides a flexibility not existing in any single domestic currency.

In the period ahead, multinational corporations will need even more capital than they have absorbed over the last decade. They will be fighting to preserve the eurodollar market, or something like it, no matter what politicians, central bankers, and government leaders may have to say against it.

Swiss banks were tardy at seeing the possibilities of eurodollars. They are conservative by nature. Money innovations seldom develop in Switzerland. Swiss bankers follow traditional methods until forced by competition to accept the new. When they did recognize the profit potential, they seized on the eurodollar as if it were the greatest invention since man shifted from clam shell to metal money.

The two countries which have benefited most from the eurodollar market are the United States and Switzerland, America as the largest borrower through its multinational corporations, Switzerland as the biggest supplier of capital through its banks. Because London is the Mecca of the eurodollar market, Britain also is a big net gainer, and the third leg on this stool.

"It is no coincidence that the Swiss banks, with such substantial foreign balances, are the largest net suppliers of the euromarket, just as Switzerland is the only country that has consistently been a net lender on that market," said R. H. Lutz, a key member of Swiss Credit Bank's management team.

About half of the deposits placed with Switzerland's big banks are short-term funds, money which must be put to work, quickly, outside the country. The eurodollar market is an ideal place for doing just that, at a return which has ranged as high as over II percent in good lending times. According to some estimates, this little nation accounts for more than 60 percent of the short-term money which goes into the eurodollar market, while accounting for from 40 to 50 percent, and sometimes more, of all eurobond placements.

The market on the loan side breaks into two segments, euroloans and eurobonds. Euroloans range from overnight loans through loans of thirty, sixty, and ninety days to a year or more in the short-term field. Medium-term loans are reckoned as three- to five-year loans by conservatives, though venturous bankers sometimes offer a term of up to ten years. Most bond issues are in the fifteen- to twenty-five-year range.

Short-term loan volume in eurodollars is astronomical, for money may be loaned over and over again on an overnight basis. Certainly, most of that $70 billion in the market always is at work in some fashion. Estimates are that the volume of medium-term lending alone added up to about $10 billion in 1971.

The total amount of eurobonds outstanding amounted to about $20 billion in the spring of 1973. The total volume of all eurobonds floated in 1972 amounted to $5.7 billion compared with $3.6 billion in the preceding year. Dollar issues amounted to $3.3 billion against $2.2 billion in 1971.

In early years of the eurodollar, Swiss banks were satisfied with playing a passive role in the field. They helped shift deposits to London banks. They merely placed underwriting issues and paper with portfolio customers. But as competition increased in the market, all three of the big Swiss banks organized offshore subsidiaries to bid directly for some of the underwriting business.

Tax avoidance has played a part in creation of these subsidiaries. Switzerland has a 30 percent withholding tax on dividends and on interest payments made to foreign investors in its domain. Where double taxation agreements are in effect, investors may recoup all or part of this tax. Where such agreements are not in effect, the investor loses his 30 percent. By working through their subsidiaries in the Bahamas or Bermuda, Big Three banks can handle eurobonds for their customers without making them subject to the withholding tax.

In 1972, Switzerland's Big Three were among the top managers and co-managers of eurodollar issues, according to White, Weld & Co., the New York headquartered bond firm which keeps statistical records of European bond trading. Union Bank ranked number one in the dollar field of the eurodollar market, with a total of $827.5 million in issues.

When all types of currencies were tabulated, Union Bank had forty issues for a total of $1.2 billion. Swiss Bank Corp. (Overseas) accounted for sixteen issues totaling $558.4 million. Credit Suisse (Bahamas) had a role in fourteen issues amounting to $290.5 million. This, of course, is only part of the total volume of issues in which Swiss banks participated.

Dow Bank, for instance, participated in eighteen money-raising issues from March 1 through December 31, 1971, through its Luxembourg-based affiliate, Eurocapital S.A. These ranged from a $25 million private placement of 8 3/4 percent bonds for the National Bank of Hungary to floating $20 million worth of 8 3/4 percent guaranteed debentures for Scott Paper Overseas Finance N.V. Meanwhile, private banks were placing various issues through their Geneva and Zurich associations.

Admittedly, in any statistical tabulation such as this, some overlap occurs. Nevertheless, it is apparent that Swiss banks have become a very big factor in the vital eurodollar market.

When most people think of a bank, they visualize depositors standing before a teller's window, probably in a queue, waiting to bank some money. In the rear of the bank, borrowers will be in quiet conversations with bank officers.

A eurobank is not like that at all. Most deposits and many of the loans are made via telephone and telex machines. Foreign exchange and eurodollar departments are likely to be together. Such a department looks like a bookie joint in a big city on a summer morning when races are scheduled in a dozen places for that day.

It is a place of animated activity and apparent disorder. Telephones ring constantly. Telex machines clatter. At Swiss Credit Bank a girl clutches two telephones, one to each ear, and seems to be talking to both at the same time. Over a dozen other men sit at small tables holding telephones, too. Office boys scurry around.

At Union Bank, just up Bahnhofstrasse in Zurich, activity is just as brisk and apparently disjointed. There may be a bit more bustle, since Union Bank is the biggest financial institu-' tion in the country. Things are on a smaller scale down the street toward Lake Zurich at Dow Bank where Bruno Huser is in charge of the money department. He is a slender, mustached Swiss in his twenties who has the self-assurance of a youth who knows how to handle his job. In a Swiss bank, he might be considered too young for that job. But this is an American bank.

Still, he admits: "You have to know what you are doing in this business." His eight traders may complete more than two hundred telephone and telex contacts in a day. This may result in the closing of fifty to one hundred deals involving $25 million to $50 million.

First, of course, there must be deposits if any bank is to operate. Much business is of an interbank nature. A bank in Frankfurt or London or Brussels has an excess of marks, pounds, or francs and wants to deposit them in Switzerland for three days, thirty, sixty, or ninety days or longer. Or perhaps the distant bank has a customer who wants to purchase some certificates of deposit, which for some reason the distant bank can't sell. Certificates of deposit are deposits made for specified periods of time, often for six months or a year, at a specified rate of interest. The certificate of ownership may be negotiable for the holder.

Order begins to appear in the confusion, as a visitor listens to the comments being made by traders in the money department of the typical bank. A bank in London has $1 million in dollars to deposit for thirty days. What's the rate?

"Four and three-quarters, five and a quarter," responds a shirtsleeved trader at the telephone. He clutches a pad and pencil in his right hand, ready to note the deposit should the deal be closed. The first figure he has cited is the bank's deposit rate this April, 1972, morning for one-month deposits. The second is for a one-month loan. Naturally, traders know the people with whom they are dealing over the telephone and telex.

"Okay," says the trader, and the smile on his face indicates that he has obtained the million-dollar deposit from the London bank. He has scarcely finished writing when another phone call is shifted to him. An American customer in Germany has $5 million he doesn't need for six months. What's the deposit rate?

The trader doesn't have to scan the rate on a blackboard on the wall, a table which may be changed many times during the day as free market forces move the rates. Still, for the very reason that changes sometimes come fast, the trader glances at that board, even as he blurts out the rate from memory. There has been no change since the last six-month deal. He says: "Five and three-quarters, six and a quarter."

It is again accepted. A $5 million deposit. The trader lifts a hand, catches the eye of the chief trader. Money is coming in easily. Perhaps the bank's rates are higher than the market. The chief trader hurriedly checks the deposit volume now on hand, compares it with the new loans being written by other traders or by loan officers elsewhere on the floor. The ideal situation is to have these in balance.

The chief trader erases the figures on the blackboard, cuts the deposit rate by an eighth of a percent, bringing the loan rate down, too. If the bank's rate still is higher than the market, deposit money will continue to be heavy. The rate may be reduced again. If the bank's deposit rate slips below the market, potential depositors probably will take business elsewhere. Meanwhile, if the loan rate is attractive, new loans probably will clean up the surplus of deposits.

An AP-DJ business news ticker clicks in a corner. Traders must follow news developments which might affect the market. Through the day they exchange information with friends at other banks. Business is not geared to making a killing at the expense of a client or bank elsewhere, for the differential between the deposit rate and the loan rate should provide a profit for the well-operated bank.

Comradeship of banks might lead the ignorant to think that banks act in collusion to set rates. The truth is, the market, not banks, usually sets rates, and nowhere is this more true than in the euro field. Sometimes governments may intercede to force rates in one direction. They do not succeed very well if goals are counter to the market, for any apparent success may beget serious troubles in other economic spheres.

All the while that deposits are coming in, loan officers and traders will be seeking to place money. Some of that money may form pieces of bond issues. Some may back up credit lines. The surplus may be deposited in another bank.

Complex deals are an everyday occurrence. A euro-money department may find itself with ten million German deutsche marks for ninety days with no borrowers, whereas it has a request for a million pounds sterling from a nearby Swiss bank. A Brussels bank may be found which is short of marks and the German currency may be deposited there. A Paris broker may have more sterling than he wants on hand. Funds may be borrowed from him to meet the sterling loan request from the nearby bank.

Many of the deposits in the euromarket are for short periods, overnight, three days, thirty days, or ninety days. Meanwhile, borrowers are apt to be requesting longer loan periods than the periods for which depositors are willing to immobilize their money. This is a fact of life in the euromarket which frightens the traditional banker, for the euro-bank finds itself compelled by necessity to violate a cardinal rule of banking: Never borrow short to lend long.

The typical euro-banker accepts that three-, thirty-, ninety-, and one hundred eighty-day money, and he often reloans it for periods of three to ten years. He gambles on the fact that in three, thirty, ninety, and one hundred eighty days there may be more short-term deposits coming into his bank, and more after that again and again until the medium-term loan is fully covered. Some incorrigible in the class may ask: "But what happens if all of those short-term depositors want their money back at the same time?"

Good question, and it is one being asked among conservative bankers, especially since roll over credits have developed as a big business in the euro field. Roll over credits are medium-term credits for a fixed period of three to ten years, with the interest rate adjusted every six months or so in accordance with the market rate at that time. The lender keeps refinancing himself on the euromarket with short-term credit through the life of the roll over credit.

"It is understandable that a banker of the traditional school, who has seen many a modernistic experiment collapse, should ask himself whether this deliberate violation of time-honored banking principles may not in the future become once more a source of serious disruption," said Mr. Lutz of Swiss Credit Bank.

The best answer to the problem of risk is to apply strict credit standards in the granting of loans, say most Swiss bankers who are in the eurodollar market. Banks also are advised to maintain a well-balanced liquidity structure for loans, and to spread the risks as much as possible. Thus, large loans may have from twenty to forty banks participating. If such a loan turns bad, no one bank would be hit seriously.

The multiplier effect of euroloans also is often criticized. A deposit of say $1 million may be lent from Bank A to B, from B to C, from C to D, and from D to F. In this example, the $1 million liability of the first bank is stretched to a liability of $5 million for all the banks as the money moves through the daisy chain.

Union Bank's Dr. Schaefer, after praising eurodollars, expressed a cautionary note. "One should," he said, "not lose sight of the fact that the euromarket also has its shortcomings, particularly the alteration of credit maturities. It is a very complex phenomenon. Often, the first creditor knows neither the use to which his loan is put nor the last debtor. He has to reckon with the possibility that, in the process of a long chain of transactions, the duration of credits will be lengthened, and that short term becomes long term."

Dr. Guido Carli, governor of the Bank of Italy, the Rome-based Italian central bank, has become one of the most vociferous critics of certain aspects of the eurodollar market. Carli is a slender, firm-muscled man of fifty-eight who thinks nothing of a two-mile swim in the Mediterranean before breakfast. In conversation, he is vibrant and intense, his angular features set in serious lines whenever he talks about the dangers of inflation, of possible international troubles stemming from the eurodollar, or about the necessity for the U.S. to correct its balance of payments deficits. He is one of the most brilliant men in Italy when it comes to finance. It isn't easy to be a central banker in Italy, where the people sometimes seem determined to commit economic suicide through strikes, plant riots, product sabotage, and slowdowns. Yet Carli has headed Italy's central bank since 1960.

"There is no system of restraints set up by monetary authorities on the operation of this market, which is thus theoretically capable of expanding itself without any limits except discretionary fractional reserves," he said.

He advocates controls on the euromarket to contain its most dangerous features. It is a suggestion made by others at various times. It is a view not shared by Sir Leslie O'Brien, G.B.E., governor of the Bank of England. Sir Leslie has a personality opposite to Carli's. He is a venerable, gray-haired banker who spent most of his career in the quiet confines of the bank, where the rustle of paper has all heads looking up. Nothing ever seems to ruffle Sir Leslie himself though. He is the unflappable pilot at the helm of Britain's pound sterling, steering it through shoals which might wreck its parity.

"If we attempted to solve the problems of international adjustment by legislating the eurodollar market out of existence, we should discover one of two things," said he. "Either the attempt would be largely ineffective, because the eurodollar market would simply shift its location to an unregulated center; or its effects would be quickly undone, as other mechanisms came into being to take its place."

Criticism of the eurodollar mounted in 1971 with the flareup of another monetary crisis. There is no doubt but what eurodollars may defeat interest rate policies and anti-inflation programs of governments. A nation which introduces a high interest rate to control inflation may find that the rate attracts foreign currencies, as was the case in West Germany in 1971. The inflow then contributes to the very inflation the government seeks to fight.

The eurodollar market is so flexible that a good credit risk does not even need any money to shift funds into a strong currency country. He can borrow money on the eurodollar market and dispatch that to the strong currency land.

Conversely, when a nation seeks to stimulate its economy through a low interest system, as was the case in the U.S. in 1970, 1971, and 1972, money may be discouraged from entering from abroad and may flow out. With interest rates higher abroad, the tendency was to keep money there, rather than shift it to the U.S. The throbbing, active eurodollar market provided that higher interest foreign market which holders of funds are ever seeking. This intensified America's balance of payments problems.

But the euromarket is only a mechanism which reflects the troubles which may be inherent in the monetary system because of abuses elsewhere. Being a mechanism, it may amplify some of those troubles, just as does a microphone in an auditorium. If there isn't any speaker at the microphone, however, no voice will emit from the loud speaker.

"As far as the alleged powder keg for monetary vicissitudes is concerned, I feel that the international money market is certainly not the crisis area," Guido Hanselmann, a Union Bank general manager, told the Financial Times-Investors Chronicle Conference on eurodollars at the London Hilton Hotel in London, March 21, 1972. "The speculative ammunition potentially available in the market can go off only if there is already a fundamental reason for it doing so. Any measures against this speculation would, therefore, have only an accessory character and would distract attention from the real evils of the international maladjustment."

Most Swiss bankers argue that the problems of the monetary system may be traced back to the problems of the U.S. dollar. Too many of them were printed in the 1960's, without enough thought given to the backing behind those dollars. Admittedly, those surplus dollars helped create the eurodollar market, certainly a good thing. Still, the more dollars there were abroad, the more people abroad worried about the worth of that dollar.

As long ago as 1817, David Ricardo wrote in his *Principles of Political Economy and Taxation*: "There is no point more important in issuing paper money than to be fully impressed with the effect that follows from the principle of limitation of quantity. It is not necessary that paper should be payable in specie [coin] to secure its value. It is only necessary that its quantity should be regulated."

There are those who contend that American restraint on the expansion of currency at home would kill the eurodollar market, since deficits help stimulate that market. Truth is, that market doesn't need any net additions at the present time. It already is large enough to do a capable job for a long time to come, with likelihood of other currencies being attracted to it as the need arises. Thus, if America's balance of payments did come into balance, the euromarket probably would continue to flourish. If America developed huge surpluses, it would be another story.

Certainly, multinational companies like that market. Speaking at the first annual Business Financing Conference in New York City, December 15, 1971, C. A. Gerstacker, chairman, Dow Chemical Co., Midland, Michigan, said: "While the eurodollar has been much maligned during recent years and even more so in recent months, this pool of expatriate dollars has furnished the world with the one largest capital market available to finance a large part of both private and public capital expansion. It is interesting to note that outside the U.S. capital markets, the eurodollar market has furnished the largest volume of long-term debt issues in recent years, and this is indicative of the vital role these dollars have played."

In the late months of 1971, the eurodollar was much maligned, often unjustly. But it was the dollar directly rather than the eurodollar market which fell on hard times. The Gnomes of Zurich were in the background in that currency crisis, just as they have been in the background in every crisis in recent years in the monetary field. Events indicated that they were there as bit players, not as lead characters. Those events should have destroyed once and for all that illusion that the Gnomes of Zurich can bring down a currency.

CHAPTER IX

MONEY GNOMES

The Bank for International Settlements in Basle sits opposite the railroad station on a busy street down which trolley cars clatter. Once through the bank's heavy metal doors, the atmosphere changes. The door blots out street noises. A librarylike hush hangs over the interior. A porter at a desk rises courteously to ascertain your business.

This is the home of the Basle Central Bankers' Club, scene of their monthly meetings. These are held in a book-lined conference room which seems designed for reflective thinking rather than for precipitate action.

Sunday nights before monthly meetings, bankers are likely to gather in a small banqueting room of the Hotel Euler's restau-

rant, just around the corner. It has more than proximity to offer.
The Euler Restaurant is one of the best eating places in Switzerland. Its numerous ways of preparing sole are renowned. Its
viande de Grisons or *viande sechée* is so delicate that the diner soon
understands why this dried meat is such a favorite in Switzerland, especially when washed down with a bottle of Dôle from
the Valais.

Central bankers don't come here to eat. They gather to
consider weighty problems of the world's monetary system. In
the spring of 1971, a most momentous time for that system, the
troubles of the United States dollar outshone all others.
Monthly meetings of the Basle club assumed an importance far
beyond anything which these bankers had ever encountered
before, and they were used to epic money battles.

They had fought the battle of the pound sterling from 1964
to November, 1967. They had skirmished in the gold market in
late 1967 and early 1968. They had sympathized with France
when that country devalued its franc by 11.1 percent in August,
1969. They had assisted West Germany when that country tried
futilely to avoid revaluation in the fall of 1969.

Now they were involved in the toughest battle of all. They
had to save the American dollar, and prevent the entire monetary system from collapsing. For years, under the Bretton
Woods monetary system introduced at end of World War II, the
world had been on a dollar-gold system, with the pound sterling
providing assistance as a reserve currency. The dollar was as
good as gold, exchangeable into the yellow metal at $35 an ounce.
In recent years, however, as America's balance of payments
deficits mounted, the U.S. Treasury and Federal Reserve spent
an increasing amount of time persuading central banks not to
cash dollars for gold.

A central bank is a government agency detailed to protect
a nation's currency through controls over credit and the money
supply. Customarily it operates with a secrecy which might be
the envy of Swiss bankers. But a central bankers' secret was
leaking in the spring of 1971, much to their embarrassment. It
appeared that, since 1969, central bankers had been investing
considerable sums in the eurodollar market. In effect, they had
been increasing the strains on the U.S. dollar.

Dollars which had been deposited at a central bank by private holders were invested by banks in the euromarket. Those dollars were put to work by commercial sources, ultimately returning to central banks as if they were new dollars. Banks noted dollars on books and again recycled them in the eurodollar market. Money returned as new dollars. Before the banks finished, they may have counted the same dollars over and over again. Each count added to the foreign claims against the U.S.

Actions of European central banks and BIS added billions to those bank claims. The German Bundesbank annual report for 1970, issued in April, 1971, says: "A considerable part of the rise in foreign exchange reserves—probably more than $5 billion in 1970—can only be explained by a reserve creation via the euromoney market independently of the U.S. payments deficit. During the period under review [1970], central banks invested a fairly large amount of dollar reserves not in the United States but directly or indirectly in the euromoney market, from where they flowed back to the central banks via the commercial banks of the countries involved; thus the same sum of dollars was added to the monetary reserves several times over."

Dr. Max Iklé, former general manager of the Swiss National Bank, estimated that the total may have amounted to about $11 billion by August, 1971. The German Bundesbank 1971 annual report, issued in April, 1972, estimated that the figure had mounted to about $13 billion by the end of 1971.

In that report for 1971, the Bundesbank claimed that central banks of the Group of Ten had ceased to invest reserves in eurodollars. However, by the spring of 1971, much of the damage already had been done. The same banks which were expected to be in the front line defending the dollar were busily investing their own dollars in a way that undercut it.

Admittedly, it would be wrong to claim that these banks brought down the dollar. Mismanagement in Washington did that. But dealings in the eurodollar market by central banks may have hastened the crisis. For years, the Gnomes of Zurich had been criticized by outsiders in every currency run. This time they remained in the background, behind the Gnomes of Basle.

Blaming Zurich bankers for currency crises is about like

blaming the umbrella for the rain. It was evident before much of 1971 had passed that a monetary umbrella was going to be needed in the year by the U.S. dollar. The U.S. had emerged from 1970 with a balance of payments deficit of $9.8 billion on an official settlements basis. This measures the deficit which has been accumulated with foreign central banks, many of which had helped increase that deficit by their activities on the euro-dollar market.

Every one of those $9.8 billion dollars was a claim against America's holdings of gold, for the U.S. then still was insisting that each dollar was worth 1/35 of an ounce of gold. The total claims against the dollar had mounted to the point where they were three times greater than the entire gold hoard which the U.S. has at Fort Knox, Kentucky, and in vaults of the Federal Reserve Bank in New York.

The Nixon Administration adopted a brave front. Admittedly, the country was in a recession, but the second half would be seeing a pickup, it was claimed. The economy had to be stimulated, even if this meant low interest rates and a continued outflow of money to Europe. There wasn't much the Europeans could do about it. The policy for defense of the dollar would be one of benign neglect, letting the dollar take care of itself. Dollars would start coming home once the U.S. economy improved, claimed the U.S. government.

That policy convinced Europeans that America really didn't care how many dollars flowed to Europe. They uneasily claimed that Europe had reached the limit of its ability to absorb dollars. Washington paid little heed to their complaints.

Still, there were some grounds for U.S. satisfaction. The U.S. spent $1.8 billion in military expenditures in Western Europe in 1970, yet was able to attain near equilibrium in its transactions with that area. Japan and Canada contributed most to the 1970 payments deficit. Meanwhile, net investment income from American companies abroad showed a rising trend which led sources in Washington to believe that income from capital investments might replace lost export income.

Reviewing events of 1971, it appears that the developing money crisis was different from any which had occurred in the past. Short-term capital movements played a most important role.

At root were the Gnomes of New York, of Detroit, of Chicago, and of other places offering bases to multinational corporations. Assists came from big international banks, and from the Gnomes of Basle.

Admittedly, corporation officials merely followed consciences in protecting funds of stockholders. They sought to minimize the effects of a possible dollar devaluation. In the process, they made that devaluation more certain.

In February and March, 1971, money markets reacted uneasily to any news of dollar troubles. A steady and growing movement of money developed from America to Europe. Some of this was worry money, funds owned by people who thought that strong European currencies might be better than the American dollar. Some represented money flowing to Europe for a better return. At the end of March, 1971, three-month U.S. Treasury bills paid 3.3 percent. The three-month eurodollar rate was 5.25 percent. The three-month interest rate in West Germany was 7.5 percent.

Some money belonged to American banks repaying debts. And thereby hangs a tale which should have warned Washington very early in 1971 that trouble was ahead for the dollar.

The tale goes back to 1969, when the U.S. followed such a tight money policy that corporations were strapped for cash. To help, American banks borrowed on the eurodollar market through European branches, and funneled the money to American customers. In 1969, banks raised $15 billion this way versus only $6 billion the preceding year. In the process, they pushed eurodollar interest rates to an all-time high of 11 percent for three-month deposits.

Bank officials were heroes to financially pressed American companies. The inflow of money into the U.S. created an appearance of improvement in the balance of payments which was deceptive. Moreover, debts must be repaid. In the summer of 1970 banks started repaying. Through the rest of the year and into May, 1971, debt repayments swelled the movement of money to Europe by $10 billion.

In the spring of 1971, money markets were ready for trouble, when, on March 11, Chase Manhattan Bank, New York, cut its prime lending rate by a half point to 5.25 percent. This created a chain reaction among other banks. John C. Holman, executive

vice president of Wells Fargo Bank, conceded at a press conference that the prime rate "could go as low as 5 percent."

That warned everybody that America was more concerned
about its recession than about the dollar. The flow of money
from the U.S. accelerated. West Germany's currency reserves
were rising at an average of $270 million a week. Money traders
were convinced that the Germans were financial supermen,
with a strong mark that would weather any storm.

As economic clouds gathered, Swiss bankers glumly expected trouble. Dr. Schaefer of Union Bank told stockholders in
Zurich, March 12, that the "dollar is exposed to the instability
generated by capital movements across national borders. . . .
Money has a tendency to evade controls and restrictions, and
neither of these types of barriers can brake the flight of capital
for extended periods."

Schaefer leavens his speeches with classical quotations and
with enough intellectualism to satisfy a college president's
forum. In this speech, he mentioned that reforms were necessary, then quoted Paracelsus: "The dosage alone decides if the
medicine will effect a cure or prove worse than the malady."

The overall tone of the lecture was sobering, the sort of
address which prompts listeners to cancel orders for new automobiles, postpone vacations, sell all speculative stocks, and ask
wives if they can find jobs somewhere to bolster finances
through a storm.

On March 31, the West German Bundesbank in Frankfurt
cut its discount rate by a full point to 5 percent. "Heavy inflows
into West Germany of international hot money, accelerating
since the recent U.S. prime rate cuts, made a reduction in the
German discount rate inevitable," a banking source in Frankfurt said.

Hot money is money which moves across borders seeking
higher interest rates or strong currency havens. It may sound as
if it involves crookery. Not so. If you, or a big American corporation, transferred money to Switzerland because you would
prefer to hold the funds in Swiss francs rather than dollars, this
would be hot money.

Such money poured into Germany, stimulating inflation
even as Economics Minister Schiller was fighting to contain it.

Schiller is a bespectacled, scholarly economist and university professor who is sometimes described as the Callas of the Social Democratic Party. He is brilliant and temperamental, an undoctrinaire socialist who spends fourteen hours a day at his desk and expects aides to do likewise. A friend says: "He has all the intellectual arrogance of the true egghead, but he is superbly efficient and a complete master of the whole field of economics."

For weeks, Schiller had been resisting pressure to float the mark. He preferred fixed parities. Now, with the flood of dollars into Germany, he wavered. Germany could not absorb many more dollars.

Meanwhile, the American public seemed ignorant of dangers. Monetary machinations often are little understood by the laity, not because they are so complex, but because high priests of the monetary cult insist on conducting rites in absolute secrecy. Their general attitude is: the less the public knows, the better.

Sometimes they are right. Nevertheless, if politicians talked more freely about causes of money depreciation, perhaps more people would understand the language of money. If people did, however, few politicians who favor inflation would ever be elected. So, for them silence or misstatement is a virtue. Right after Britain's pound devaluation in 1967, for example, Prime Minister Harold Wilson went on television to tell Britishers that the action didn't change the pounds in their pockets by one iota.

Wilson, now just plain Mr. Wilson as leader of the opposition British Labor Party, is a silver-haired, suave politician with rosy cheeks who usually looks as if he had spent the last hour in a barber shop. He can remember anything he ever said in the last twenty years if the statement proved true, citing time, place, and speech page number for benefit of enterprising Wilsonian researchers. This retentive facility fades quickly when a speech of his proves wrong.

Truth is, anytime a currency is debased, anyone holding that currency suffers, even though damage may not be apparent at the moment. If the man-in-the-street in America did not recognize this in the spring of 1971, treasurers of multinational corporations did. They used every foreign exchange gimmick available to make certain that overseas operations would have few dollars on hand when devaluation came.

In international dealings, money is a commodity which reacts to supply and demand in about the same way as do beans, potatoes, or copper. If supply is short, demand pushes prices up. If supply is ample, demand slackens and prices fall.

By agreement, currencies have parities, or center rates. Because demand for currencies rises and falls, bands are established on each side of the parities. In 1971, this usually represented a 1 percent margin on each side of that parity. Thus, in 1971, the British pound had a parity of $2.40. But the rate could vary from $2.38 to $2.42, for a side margin of 0.833 percent.

The dollar was the exception. This was the pivotal currency around which the monetary system orbited. It remained fixed in relationship to gold, one dollar equaling 1/35 of an ounce of monetary gold. If the dollar weakened, as it did in the spring of 1971, it stayed at one dollar equals 1/35 of an ounce of gold. But values of other currencies would rise in foreign exchange markets in relationship to the dollar, while the free gold price might climb too.

Confusion in money markets is sometimes compounded for laymen because markets quote rates in two ways: in U.S. cents per foreign currency, and in units of the foreign currency which equal a U.S. dollar. Thus, the pound in early 1971 was officially set at $2.40. If the dollar weakened, the rate might go to $2.41 or $2.42, indicating that you needed more cents every time you purchased a British pound with American currency on the foreign exchange market.

The German mark had a parity of 3.66 marks to the dollar. When the dollar weakened, the mark rate would go down, perhaps to 3.65 or 3.64. This meant that any time you exchanged dollars for marks you were getting fewer marks for your money.

Money markets may be controlled by feeding dollars into them, or by withholding dollars. Dollars were, and still are, the favored intervention currency. In 1971, the dollar was fixed at 1/35 of an ounce of gold, so it represented a fixed entity, just as a foot rule or a quart container provides the unchanging unit for measuring a length or quantity.

Often, in the U.S., the importance of gold is downgraded.

Most Europeans think differently. Not only do they realize its value as a monetary measuring stick, they treasure it in reserves as something which is likely to retain value no matter what happens to paper currencies.

"There is every indication that gold has far from played out its role as a reserve element," said Dr. Samuel Schweizer, then chairman of Swiss Bank Corp. "On the contrary, it is likely to consolidate its privileged status, the greater the glut of other reserve media becomes."

Gold is so valued by central banks that they never even consider using it as an intervention unit in foreign exchange markets. The task of intervening in those markets within its territory belongs to a central bank. If it appears that the dollar rate is falling too fast on a market, the central bank may buy dollars, reducing the supply available. This pushes the price of the dollar up in normal markets. If the dollar price rises higher than is considered best for the country's economy, the central bank sells dollars on its market. The added supply pushes the dollar price down.

In the spring of 1971, so many dollars were pouring into key European countries like Germany, Switzerland, and Britain that central banks could not buy enough dollars to push the dollar rate upward. On April 1, the U.S. Treasury announced in Washington that it would offer a special issue of $1.5 billion worth of securities to plug the drain of dollars into the eurodollar market. It was an April Fools' Day gesture which did little to change events.

That same day in London, the Bank of England followed its traditional practice whenever it has a momentous announcement. It dispatched one of its top-hatted messengers to the London Stock Exchange to announce that the bank was cutting its discount rate a full point to 6 percent.

The discount rate of a nation is the central bank's charge on loans to commercial banks. The rate influences the general level of interest rates. A lower rate often stimulates domestic lending and may improve economic prospects. A lower rate also may discourage the inflow of capital from foreigners, since it reduces returns on their money.

Sometimes internal policy conflicts with a nation's external desire. It may prefer low domestic interest rates to stimulate the economy, whereas higher rates might be desirable to keep funds from flowing outward. Generally, whenever internal and external policies conflict, the internal wins the argument. Politicians worry more about voters at home than about what foreigners might say about the nation's currency.

At the Bank of England on that April Fools' Day, a spokesman said: "Interest rates overseas have been falling for some months, and further reductions have taken place just recently. Today's change in the discount rate is in harmony with this trend, and is intended to avoid a further widening of the margin between rates in Britain and abroad."

Off the record, officials at the Treasury expressed concern about the weaknesses of the U.S. dollar. A flood of money was pouring into Britain, pushing the pound close to its $2.42 ceiling. This meant, of course, that the dollar was on the floor.

Three days later, in Washington, a U.S. Treasury spokesman, Cal Brumley, was insisting that the influx of dollars into Europe did not mean any exchange rate changes were coming. Brumley, then forty-eight, had spent most of his career with the *Wall Street Journal* and with the *Journal*'s affiliate, Associated Press–Dow Jones Economic News Service. He understood monetary and financial matters and he was a fellow who didn't like to dissemble. But the Nixon Administration firmly believed that Europeans couldn't do much about the dollar's weaknesses no matter how much they squealed.

In Zurich, bankers complained about how short-term capital flows were disrupting money markets. Dr. Hans J. Mast, knowledgeable chief economist of Swiss Credit Bank, is a thin-haired, straightforward man who carries enough monetary data in his head to dictate a book. Sitting behind a desk piled high with reports in three languages, he worried about the casual manner with which America was treating its dollar problem.

"Something should be done to control capital movements," he said. "Your American companies are investing so much money abroad that they are upsetting the monetary system."

Nearly every American corporation doing business abroad was trying to maintain overseas liquidity to the maximum allowed by the U.S. Office of Foreign Direct Investment. It is standard corporate practice today to reduce holdings of a weak currency to the lowest possible limit. This meant that overseas dollar holdings were being sold for marks, pounds, francs, and to a growing extent, Japanese yen.

Multinational corporations were hedging, playing leads and lags and shorting the dollar, often using eurodollars to do it. Hedging is common in international trade to protect a company against foreign exchange losses. Thus, an American company subsidiary located in Britain may sell some of its products on a deal which calls for payment of $1 million in dollars in six months' time from a firm in Germany. But the U.S. subsidiary doesn't know what the dollar will be worth in six months. Should a devaluation occur before payment, the company loses.

To protect ("cover" is the term used in foreign exchange) itself, the company sells $1 million worth of dollars forward for delivery in six months' time. This hedges the risk. If the dollar were devalued, there would be a loss on the payment from Germany. This would be balanced by the profit from the foreign exchange deal.

Meanwhile, companies were playing leads and lags to the limit. This means that they lagged in the payment of any bills owed internationally in dollars, hoping bills could be repaid with cheaper, devalued dollars later. They lead, or hurried payments, to Germany, Switzerland, Japan, and other nations with strong currencies, lest a dollar devaluation increase costs of those bills.

Professional speculators may deal in foreign exchange for profit, too. In times of monetary unease, the foreign exchange market becomes like a giant casino. It's no place for the little guy, though. By custom, banks and foreign exchange dealers use the interbank rate for measuring foreign exchange commissions, and that applies to amounts of $250,000 and up. Money changing charges rise fast when small amounts are involved, as anyone knows who has ever cashed travelers checks during a money crisis.

Of course, if you are a little guy with $250,000 and up in your pocket, well. . . . In recent years, fortunes have been made in every currency crisis by speculators who knew how to sell the pound short in 1967, the French franc short in 1969, and the dollar short in 1971.

All through 1971 the *International Harry Schultz Letter* and similar investing newsletters were telling people how they could short the dollar, or increase assets by getting out of it. Schultz is a diminutive, Milwaukee-born writer who has the distinction of being an introvert promoter. He seems ill at ease in a crowd, yet he is a whiz at promoting himself and the letter which he distributes at $125 a year on a twenty-five-times-a-year basis.

The true speculator sees nothing immoral about his activity, for to him all markets are amoral. Markets react the way they do because of laws of supply and demand, not because of the immorality of the participating speculators.

In April, 1971, a speculator had no trouble selling the dollar on three months' forward contracts with 10 percent or less margin. Many operators made an 80 percent profit on their money that spring and summer through shorting the dollar.

The foreign exchange department of a bank looks exactly like the eurodollar department. In fact, in most banks, both operations are carried on together. Nearly all foreign exchange transactions are handled via telegraph, telex, and telephone. On one visit to Swiss Credit Bank's foreign exchange department, twenty-four traders hung onto telephones, or leaned over telex machines. The babble of voices produced a constant hum of sound, with the clack of the telexes forming a sonorous background. The volume of business handled by a department like this is staggering.

"We do about $250 billion worth of foreign exchange business in a year here," said Ernst Bigler, manager of the bank's gold and foreign exchange departments. He is a man of medium build, fair hair, and brisk manner, who seems undisturbed by the scope for losses represented by the business going through the bank.

"Did you say billion?" The visitor found the figure hard to believe.

"Yes, $250 billion," said Bigler. "As you know, the dollar is the only real market which exists in the foreign exchange field, so all our trading is against the dollar."

In trading, the bank may take two orders from the same customer, $5 million to buy and $5 million to sell a currency forward against the dollar, for instance. This provides the client with currency protection no matter what happens, and the contracts add up to $10 million. But the only amount changing hands will be the difference between the two contracts when it comes time to settle. Thus, the $250 billion figure does not mean that this amount of cash is flowing in and out of the department.

In the foreign exchange field a figure of .001 may have a lot of meaning to a trader. For instance, at the start of a day, a trader may purchase $10 million with Swiss francs. Should the dollar weaken to bring the rate down by .005, that would mean the dealer has lost 50,000 Swiss francs on that purchase, or about $13,000. Then, suppose another $10 million worth of dollars are purchased and the rate declines another .005. That's $26,000 down, with the day barely started.

This is only a paper loss as long as dollars are unsold. Still, it probably would cause a hurried conference. With the bank buying, the rate is slumping. Is someone unloading dollars? Are there adverse factors for the dollar which the bank hadn't known about when it established its morning quotes?

"Sometimes, it takes strong nerves to sit out a situation," says Bigler.

In the above example, this may have been a case of a bank dumping dollars for internal reasons, with Swiss Credit getting the brunt of the offloading. The dollar rate may pick up. Before the day is over, those dollars acquired in the morning for an apparent loss may be sold for a profit.

Foreign exchange departments in all major banks worked overtime in the black April of 1971. London is far and away the biggest foreign exchange center, reflecting the city's importance as a trade and shipping center. Other key foreign exchange centers are New York City, Zurich, Geneva, Frankfurt, Brussels, Milan, and Amsterdam, not necessarily in that order. Prior to 1961 when the U.S. Treasury started dealing in foreign exchange, New York definitely was in the minor league in foreign exchange.

Until the dollar developed troubles, most American corporations dealt almost exclusively in dollars, no matter where they traded. Only the big multinationals had foreign exchange departments of any consequence. Now, dollar troubles were changing that.

"You name any American company with international operations and you can be pretty sure that its financial people somewhere along the line are shifting funds into marks, Swiss francs, or Japanese yen," said a Swiss-based official of one big New York bank, in early April, 1971.

Many Europeans wondered uneasily if central banks could continue accepting dollars. The German Bundesbank reported that its reserves of gold and foreign exchange had soared to a March-end $15.6 billion, a doubling of the total in fifteen months. Meanwhile, the United States experienced a first-quarter deficit on an official settlements basis of over $5 billion, $3.5 billion of it due to the outflow of short-term capital. The American hemorrhage in that one quarter exceeded what had been anticipated for the entire year.

On April 19, when central bankers met in Basle for their monthly meeting at BIS, they pressed the U.S. to limit the growth of the dollar supply. But the American position was clear. First emphasis had to be placed on stimulating the American economy. Europeans should relax. The money crisis would peter out as had earlier threats to the dollar. If Europeans didn't want to attract any more dollars, nations with strong currencies such as Germany and Switzerland could revalue them.

There were some red faces when bankers discussed eurodollars and the way central banks and the BIS had contributed to America's deficit through that market. It was agreed that central banks would no longer invest in eurodollars. A committee was established to examine how controls might be introduced to fetter the euromarket. Some bankers argued that it was becoming a financial monster.

Valéry Giscard d'Estaing, France's brilliant and scholarly finance minister, took this position. The next day in Paris he publicly called for international regulation of eurodollars. France always has been the most control-minded of continental nations, ready to establish an army of bureaucrats over industry at the first strains of *La Marseillaise*. As for the eurodollar, French hated this as an instrument which was enabling the American dollar to dominate Europe.

Wednesday, April 21, Germany's then economics minister Schiller made an appearance among the gaudy-painted buildings of the Hanover Fair. Flags waved gaily in the wind before pavilions. Crowds clustered around displays of derricks, mine conveyors, coal shovels, and other industrial equipment which Germans build so well.

In one of the pavilions, Schiller took the rostrum, told businessmen that he firmly opposed any revaluation of the German mark. He called for a more elastic monetary system. The crowd listened and applauded. Some interpreted that speech to mean that the government was considering a mark float.

A currency is floated when the central bank suspends its intervention in the money market, allowing supply and demand of currencies to set the rates. Germany's parity of 3.66 to the dollar had an upper limit of 3.69 and a lower limit of 3.63. Under a float, if the heavy dollar inflow continued, this would cheapen the dollar against the mark.

In effect, the mark and dollar were like two kids at each end of a teeter-totter. When the dollar went down, the mark went up. The U.S. government urged Germany to recognize that it had a super-strong currency and to revalue it. Revaluation, however, is never popular. When the value of a currency rises, the export prices of that country may rise, too. This makes it harder for companies to sell abroad. Meanwhile, import prices drop in foreign exchange terms. This increases import competition.

Moreover, it is difficult for a nation to determine the exact revaluation figure. Should it be 2 percent or 4 percent? Or what? If set too low, the revaluation encourages speculators to gamble that another may follow the first. Ah, so someone might say, the answer is to select a high figure which would discourage such speculation.

That's not good either. The higher the revaluation figure, the higher may be export prices. The higher that level, the harder will it be for the nation's exporters to sell in competitive foreign trade markets.

Academics and economists on both sides of the Atlantic had been saying for months that the answer to this problem lay in floating a currency such as the German mark. The free market then would determine the level to which the mark should rise. Curiously, few exporters, foreign trade experts, or bankers in foreign commerce favored floating rates. They prefer to know what a foreign exchange rate may be in the future, hedging to protect themselves if any changes are expected. With a floating rate, that rate might be changing every minute of the day.

"Much of the pressure for floating rates comes from professors and scholars who have never handled a foreign trade contract in their lives," said one official of Union Bank in Zurich.

Economics Minister Schiller, a fixed rate proponent, now was leaning in the direction of floating rates. He needed only a slight push to nudge him across the line of decision. That push was being readied by five of Germany's prestigious research organizations.

Meanwhile, in Switzerland, a new law took effect on April 1 that was akin to buying an umbrella just before a rain. It revised the country's mint law, giving the government authority to revise the parity of the Swiss franc. Previously, any change of the parity had to be considered by parliament, and might have been made subject to a national referendum within a three-month period. It would have been difficult to change the parity in any crisis without risking chaos for up to three months.

Almost nobody wanted to change the value of the franc. Yet, Swiss bankers breathed easier when the mint law revision finally cleared parliament, just in time as events proved.

In Washington, Pierre-Paul Schweitzer, managing director of the International Monetary Fund, had been watching the developing storm with growing unease. At fifty-nine, he had been boss of IMF for eight years, a conscientious public servant who had won the French Croix de Guerre as a resistance fighter in World War II. Now he could see another battle ahead, a battle to save the U.S. dollar and the whole monetary system.

The IMF had been created at Bretton Woods in 1944. Its objectives were to facilitate expansion and balanced growth of international trade, to promote exchange stability, to maintain orderly exchange arrangements among members, to oppose competitive exchange depreciation, and to make fund resources available to needy members. In effect, it is an international bank, a monetary policeman without a club, an information forum for monetary data and a medium for furthering international financial cooperation.

It is also an agency for crying wolf in time of monetary danger. Schweitzer considered this to be such a time. He called on the U.S. to check its inflation and tried to alert people to dangers posed by the weak dollar. His voice was lost in the storm.

In the last week of April, David Kennedy, the ex-Chicago banker who was President Nixon's special ambassador, flew to Tokyo to try to persuade Japan to revalue its superstrong yen. Tadasu Sasaki, governor of the Bank of Japan, coolly brushed the suggestion aside.

Later, Japanese and European statesmen were to claim that Treasury Secretary Connally was a brutal diplomat who ignored foreign sensibilities. In retrospect, it appears that some countries were unwilling to take even token steps to help the dollar during its crisis.

By the end of April, West Germany's reserves had climbed to $15.8 billion, a total comfortably larger than the reserves of the U.S. Japan's reserves totaled about $6 billion, up from $4.8 billion at the end of 1970. The free gold price finished the month of April at $39.75, inching up about twenty cents on the last trading day of the month.

Saturday, May 1, was a holiday on the Continent, the European equivalent of Labor Day. Few bankers enjoyed that holiday. The air of crisis hung over money markets. Still, most sources felt that somehow the monetary system would surmount this flurry, just as it had survived earlier ones.

That certainly seemed to be the view at the Bundesbank in Frankfurt. Frankfurt, a much bombed city in World War II, is a rebuilt prosperous metropolis of modern buildings and well-stocked stores. This is a city of money, where the financiers of Germany raise capital for new Volkswagen plants or Thyssen steel mills, discussing their deals over *schnitzel und spätzle* when lunching at the Frankfurter Hof or at the Kaiserkeller mit Arnoldgrill. The Bundesbank on Taunus Anlage is as solid as the German character is supposed to be, a building for guarding the treasures of an empire, or the good name of the American dollar.

The dollar's reputation, indeed, came under attack as soon as the Bundesbank opened for business on Monday, May 3. Speculators were trading dollars for marks at Germany's commercial banks. Dollars came to the Bundesbank, which returned good marks to the commercial banks. Yet officials were heartened that the inflow didn't exceed $100 million that day. The preceding week the inflow had averaged about $200 million a day.

Trouble arrived near the end of the business day. West German business and industry leaders heeded economic reports prepared by key economic institutes. Five of these institutes had been cooperating in an intensive study of the economy and of the ultra-strong mark. Institutes released the report on this Monday. It created a bombshell.

Four of the institutes, those in Hamburg, Kiel, Munich, and Essen, advised the government to float the DM. The fifth institute, that in West Berlin, suggested that the government should either revalue the mark or float it.

A key graph of the joint report said: "All weapons used by the government to stabilize the economy are worn out, and new restrictions would do little to improve the situation. Therefore, there is no alternative to a free float of the currency for an indefinite period."

Markets closed too soon on Monday for the report to have much effect. An attempt at reassurance came from Chicago, from Paul W. McCracken, chairman of President Nixon's Council of Economic Advisors. Dr. McCracken, a learned university professor, had the unenviable task of exhibiting a cheery public front concerning the American economy. This day, he donned his Good Humor Man role before the International Economics Forum in the Windy City.

He claimed that the interest rate differential between Europe and the U.S. was changing for the better. "If the trend continues, we can reasonably anticipate a significant reduction of short-term capital flows," he said. "There are heartening signs that the worst may be over."

Next day, a record $1 billion poured into the Bundesbank in Frankfurt. Every foreign exchange speculator on both sides of the Atlantic put more faith in the report of Germany's economic institutes than in Dr. McCracken.

In Zurich, foreign exchange departments of banks faced near-panic markets. Orders came to sell dollars. Sell. Sell. Sell.

The National Bank desperately supported the dollar at its 4.295 francs per dollar floor.

Before, the National Bank had remained almost aloof from the money market. Switzerland has such a well-oiled money machine that, as dollars poured in, bankers shunted them quickly into eurodollars, into the American market, into dozens of other investment opportunities. The inflow merely meant that bankers had to work harder and faster.

The National Bank of Switzerland occupies a whole block at the foot of Bahnhofstrasse in Zurich, just before the street ends on the shores of the Lake of Zurich. The building has the heavy, formidable appearance of a fortress erected for defense of some cherished liberty. This isn't far from fact for the franc is considered by Swiss to be an element of democracy worth defending to the last gold bar in vaults of the National Bank.

By a characteristic oddity, the Zurich building is only one of the headquarters of the bank. When the National Bank was created in 1905, Berne claimed the headquarters as its right. Even then, Zurich was becoming an important financial center. Financial moguls of Zurich didn't see why the thick-headed Bernese should lay any claims to a financial institution which would do most of its business in Zurich.

In olden days, such arguments resulted in wars. Swiss solved the impasse in a typically Swiss, civilized fashion. Two headquarters were created. The administrative headquarters and the mint were placed in Berne. The operational headquarters was located in Zurich. This means that the task of intervening in money markets is handled in Zurich where the bulk of the country's foreign exchange business is conducted.

With the dollar slipping downward, the National Bank entered the market, beginning to buy dollars. It protected the dollar from falling through the parity floor, but only at a price of about $100 million on that Tuesday.

By now it was apparent that this was no ordinary crisis. Phone lines hummed between Frankfurt and Zurich after the close of markets. Bankers talked with bankers. How did the situation look? Could parity floors be held? Swiss bankers disliked asking the question which bothered many of them: Would the Bundesbank open for business the next day?

The Bundesbank would, it was made evident. This was no time for lack of will. Speculators had taken enormous loans in the eurodollar market to finance some of their buying of marks and Swiss francs. The Bundesbank thought that a solid front of central bankers would defeat them. Loans would come due shortly, and speculators would have to cover.

Nevertheless, it was a tense crew which opened the Bundesbank for business on Wednesday, May 5. If the day passed with the rate held at 3.63 marks to the dollar, the worst might be over. The U.S. Federal Reserve had expressed their intention to sop up some of the surplus dollars with a securities issue. The heavy movement of money from American banks in the U.S. to branches abroad was expected to ease before long. Central banks had committed themselves not only to ending investments in the eurodollar market, but to withdrawing some of their investments from it. All in all, it did seem as if speculators might lose courage, if the bank could win the battle this day.

Vain hope.

Orders for sale of dollars had piled up all night on telex machines in commercial banks and finance houses around the country. When the Bundesbank opened its doors at 9:30 A.M., traders were hit by an inpouring of these orders. Telephones clamored for attention. Telex machines clacked away with fresh sell orders. A million dollars here. Ten million dollars there. Twenty million dollars in another order. Every order specified sale of dollars, with no regard for the price.

In fifty-five minutes of trading, the Bundesbank accepted a fantastic $1 billion. At that pace, the bank might have absorbed the equivalent of America's total gold and foreign exchange reserves in two days flat.

At 10:30 A.M. the bank surrendered, closed its doors. Stunned officials wondered what this meant. It meant, of course, that the Bretton Woods monetary system had entered its death agonies.

Money markets in Zurich operated for another half hour. News of the closing of the Frankfurt money exchange reached Zurich almost immediately. But human reflexes don't react as fast as electronic impulses over communications networks. Swiss banks had no contingency plans for such an emergency.

Traders continued to accept dollars, immediately resold them to the Central Bank.

There was no chance of putting those dollars into euro markets, or anywhere else. Nobody wanted dollars. They were mere accounting tabulations, which only the Central Bank would honor. The Central Bank bought and bought. A total of $600 million engulfed the bank before it, too, closed its markets.

By a coincidence, Dr. Fritz Leutwiler, a Swiss Central Bank director in Zurich, had scheduled an address that same day before the Sound Money Association. This is a group composed mainly of bankers, who are just as conservative as the title of their association signifies. The meeting gave Dr. Leutwiler an opportunity to report that the bank had accepted $100 million in dollars on Tuesday, $600 million on its shortened Wednesday, and about $1.3 billion over the preceding six weeks.

Netherlands, Belgium, and Austria closed their money markets immediately behind the Swiss. That same morning in Paris, a high official of the French Finance Ministry talked in his offices adjacent to the Louvre Museum, with a reporter from the *Wall Street Journal*. An aide rushed in to say that the German Bundesbank had stopped buying dollars. Surprise marked the official's face. There had been no consultation between Germany and France. Everybody had been surprised by the enormity of the speculative wave which had engulfed the German money market.

Willy Brandt, West Germany's square-jawed chancellor, wasn't even in Germany. He was in London making a good-will appearance before the House of Commons. That Wednesday evening he hurried home to a Germany with paralyzed markets.

At height of the crisis, U.S. Treasury Secretary John Connally declared that it would not cause any change in U.S. policies. This was a European, not a dollar problem, he said. This wasn't very reassuring to Europeans. Most of them believed that the free spending, low interest policies of the U.S. were responsible for the crisis.

The American government hoped that the monetary impasse would force other industrial nations to revalue currencies. This would leave the dollar untouched, but worth less measured against German marks, Japanese yen, Swiss francs, French

francs, Dutch guilders, and maybe the British pound sterling.
America would have the benefits of a dollar devaluation without
devaluation's political onus. A politician dislikes a devaluation,
for voter reaction may boot him out of office come the next
election. So it was easier for America to press for revaluations
elsewhere, hoping for the same result, lower prices on American
exports and higher prices on imports into the U.S.

Dealings in West German marks had stopped. Trading of
dollars continued in isolated markets, but with dollar holders
receiving only ninety cents and less on the dollar. In Brussels,
the Hilton Hotel refused to cash dollars. In London, the Savoy,
Claridges, and other deluxe hotels cashed dollar travelers checks
only in amounts of up to $100 a transaction. The discounts
ranged from 10 to 20 percent. Confused American travelers
spent more time trying to cash money than in sightseeing.

In Bonn, Conrad Ahlers, the official spokesman for the
Brandt government, went on television on Thursday, May 6, to
say that Germany would not revalue. The only alternatives
were to float the mark, or to reopen money exchanges with
stringent money controls to bar dollar inflows.

In New York, the Federal Reserve Bank, America's equivalent of a central bank, reported that it had spent about $1.3
billion trying to calm money markets. It had, for instance, purchased $1 billion of government securities which holders
dumped in panic.

That same day in Washington, Treasury Secretary Connally told a press conference that the problem "can't be at-
tributed to any action of the U.S., or to a weakness of the dollar."
The Treasury Secretary was laying the foundation for some of
the resentment among Europeans which was to affect events
later in the year.

Connally is a breezy, boisterous Texan with silver hair and
the good looks of a middle-aged matinee idol. And like an actor,
he seems to be continually emoting for fans in the upper galler-
ies. He plays the game of politics with shrewdness and daring,
a man to esteem if he is on your side. Though nominally a
Democrat (one-time democratic governor of Texas), he was
added to the Nixon team not because of his financial expertise,
but for his command ability in tough situations.

"Neither Nixon nor John Connally understands this sort of thing [the monetary crisis]," one Washington source told the *Wall Street Journal* during the crisis.

Connally was to learn fast. One suspects, too, that the President also had a much better understanding of monetary matters before 1971 ended.

Germany's closure of its money markets irritated Common Market partners. Theoretically, a Common Market nation must consult partners before taking any drastic actions. Germany claimed that the suddenness of the money onslaught had caught it unaware. Still, other nations, particularly France, thought that it should have received at least a little warning, if only to preserve a fantasy of mutual cooperation within the European Communities.

France was particularly concerned now. The agricultural price system in EC is pegged to a "unit of account," which had the same value as the dollar. If any EC nation changed the value of its currency, this would upset the whole farm price system which had been negotiated only after much bickering. France was the biggest net gainer under that system. It had the most to lose if the program went down the drain.

A Council of Ministers meeting of EC was hurriedly called for Saturday, May 8, in Brussels. The purpose was to develop a common monetary policy for the bloc, one which would resolve the crisis without destroying the agricultural price system.

Brussels is a bourgeois city built around its opera setting Grand Place, where a fifteenth-century City Hall sits on a square of fifteenth- and sixteenth-century-styled buildings. Most of the buildings had been destroyed in 1695 by the French. The good burghers of the town stubbornly insisted on rebuilding the square in original style, with a few baroque embellishments. Obstinacy is a Belgian trait, still found in Belgium. Nobody ever wins an argument with a Belgian, something modern visitors discover every time they are overcharged by a Belgian taxi driver (which is just about everytime).

The city experienced a rejuvenation when the Commission of the European Communities established its headquarters here. Now, as the capital of the Common Market, Brussels fancies itself to be quite a metropolis. But the men who really run the

Common Market are on its Council of Ministers, the foreign, finance, and agricultural ministers of the member countries. Except for the Belgians who live in Brussels, these men breeze into the city for a council meeting, raise some journalistic smoke, then depart for home capitals after a brief taste of the city's justly renowned cuisine. The Proçencaux, the Carlton, the Villa Lorraine, and various other restaurants are usually what statesmen talk about when rehashing days spent in Brussels, not about the harmonization of taxes in EC or the price of pig meat in Community meat packing plants.

In Zurich, those gnomes who allegedly are at the heart of every money crisis, sat on the sidelines. Events were emphasizing quite clearly that the Gnomes of Zurich are only part of the machinery in a money crisis, not the power supply for it. Yet they had a big stake in developments, too. Banks and clients held enormous sums in eurodollar loans, in investments in the American market, and in dollar-denominated bonds.

On that Saturday, as Common Market ministers assembled in Brussels, one executive of a Big Three bank said in Zurich: "If Switzerland doesn't revalue, the speculators will shift their attention from Germany to us. We will be overwhelmed by the flood of dollars."

Soundings made among banks indicated that nobody wanted a floating Swiss franc. Switzerland's prosperity had been built on a basis of stability, not only of the economy, but of the franc itself. People who invested in Switzerland from outside wanted to know what their francs might be worth come time to take them out.

Eyes focused on Brussels. Swiss newsmen joined the throng of journalists who converged on the Common Market capital for what some felt might be a historic meeting. Perhaps all the Common Market nations might revalue their currencies together against the U.S. dollar. Impetus might even be started toward establishment of a European monetary bloc which might rival a dollar bloc.

That meeting opened at 10:30 A.M. as an encounter between Germany's Schiller and France's Giscard d'Estaing. Neither man likes the other. They are two intellectuals who flash sparks at every encounter. Giscard d'Estaing chaired the session, in a position to use the rules of order to further France's interests.

Germany had about decided to float its mark alone, unless all the EC nations revalued currencies together. France opposed revaluation of its franc. It favored a complex series of money controls which would have hamstrung most people and corporations who tried to shift dollars into the Common Market.

The meeting lasted for twenty hours, finally ending in the early hours of morning.

Even when EC ministers fail to agree, they feel compelled to prepare communiqués which indicate that the Council has jointly agreed to disagree. Euphemisms often patch quarrels. This communiqué said Germany would be allowed to float its currency.

But in a statement after the meeting, Giscard d'Estaing icily said: "Flexible exchange rates are not compatible with the spirit of the Community."

Schiller hurried home to Bonn for an 11 A.M. cabinet meeting on Sunday, May 9. Nothing much ever happens in Bonn on a Sunday, except for mass in the twelfth-century Munster. This Sunday was an exception. Brandt called his cabinet to order promptly and the discussion started. There was no argument. Germany would reopen its money markets the next day, and the mark would float. Free markets would determine how that mark rated against the dollar.

Schiller appeared on television to announce the action. The official rate of the mark, he declared, would remain at 3.66 to the dollar. This was a fiction which Germany maintained for some weeks, as if speculators would somehow be convinced of it. Nobody in Switzerland believed the mark would again see that 3.66 rate.

In Berne, the Federal Council met on Sunday afternoon immediately on receipt of the news from Germany. Consultations already were underway with the National Bank. Nello Celio, Switzerland's finance minister, announced that the Swiss franc was being revalued by 7 percent. The parity rate against the dollar dropped from 4.37 francs to the dollar to 4.08. This was the first change in the nation's currency since 1936. "It was not with a light heart that we took this decision," said Celio.

Austria quickly followed with a 5.05 percent revaluation.

That evening, central bankers were collecting in Basle for another of their monthly meetings at BIS. Their meeting was
somewhat of an anticlimax. Matters had moved from hands of
central bankers to those of politicians.

In Frankfurt, the German money market reopened, with
the dollar dropping to 3.5350 in the day. This represented about
a 3 1/2 percent revaluation of the mark. In Zurich, the dollar
opened at 4.12 in first trading, then slid gently down to 4.0975 at
close. The Netherlands, which has close trade ties with Germany, floated its guilder. Belgium established a complex two-
tier money market. There was no rush of trading in currencies
anywhere. Apparently, the heat had been removed from the
crisis.

In Washington, Nixon Administration folk were smugly
satisfied. The higher the mark floated, the better for the U.S.
The reaction of markets raised hope that things were returning
to normal. The U.S. could continue its policy of stimulating the
domestic economy and allowing foreign nations to solve the
dollar problem through revaluations of their currencies.

Nations like France might protest that gold's price should
be raised to solve the problem. No matter. France could not
force America to raise the price of gold, and thus to devalue the
dollar.

All in all, it seemed to be a narrow escape for the dollar
from what might have been a very tricky situation. But was it
really an escape? Two things developed in that week of May 9
which raised questions. The free price of gold started climbing,
reaching $41.30 on May 14. And heavy buying of the Japanese
yen developed, indicating that speculators, now apparently
blocked in Europe, were seeking another strong currency haven.

CHAPTER X

BATTLE FOR SURVIVAL

One Saturday spring day of 1971, 7,000 young people converged on Wetzikon, a village in the Zurich area for a pop festival called Pop-Monster '71. The event started at 2 P.M. and lasted until midnight, which is late by Zurich standards. The festival made enough noise to be heard five miles away. Organizers tempered hostility by presenting roses to residents of the area in typical flower children fashion. Three dozen of Switzerland's Hell's Angels parked motorcycles and became leather-jacketed policemen. Nobody got hurt. "Loving" sessions developed in dark corners or in bushes on the fringes of the floodlights. Some pot may have been smoked.

All in all, it was a most happy event. Later, in Zurich, one

Swiss banker was asked jestingly if he had attended the affair. He took the question seriously.

"Oh," he said, "it wouldn't have looked right for me to be there, even as a spectator." He shook his head and sighed. "You know, foreigners put their money into Switzerland to get away from pop festivals and things like that. It will be a sad day for Switzerland if the world thinks that pop and long hair have arrived here, too."

Apparently, such word had not reached the wealthy. In June, 1971, money was pouring into Switzerland as if the whole country were a massive bank. Dollars arrived to be changed into Swiss francs, and banked. If the dollar were devalued, speculators would be holding not cheap dollars but strong Swiss francs.

Dollars were either forwarded by anxious Americans and foreigners or shifted by treasurers of American corporations. Obviously, many people were not convinced that the dollar was emerging strongly from the May crisis. The battle for survival of the dollar at 1/35 of an ounce of gold was entering its final phase.

Some sources drew comfort from the apparent success of the German float. Through May, the mark fluctuated in a range equivalent to a 2.5 to 3.5 percent revaluation. At the Bundesbank in Frankfurt, officials talked guardedly of finally establishing a new fixed parity only 3 or 4 percent above the 3.66 rate which Germans still insisted was their official parity. When the Bundesbank opened for business on Wednesday, June 2, it established a mark floor equivalent to a revaluation of only 2.52 percent.

"I would have thought that the mark would be much stronger than that," said one Zurich banker that morning.

To confuse speculators, the Bundesbank bought dollars and sold dollars with no recognizable pattern. Meanwhile, Schiller became economic czar of Germany, adding the finance ministry portfolio to that of economics minister when ailing Alex Möller resigned the finance job. German industrialists were complaining that the Social Democratic coalition government was leading the country into recession. Order books showed a declining trend in industry. The government was urged to contain the revaluation of the mark to 4 percent.

There were some signs that the Bundesbank's policies might pay off. Some of the funds shunted into the country in May departed.

Meanwhile, in Tokyo, the Japanese government insisted that it would not revalue the yen under any circumstance. Everybody but the Japanese thought that the yen was grossly undervalued, not only in relationship to the dollar, but against other currencies as well. The 360 yen to the dollar rate had been established shortly after World War II when Japanese industry was prostrate. Now its powerful economy shipped radios, television sets, automobiles, and dozens of other products into markets of the world to outsell competitors with ridiculous ease.

Japan's reserves of gold and foreign exchange had been climbing steadily. After the German float, those reserves soared. Switzerland and Britain were the other strong currency havens in the monetary battle underway.

On June 2, Britain announced that its reserves rose in May by $103 million, pushing the total to $3.5 billion. In Basle, at the headquarters of BIS, a special committee studied the eurodollar market, but couldn't agree concerning how that market should be controlled.

On June 9, Switzerland banned interest payments on foreign deposits. This made only a marginal difference to the currency inflow. Fright money arrived in Switzerland because holders felt the Swiss franc offered one of the best currency havens to be found. Interest rates didn't matter.

People who had never had Swiss bank accounts were dispatching letters to Swiss banks, with checks enclosed. They wanted Swiss bank accounts to protect their savings.

Central bankers gathered in Basle on Sunday, June 13, for the annual meeting of BIS, a conclave which brings together bankers from Hungary to Sweden and from the New York Federal Reserve Bank to the Bank of Japan. By early evening, the bar of the Euler Hotel hummed with sounds, bankers' sounds, talk about the dollar, currency floats, interest rates, and margin bands.

Next day, BIS issued its forty-first annual report, a document which clearly outlined troubles convulsing the world's monetary system. "The U.S. basic deficit is certainly a continu-

ing weakness of the international monetary situation," said
René Larre, BIS general manager and writer of the report. That
report also reflected the thinking of Dr. Milton Gilbert, American economic adviser to BIS, who has long insisted that America
could correct its dollar problems by increasing the monetary
price of gold.

Jelle Zijlstra, head of the Dutch Central Bank and BIS
chairman, reported that central banks had agreed to withdraw
$3 billion of their funds from the eurodollar market. He, too, was
critical of the way in which the dollar was upsetting the monetary system.

"The dollar cannot remain the basic currency of the international monetary system if the U.S. doesn't participate fully in
the adjustment process," he said.

Corridor conversations indicated that Switzerland had purchased $50 million in gold from the U.S. In March, that coun-
try's National Bank had purchased $75 million worth of gold
from America. Switzerland had the dollars for it. In the month
of June, its reserves of gold and foreign exchange jumped from
$4.6 billion to $5.1 billion.

The Swiss National Bank encouraged commercial banks to
increase money transfers to foreign markets to dampen wild
inflation at home. Article 8 of the Swiss Federal Banking Law
specifies that any foreign loan exceeding Sfr 10 million issued in
Switzerland is subject to the approval of the National Bank. The
bank limit may be lowered, if market conditions warrant. Thus,
the Bank may control the flow of foreign issues. Now, in 1971,
the Bank followed an extremely liberal policy any time banks
wanted permission to float a foreign loan.

Figures show that in 1971, the volume of foreign loans
floated in Switzerland set a record, surpassing the peak set in
1968. In 1971, thirty-eight foreign issues were authorized with a
total nominal value of Sfr 2 billion or just over $500 million. This
compared with eighteen loans registered with a par value of Sfr
871 million in 1970.

"The aim was to encourage the outflow of capital which
had poured into Switzerland as a result of the monetary crisis,"
said an official of Swiss Bank Corp., Basle.

That program seemed to be succeeding. In July, 1971, the

total Swiss reserves dropped by $500 million to $4.6 billion. This decline reflected the ability of the Swiss money machine to transfer funds to outside investments rather than any waning interest among foreigners concerning banking in the country.

July opened with a Council of Ministers meeting in Brussels. France still stood on one side of the table, and Germany on the other. Valéry Giscard d'Estaing, France's finance minister, had been talking about the German float for weeks as if it would end on July 1. At the Brussels session, Germany's economics boss Schiller made it clear that Germany intended to continue its float indefinitely.

At that time, the mark had floated to the equivalent of a 4.4 percent revaluation. Now, sources in Germany were saying that ultimately the rate would settle at about a 6 percent revaluation. In Washington, the Nixon Administration seemed to be happily watching events. The stronger the mark got, the tougher it would be for Volkswagen, Mannesmann, Siemens, and other German companies to sell their products on the American market. Meanwhile, differences in the Common Market played into U.S. hands. As long as Germany and France bickered, there was no possibility of EC organizing a monetary bloc which might counter American policy. The hope was that ultimately France would join Germany either with a float or with an outright revaluation of the French franc.

"If that happens, the Japanese won't be able to hold out. They'll revalue, too, and we'll be out of the woods," one American diplomat in Europe said in that first week of July.

Rumors swept money markets suggesting that France might revalue. A flood of money poured into Paris. If the French franc were due to rise, substantial profits might be made by anyone buying those francs before the revaluation.

One Middle Eastern businessman recently bragged that he made more money in foreign exchange dealings the last few years than he has from his very profitable export-import business. In October, 1967, he used $100,000 in dollars, for instance, to short the pound sterling at a Swiss bank on 10 percent margin. This meant that he was promising to deliver to the bank, on a contract of three months, the same number of pounds as $1 million would purchase on that October date. At the time the pound's parity was $2.80, though the market price was closer to $2.78. The next month the pound was devalued by 14.3 percent to $2.40.

That speculator repaid his obligation with $2.40 pounds instead of $2.78 units. After devaluation his million dollars was worth £416,666, whereas before devaluation it had been worth only £359,700. The difference ($136,000), less commission, represented his profit.

Thus do speculators grow rich. In 1971, those speculators were shorting the dollar, not the pound. And they had company in multinational corporations. MNC's always claim that they are "defending" company money against losses whenever money crises trigger currency transfers. A treasurer doesn't complain, however, if a transaction earns an exchange profit. From the volume of money transfers made by corporations in 1971, it appears that many companies were trying to do more than break even. The U.S. dollar suffered in the process.

Curiously, some people regard it as "unpatriotic" when an individual shorts dollars to make a profit. It is considered good business when a corporation does the same thing, only in much larger amounts. Of course, there isn't any law against such activities, for the individual or for the corporation. Moreover, the businessman, like the individual speculator, may comfort himself with the rationalization that the dollar's weakness is not really his fault. Past government errors placed the dollar where it was in 1971.

Meanwhile, Germany continued its fool-the-speculator campaign. The Bundesbank intervened to buy dollars when the mark rate seemed ready to soar. It quietly sold dollars when this could be done without driving the mark upward. Such intervention is understandable. No matter what the university academics, liberal capitalists, and others say about the advantages of the free currency float, no government wants its own currency to become the plaything of money speculators.

The parity of a currency helps determine the rate of internal prosperity, the employment level, the export total, and other economic factors. A government prizes its sovereignty too much to allow the free market to take total control of these factors. So its central bank will intervene to steer money policy in whatever direction seems best for the nation.

Admittedly, money is like water, always seeking its own level. A case may be made by the free enterpriser showing that ultimately markets will assert themselves, no matter what governments do. But governments want to be in position to adjust to those pressures at a time of their own choosing, not at the whims of international money speculators.

If only commercial and trade transactions decided the parity of a currency, perhaps the free-floating money system would work. Then the laws of supply and demand would determine whether or not a currency were over- or undervalued. In time, markets would adjust to, and would help set the parity, or value of the currency. There would be no problem of surpluses or deficits. If a nation headed toward deficit, the value of its currency would decline until a balance resulted. The same thing would happen in reverse with a nation in surplus.

But many rigidities are built into the system, inability of manufacturers to reduce wages for one thing. Moreover, capital flows of currencies have become an important part of the monetary scene since the birth of the MNC.

There have been foreign investments, without currency crises, almost since the dawn of history. The Phoenicians were establishing overseas trading posts in the second millennium before Christ. Tomb paintings in Egypt show that ancient Egyptians were trading in such places as the Land of Punt perhaps a thousand years earlier.

In those days, however, foreign investors didn't have giant networks of banks joined by telex, cable, and telephone systems. Today, American and foreign banks do have such networks, allowing transfers of funds with the speed of electronic impulses. Massive amounts of short-term funds are poised over money markets, ready to be shifted across borders within minutes, at the first rumor (right or wrong) of currency trouble. Sometimes funds seem directed by mass panic rather than by normal economic considerations. Overnight, the slight weakness in a currency may become a grave weakness due to speculation which breeds more speculation.

Faced with that massive overhang of short-term funds, most governments prefer to intervene in their money markets to guard economies from adverse effects of lemming-like currency flows.

From June 2 to early July, the German Bundesbank cleverly manipulated the float, apparently convincing many speculators that better profit opportunities existed elsewhere. Bank officials reported in early July that Germany had experienced an inflow of $5.5 billion in foreign funds, chiefly dollars, immediately prior to floating the mark in early May. From June 2 to early July, it managed to export $3.3 billion worth of those dollars, while another $2 billion arrived, for a net reduction of $1.3 billion.

This looked good for Germany, not for some other nations. Those dollars refused to go home. When speculators transferred money from Germany, the funds went into Switzerland, Japan, Britain, and, in July, into France.

The movement of money into France amazed many people, especially the French. Nobody with any real understanding of the monetary situation believed that the French franc was a candidate for revaluation. It had been devalued only two years before. Authorities still wanted to gain more benefits from that currency change.

But speculators had to put their money somewhere. So money began to flow into France. France's reserves increased in July from $5.7 billion to $6.2 billion. Finance Minister Giscard d'Estaing appeared on television July 13 to ridicule the idea that France might revalue its currency.

The speech didn't change the money flow by much. Speeches seldom do. Government officials always deny any currency parity changes right up to the moment that they make such changes.

Alarmed Swiss bankers met with officials of the National Bank near the end of July. Standby measures to keep out dollars were scheduled to take effect August 20. These provided that, if the crisis grew worse, incoming funds would be deposited without interest at the National Bank.

The month closed with the German mark at the equivalent of a 5.47 percent revaluation from its 3.66 parity, which Germans still claimed was the "official" parity. The U.S. dollar was at the opposite end of the German teeter-totter. As the value of the mark floated upward, the value of the dollar sagged.

August 1 dawned with a feeling of growing unease in Europe. In Washington, there was a deceptive outer façade of serenity. Officially, the policy still was "benign neglect" insofar as the dollar was concerned. Actually, people at the U.S. Treasury, at the Federal Reserve, and at the White House were worried, not only about the dollar, but about the U.S. economy.

A series of quiet meetings were held at Camp David near Washington and elsewhere. Officials weighed various economic suggestions. Contingency planning assignments were delegated. In Frankfurt, one highly placed banker said later: "We knew in July, 1971, that America had a contingency plan for establishing import controls."

August 1 is Switzerland's national holiday, the anniversary of the creation of the Four Cantons Alliance in 1291. Civic functionaries parade down main streets of towns and villages. Brass bands play. A carnival atmosphere reigns. At night, bonfires blaze on mountain tops. Fireworks explode.

This holiday was a Sunday, with tourists jamming every resort from Lugano to Lake Constance. Many of them were American, for Switzerland always has been popular with footloose Americans. These travelers encountered some disquieting signs of the times. Most hotels were cashing travelers checks at four Swiss francs to the dollar and less. That good old American dollar was worth ninety cents in this climate.

Speculators seemed convinced that the dollar might be worth less than that. Money poured into France, Switzerland, Japan, Germany, and Britain.

Economic news in the U.S. was bad. The U.S. trade deficit was widening. Imports poured into the country. Exports showed little bounce. America faced the first adverse trade balance since 1893.

Some foreign nations queried the U.S. Treasury about transfer of some of their dollar holdings into gold. And the dwindling U.S. gold stock declined toward the $10 billion level, rock bottom for U.S. defense purposes. Pentagon officials knew well that, in the unlikely event of war, no neutral nation would accept bits of paper as payment for munitions and supplies. Only gold would serve.

Total claims against the U.S. dollar that August 1 amounted to $57 billion. Yet the U.S. reserves available for paying those claims had declined to the lowest level since 1938. America was like a rich movie star who finds himself in bankruptcy court because of his own profligacy.

On Tuesday, August 3, Britain announced that its reserves reached a postwar high of $3.87 billion. Meanwhile, authorities at the Bank of France and the Finance Ministry in Paris worked into the late hours of that night preparing a wall against unwanted dollars.

On Wall Street, the Dow Jones average slumped fifteen points that same day. Unemployment was rising in the U.S. A wage settlement announced by the steel industry convinced many that inflation was running wild.

On Wednesday, August 4, the U.S. dollar plunged precipitously in European money markets. The Bank of France disrupted markets that morning when it told French banks that henceforth they should accept dollars for commercial purposes only. It was the first step toward creation of a two-tier dollar market. But nobody knew exactly what this meant.

Swiss money markets closed for an hour and a half to study the situation. Demand for gold soared. The free market price hit $42.80 in Zurich.

Now people talked openly of a possible U.S. dollar devaluation. "The growing American balance of payments deficit is a sure sign that the currency is overvalued relative to other currencies," asserted an official of the Amsterdam-Rotterdam Bank in Amsterdam, Holland.

In London, an executive of Hambros Bank, one of the city's big merchant banks, said: "Everything points to a further currency crisis." In Zurich, bankers disliked commenting. Any such comment invited criticism about Gnomes of Zurich trying to upset the dollar.

In Paris, the Bank of France clarified its actions. France intended looking at the U.S. dollar as if there were two types of them. The commercial dollar would be that which entered the country through normal foreign trade procedures. This dollar would be redeemed by the Bank of France at the established parity of 5.55 francs to the dollar. Dollars which entered the country for tourism or capital purposes would be classed as financial dollars. Initially, banks were told not to take them at all. Shortly, it became clear that the free market would set a value on these dollars, with that value lower than the value on the commercial dollar.

"These new measures are aimed only at the speculator," said a Bank of France official.

That Wednesday P.M. the dollar hit a record low in Frankfurt, equivalent to a 6 percent mark revaluation. In Paris, the dollar finished at 5.5125. In Zurich, even with support of the National Bank, the dollar closed at its floor of 4.06. In Tokyo, banks noted a heavy influx of dollars. Everybody who owed money to Japanese firms sought to pay dollars in advance. Payments of Japanese yen to outsiders slowed to a trickle.

In Frankfurt, Bundesbank vice president Otmar Emminger said: "When central banks limit spheres of transactions, then the transactions are likely to happen in another place, perhaps in another country."

Money barred from France was finding its way to Japan.

That first week of August ended with most foreign exchange traders happy for the weekend. This had been the most hectic week in the history of trading on European money exchanges. Many wondered if an American devaluation of the dollar would come over the weekend.

Nothing happened that weekend. But two reports materialized in Washington. Both helped shape events. Early in the week of August 8 a political poll was given to President Nixon, according to the Rowland Evans and Robert Novak Washington column. The poll reportedly showed that only 27 percent of people queried favored Nixon as first choice for president in 1972. Nixon was losing his appeal on economic grounds. He was viewed as another Hoover leading the country into a depression.

Meanwhile, another report surfaced, that of the Subcommittee of International Exchange and Payments of the Joint Economic Committee of the U.S. Congress. It is headed by Congressman Henry Reuss, the Wisconsin representative who is one of the most knowledgeable men in Washington in monetary affairs. His report suggested that perhaps the dollar might be devalued. This, of course, wasn't any more than bankers and businessmen already were saying on both sides of the Atlantic.

But Congressman Reuss was the first man in an official position in Washington to talk openly of devaluation. His report seemed to have a stamp of authenticity which lent far more weight to it than was being accorded to speculations of people outside government.

When money markets opened for business Monday, August 9, speculative pressure hit the dollar from all sides. In Frankfurt, the mark floated up to a rate comparable to a 7 percent revaluation. In Zurich, Swiss banks temporarily halted trading in dollars after the Swiss National Bank said it would freeze all incoming dollars in a special account. The free market price of gold jumped $1.38 to $43.94. On that black Monday, the Swiss Central Bank absorbed $400 million in dollars. The dollar fell below its 4.06 floor.

Tuesday was a repetition of Monday. The Swiss National Bank summoned banking leaders. In a sedate conference room of the bank in Zurich, Swiss money men listened as bank officials suggested ways to stem the dollar deluge. A new monetary package would take effect Monday, August 16. A reserve requirement of 100 percent would be established on all dollars sold to the Central Bank since the beginning of August. There would be no interest on foreign deposits placed for less than six months.

Soundings were made concerning a two-tier market, one for the commercial and the other for a financial franc. Bankers protested that Switzerland did not have the bureaucratic organization for it. Two-tier markets require an army of bureaucrats to control currency inflows.

That week of August 8 dollars cascaded into Europe and Japan from everywhere. MNC's sought to clear out dollar holdings. Mideast oil sheikhs dispatched worried cables to bankers in Switzerland. Individuals in America frantically sought to join the speculative parade.

Switzerland absorbed $2 billion in foreign currency in the first two weeks of August. Japan, which had $8.1 billion in its reserves at the end of July, had $12.5 billion at the end of August, with the bulk coming into the country in the first two weeks. Britain's reserves jumped from $3.9 billion to $4.8 billion. France's reserves rose from $6.2 billion to $7.6 billion.

On Friday, August 13, it was evident that the dollar at 1/35 of an ounce of gold had had it. In Washington, President Nixon

sent an urgent return-to-Washington message to a vacationing
Treasury Secretary Connally in Texas. Messages went to other
members of the President's economic and monetary team.

Officially, it was announced that the President and his team
would concentrate on problems of the U.S. budget at a weekend
meeting in Camp David, the Maryland presidential retreat. Friday afternoon President Nixon climbed into his official helicopter on the White House lawn. Accompanying him were John
Connally, Arthur F. Burns, chairman of the Federal Reserve,
Paul McCracken, head of the Council of Economic Advisors,
and George Shultz, director of Office Management and Budget.

To confuse the real purpose of the meeting, Paul Volcker,
astute Treasury undersecretary for monetary affairs, presidential aide Herbert Stein, and President Nixon's speechwriter,
William Safire, departed for Camp David from Anacostia Naval
Base, two miles from the White House on a second helicopter.
Speechwriter Safire is a man who usually is around the president just before a presidential address. His appearance with
Nixon under these circumstances would have alerted the press
that something brewed. Volcker's presence would have hinted
that the U.S. dollar was at the heart of the matter.

The team was a prestigious one. Breezy, wisecracking Connally is a shrewd politician whose talents had been recognized
by President Nixon. For weeks, his stock had been rising in the
hierarchy of the Administration. Burns, chairman of the Fed, is
an Austrian-born, naturalized American who, at sixty-eight, had
a long and illustrious career as an educator, economist, and
public servant. He is a bespectacled, courtly man who seldom
opens his mouth unless he has something to say. Conservative
by nature, he is not one to recommend the crowd-pleasing economic panacea. Shultz is recognized as a man of keen mind, with
imaginative ideas. McCracken, at fifty-six, had come a long way
as an educator and public servant from his Iowa start.

Before departing from Washington, Stein was asked what
sort of weekend might be anticipated at Camp David. Standing
beside the helicopter at Anacostia Naval Base, Stein reportedly
said: "It may be the most interesting in the world of economics
since March 4, 1933."

The Franklin Delano Roosevelt Administration took

charge on that day. Immediately on reaching Camp David President Nixon and his team went into a four-hour huddle preparing a program for stimulating the domestic economy and for controlling inflation. Everybody realized drastic remedies were necessary.

There was a break for dinner. Then, the U.S. dollar became the topic. This was a subject for the President, for Connally, for Burns, and for Paul Volcker.

Volcker is a Princeton graduate with a year at the London School of Economics, who has alternated through much of his career between the U.S. Treasury and Chase Manhattan Bank. He is over six and a half feet tall, a lean, gangling man who walks with a long stride which matches his height. A receding hairline helps frame features which often seem concentrated in thought. He has long been a proponent of special drawing rights, the paper gold units devised by the International Monetary Fund to increase world liquidity and reduce dependence of the monetary system upon gold. Volcker has a reputation for being anti-gold, so much so that believers in gold as a monetary metal refer to him as "an anti-gold nut."

Perhaps more than any other man in government, he has fought to reduce gold's importance in monetary affairs and to replace it with some man-made instruments. For this reason, the gold lobby in Europe does not like Volcker at all. This does not seem to upset Volcker very much.

It was evident that an outright devaluation of the U.S. dollar might have political repercussions. President Nixon did not want to go down in history, especially before the 1972 election, as the president who had devalued the dollar.

But suppose nations with strong currencies would revalue their money? This would have the same effect as a dollar devaluation, with none of the political problems. The development could be presented as the fault of foreign nations. They had allowed their currencies to become too strong, partly because of wrong policies and because some of these nations were not carrying their proportionate share of the free world's aid and military burdens.

It was agreed that the dollar had to be cut loose from its link with gold. There wasn't enough gold at Fort Knox and in the vaults of the New York Federal Reserve Bank to redeem dollars for gold at $35 an ounce. If convertibility were maintained, every nation with dollars would be clamoring for the exchange of those dollars for gold the following week.

The meeting ended late Friday with agreement that the president should appear on television Sunday night for what promised to be one of the most important speeches of his career. Safire, the speech writer, would write the address Saturday morning. The President would check it Saturday afternoon. Sunday it would be ready for delivery.

President Nixon went to bed, spent a few restless hours. At 3:15 A.M. he arose, reached for the dictating machine by his bedside. Then he dictated the Sunday speech and left word that he wanted it typed.

Unlike most presidents of recent vintage, President Nixon composes the basic outlines of most of his speeches. He tells speechwriters what parts to emphasize, then gives them the polishing job.

Next morning, when speechwriter Safire arrived for his task, he found a typist already putting the president's dictation on paper. Safire picked up the pages, went to work. There are few word-jugglers in Washington who can match Safire's ability to find the right word and the right phrase for the appropriate idea.

He knows all the taboo words which President Nixon hates. Included are: exacerbate, viable, meaningful, hegemony, knowledgeable, and a small dictionary of other words which the president considers vague. President Nixon scorns Humpty Dumpty semantics which seems to insist that "When I use a word, it means just what I choose it to mean—neither more nor less." He likes words that people understand.

Sunday evening President Nixon took to the air on television's prime time. A couple of hours before that speech, Treasury Secretary Connally, Secretary of State Rogers, and various other government officials were phoning world leaders, giving them capsules of the President's speech.

President Nixon told the nation that prices, wages, and dividends would be frozen for ninety days. A Cost of Living Council was being established to fight inflation. Foreign aid and government spending were being slashed. A 10 percent import surcharge was being introduced. The dollar's link with gold was being severed. Income and excise tax cuts were being effected. A job development program was being implemented.

The president's speech reverberated around the world. Japanese contended that they were given so little warning of the speech that it was an insult. Most Europeans first heard the news on radios next morning, or in newspapers which had delayed morning editions until the story could be printed.

That speech left Europe and Japan in no doubt that strong currency nations were expected to help the U.S. dollar, even if it hurt them to do it. This was almost an ultimatum.

"There can be no doubt that the United States moves are a hard blow to international monetary and economic cooperation, as well as to reciprocal confidence built up painstakingly over the years," said Felix W. Schulthess, chairman of Swiss Credit Bank, Zurich, shortly after hearing the news from Washington.

His sentiments were widely shared in Switzerland and across the continent. There were fears of recession. The 10 percent surcharge on American imports promised to hurt many of Europe's industries. The Swiss watch industry feared widespread unemployment. In Geneva, the General Agreement on Tariffs and Trade, a major tariff liberalization body, called a special meeting to consider effects of the surcharge. German newspapers expressed fears that Nixon's measures would export American unemployment to Germany.

Money markets around the world closed. Meetings were called at central banks, finance ministries, and cabinets to weigh reactions. Immediately after Nixon's speech, Treasury Secretary Connally had dispatched his aide, Volcker, to Europe. The purpose was to explain to Europeans the reasons for Nixon's moves.

Cables and telephone calls went to Bonn, to Frankfurt, to Rome, to Paris, and to London suggesting an international meeting for Monday afternoon in London. Dr. Otmar Emminger, vice president of the Bundesbank, arrived to represent Germany. He is a Shakespearean scholar with cheery features who is not afraid of new ideas. In Europe he is regarded as the father of the SDR idea.

Bernard Clappier, first vice governor of the Bank of France, represented France. He is a shrewd banker who joined the Central Bank in 1963, a man who was a close associate of Robert Schuman, one of the founders of the Common Market. With him came Claude Pierre-Brosselette, a man of forty-three who looks younger, one of France's rising technocrats who was a director of the French Treasury.

The Bank of England's representative was Jeremy Morse, an oddity among bankers for he is a philosopher by schooling, with a keen mind which he sharpens on crossword puzzles. With him came Alan Neale, forty-two, a career man with the Department of Trade and Industry before switching to the Treasury in 1968. Last man to appear was Dr. Rinaldo Ossola, vice director general of the Bank of Italy. He is a veteran of the bank since 1938, one of Italy's key monetary experts. At the time he was chairman of the deputies of the Group of Ten. His presence immediately raised speculation. Surely he was in London to prepare for a Group of Ten meeting which would tackle problems raised by America's action.

Even some of those in attendance thought this was the purpose of the meeting. Volcker didn't take long to clear up this misunderstanding. He was in London merely as the spokesman for America, to elaborate and define matters covered by the President's speech. He was not in Europe to negotiate, to plan for any Group of Ten meeting, or to suggest any other avenues for Europeans to take.

Volcker continued around Europe as a messenger for the American Administration, leaving some disappointed Europeans in his wake. Prior to its August 15 blockbuster, America had followed a policy of benign neglect toward the dollar. Now it seemed to be following the same policy toward a dollar severed from its link to gold.

The 10 percent surcharge was considered to be an especially foul blow by many Europeans. Indeed, it was a devilishly shrewd move, for it forced Europeans to face up to the dollar's problems. The United States is much less dependent upon foreign trade than are European nations and Japan. Only 4 percent of the U.S. Gross National Product stems from trade. With some European nations, that percentage is over 25 percent.

So Europe couldn't smugly relax and wait for the U.S. to

do something to solve this particular problem. Europe faced one of two things: either revalue currencies against the dollar, or float those currencies. European nations could not let their money markets remain closed for too long, for that would stifle the foreign trade which provided life for so many countries.

"This is Europe's problem, not ours," Volcker said in answer to a newsman's question at this time.

So once again battle lines were drawn. Though America could pretend that this was Europe's problem, it had a real stake in the battle. The best hope was that European nations would revalue their currencies together substantially against the dollar. Japan, then, would be forced to follow. America, and the world, might be assured of several years more of monetary peace.

France proved to be the laggard. It claimed that the dollar was overvalued, not European currencies undervalued. Therefore, a gold price hike was needed to solve the problem. In effect, this would be an American devaluation, rather than the backdoor route devised by the Nixon Administration.

Some American government officials frowned. Was France going to upset this carefully planned American program for correcting the dollar's ills?

France wasn't alone in contending that the U.S. should have taken the simple route, raising the price of gold. Swiss bankers thought so, too. Guido Hanselmann, general manager, Union Bank, said in Zurich: "It would obviously have been more elegant to seize the opportunity to realign currencies through an increase in the official gold price, and then to find an agreement on the extent to which each country would go, thereby creating the differential which market conditions obviously require."

Consensus among Swiss money men was that President Nixon allowed political expediency to sway him against a straight rise in the monetary price of gold of 15 to 25 percent. They reasoned that such an increase would have permitted a range of from 15 to 25 percent at the upper end, down to zero among other nations of the world when it came to realigning currencies. Some nations would have resisted any change from the dollar's level. Nations with strong currencies might have accepted most of the dollar's devaluation.

When the U.S. adopted what ultimately seemed to be a fanatical opposition to any change in the gold price, France seized on this to stymy the quick monetary settlement which the U.S. preferred. On Wednesday, August 18, French President Pompidou debated the situation with his cabinet in Paris. Shortly after 2 P.M. a press aide emerged to report that France would not revalue its currency. It would entrench the two-tier money system, with the commercial rate holding at 5.55 to the dollar and the financial rate being set by a free market.

If the American surcharge were a diabolical invention, as Europeans claimed, then the French two-tier system was a Machiavellian response. It gave France the best of two worlds. If speculators continued to push short-term capital funds into France in the form of dollars, those dollars would float down and down in worth. Yet decline of that dollar would not matter to French exports, for these would be geared to the 5.55 rate. The U.S. would not obtain the benefits of any revaluation of the franc in the French market.

America appeared to be losing any chance for a quick settlement of monetary questions. Still, American sources maintained a slight hope. Common Market nations had scheduled a Council of Ministers meeting in Brussels on Thursday, August 19. The purpose was to formulate what America hoped would be a mass increase of currency parities. Could France be persuaded to reconsider its position? The U.S. wisely refrained from any lobbying to press its position, realizing that this might offend more Europeans than it would convince.

Giscard d'Estaing arrived for the meeting at EC headquarters, cool and elegant. Schiller came with his brisk, no-nonsense manner. The meeting in the Charlemagne Building of EC was another with Germany on one side and France on the other. It was, however, remarkably calm considering the wide differences which existed. France opposed any change in the value of the franc and insisted it would stick to a two-tier market when its money markets opened for business the following Monday. Germany liked its float.

At 6 P.M. Thursday, EC ministers called a recess in their svelte headquarters. Anthony Barber, Britain's Chancellor of the Exchequer, had been invited to Brussels, since Britain was a member-applicant. Now, he was briefed concerning the positions of the various countries.

Barber, at fifty-one, was at the peak of his career. He is a tall, articulate man, with a daring World War II record and a subsequent brilliant record in Britain's parliament. He listened, then was asked by Schiller to comment.

"I'm not an expert," said Chancellor Barber, "but I should think that a two-tier system would be impracticable for us."

Barber departed and the EC meeting continued until 2 A.M. without result. So, the ministers laboriously drew up another one of those joint communiqués which meant that each country would be going its separate way. It read: "The council is agreed that the rates for the U.S. dollar will be left free to find their own level on a single foreign exchange market in certain member countries, while the rates will be set in others on a double market."

America had lost the first round. But this was a fifteen rounder, with America packing a horseshoe in each glove.

Still, when money markets opened on Monday, August 23, hope for a quick settlement of the monetary crisis was fading. It was every nation for itself. Germany continued its float. France had its two-tier market. Belgium and Holland opened with a joint float to keep currencies together. Britain allowed its pound to float, but indicated it would intervene to hold the rate in the $2.45 to $2.47 range, if necessary. Italy floated. Japan insisted there was nothing wrong with its yen and tried to keep an unchanged parity. Israel devalued by 16.7 percent.

Switzerland's markets remained closed that morning. Swiss wanted to watch developments before acting. Bankers kept insisting that Switzerland's 7 percent revaluation of May was adequate. Eventually, markets reopened with a float, surrounded by controls.

In Zurich, Dr. Alfred Schaefer, chairman of Union Bank, warned: "The possibility of a worldwide recession may become very real." Like most Swiss money men, he dislikes floating rates. "Any situation of floating currency," he added, "creates a great deal of uncertainty on markets, and therefore handicaps international trade. A quick solution of the present crisis with a return to fixed parities would be highly welcome."

As the weeks passed, it became evident why some Europeans disliked floating rates. Foreign traders were finding it
exceedingly difficult to obtain any foreign exchange cover for
anything beyond a year. This hampered trade deals.

Meanwhile, the U.S. pressed its allies for more help in
carrying the aid and defense load for the Western world, and for
trade concessions to help U.S. exports. And, of course, a realignment of parities had to be effected.

Pressure was low key. The Nixon Administration continued to claim that this was a European problem. Treasury
Secretary Connally, however, was anything but low key in
bluntly letting Europeans know that they were going to have to
make adjustments or the U.S. could go on indefinitely with its
import surcharge.

Would a softer Connally line have worked? Probably not.
For years, the U.S. had been complaining about Common Market trade protectionism, about the need for more defense shar-
ing, and about the necessity for nations like Japan to revalue
currencies. No amount of diplomacy produced any results.

"We had to give them a kick in the pants," one American
diplomat in Europe said.

In one area, the U.S. may have made a misjudgment. That
was in its adamant insistence that America simply would not
increase the monetary price of gold no matter what Europeans
said. Very early in the crisis which followed President Nixon's
August 15 speech, France won support in Europe for at least a
token increase in the price of gold in any settlement. Within a
month, all nine of America's partners in the Group of Ten,
plus observer Switzerland, favored an increase in the price of
gold.

America, led by Connally, kept insisting that a gold price
was immaterial, and really didn't mean anything. If this were
so, then of course the U.S. would have been surrendering nothing by agreeing to a gold price increase in order to gain a general
settlement of monetary-trade problems.

It was evident very early that the Group of Ten would be
the forum for settlement of the monetary crisis, with the Organization for Economic Cooperation and Development providing an assist through its trade and monetary experts. OECD is

a Paris-based international organization of the non-socialist industrialized world which seeks to live up to its name.

The IMF had a role to play, too. On Tuesday, August 24,
it inadvertently leaked contents of a working paper in Washington. This suggested raising the monetary gold price to $37.50 an
ounce, with revaluations of currencies. The net effect would be
to revalue the Japanese yen by 15 percent in relationship to the
dollar, the German mark by 12 to 14 percent, the French franc
and the British pound by 7 percent, with other currencies falling
into line under that level.

Publication of the paper was embarrassing. It showed that
IMF differed from the U.S. on the gold question. Subsequently,
developments indicated that this leak played a part in American
government disillusion with IMF boss Schweitzer, and to hard
lobbying for removal of the IMF chief. At the time it happened,
the leak so aggravated the IMF hierarchy that a massive hunt
was launched for the culprit. A directive from senior management warned the staff to be more discreet with newsmen. Even
to meet socially with a journalist, as for dinner or tennis, a fund
staffer would have to first inform his department head.

An IMF staffer who explained the directive mixed his metaphors when he said: "You see, we had to lock the stable door
after someone had pulled the plug out of the dam."

Maybe the old plug had escaped when the stable door was
unlocked, and then had fallen into the reservoir behind the dam.

Japan floated its yen on August 27, after stoutly insisting
that it meant to maintain the currency at its long established 360
to the dollar rate. Almost immediately, the yen floated upward
to the equivalent of a 6 percent revaluation. This still was only
a piddling change in the U.S. view.

A flurry of bilateral meetings preceded a meeting of Group
of Ten deputies in Paris on September 3 and 4. Schiller flew to
Rome to meet Italian monetary and finance officials, taking time
for a press conference. Here he declared that the future role of
the dollar would be "important, but no longer decisive."

Mario Ferrari-Aggradi, Italy's diminutive, nearly always
optimistic finance minister, admitted that "The road to monetary stability is not an easy or a quick one. It would be lacking
in realism to expect rapid and spectacular results."

Thus, forewarned, few people expected much in the way of results when the deputies of G-10 met in Paris. It was a sunny, warm day that Friday, September 3, when deputies convened at the IMF's new contemporary-styled Paris building on the avenue d'Iéna. Visiting newsmen were kept well away from the delegates. But it was possible for newsmen to see the deputy ministers at work beyond a dark, tinted wall of glass which fronted a small Japanese garden. Volcker's nasal drawl was allegedly identified by one newsmen. The fact, however, was nobody heard anything, and unfortunately there were no lip readers among the journalists.

The purpose of the meeting was to prepare the agenda for a full ministers meeting in London, September 15. The American delegation rocked deputies by reporting that the U.S. expected a $13 billion swing in its balance of payments from revaluations, trade benefits, and help with the defense burden. Thirteen billion! This could come only by drastically reducing the favorable trade balances enjoyed by Japan, Germany, and other nations. Foreign nations protested that this was a beggar-my-neighbor program.

U.S. delegates were unmoved. The U.S. had paid a high enough price in the way of unemployment and economic stagnation. Now, it was time for others to pay.

On September 13, the finance ministers of EC convened in Brussels in an attempt to formulate a joint Common Market front vis-à-vis the United States. Ministers closed ranks "against" rather than with the U.S.

Among points in the EC official communiqué of that meeting were:

—The reforms to be carried out within the international monetary system must respect the principle of fixed parities which should be adjusted as soon as it becomes apparent that they are no longer realistic. Satisfactory international payments relations based upon such principles will only be possible if differentiated realignment is introduced in parity relations between currencies of industrialized countries. Such a realignment should include the currencies of *all countries concerned, including the dollar.*

—The correct functioning of the international monetary system thus reformed would require measures affecting the international movement of capital. These measures could consist of a limited increase in fluctuation bands in order to compensate for the consequences of interest rate differences and also of appropriate measures to discourage short-term capital movements.

—International reserve assets will continue to depend upon gold and, to an increasing degree, upon reserve instruments collectively created and managed internationally. There will be a *gradual decrease in the importance of national currencies* as reserve assets.

—All countries, without exception, must respect obligations and constraints involved in balance of payments adjustments. (Italics added.)

In short, the dollar had to be devalued, which meant the price of gold had to be increased. Gold would remain in the monetary system. The U.S. dollar would be phased out as a reserve unit. The U.S. was expected to eliminate its balance of payments deficit. Common Market nations now had a joint position, and it was on the far side of the table from the U.S.

This didn't augur well for the full ministerial meeting of G-10 in London. It opened Wednesday, September 16, in the Louis Quinze decor music room of the British government's Lancaster House. The building sits on the Mall adjacent to Green Park, with Buckingham Palace only a long stone's throw away. Newsmen appropriated most of the office space on the first floor. Delegates gathered on the second floor, which was reached by a magnificent staircase. This became the favorite roost for journalists who wanted to waylay delegates.

Treasury Secretary Connally breezed into the ornate lobby of the building, accompanied by a staff which swept along with him as if tied by invisible strings. Cal Brumley, his press secretary, waved to several of the American journalists who clustered around. Connally ignored them, and pushed up the stairs.

As delegates arrived, the United States, the world's leading economic power, rated number three in at least one respect in this Group of Ten. For years, America had led the world, with the largest total of gold and foreign exchange in its reserves.

Now, with floating currencies, it was difficult to compute reserves exactly. But there was no doubt that West Germany had
the largest total, somewhere between $17 to $18 billion worth.
Japan ranked number two, with over $12.5 billion worth. The
U.S. came third.

There were forty-five delegates and aides as the meeting
opened, representing eleven countries, the BIS, the IMF, and
the OECD. Countries included the U.S., Britain, Belgium,
Canada, France, Germany, Holland, Italy, Japan, Sweden, and
Switzerland. Dr. Edwin Stopper, president of the Swiss National Bank, and Dr. F. Leutwiler, vice president of the bank,
represented Switzerland.

It was America against the rest of the Group. The prescrip-
tion advanced by U.S. allies was simple: devalue the dollar
against gold. Lift the U.S. import surcharge to make it easier for
foreign nations to estimate new parities. Include the gold hike
as part of a package to adjust currency parities.

There was agreement that wider currency bands should be
introduced to provide currency flexibility. Support was accorded for use of some man-made unit, whether the SDR or
something else, to take over the reserve tasks performed by the
U.S. dollar.

During one break in a session, a British Treasury official
said: "Nobody is advocating a big increase in the price of gold,
but it appears that everybody except America wants some increase." Nations and international agencies had about $41.25
billion worth of gold in reserves (at $35 an ounce). They weren't
as ready as was the U.S. to downplay gold's importance.

America contended that it had to return to the U.S. balance
of payments situation of the mid-1960's. This called for a $13
billion swing toward the plus side in its balance of payments.

In one behind-the-scenes interpretation of the figures,
Volcker reported that, if the deteriorating situation had been
allowed to continue, the U.S. would have had a merchandise
trade deficit of $5 billion in 1972. In 1970, the U.S. had had a
favorable trade balance of $3.26 billion. This fell away sharply
in 1971. The country headed for a deficit as the G-10 meeting was
underway.

Estimating conservatively, according to Volcker, the U.S.

government's net outflow for foreign aid payments, military expenditures, and such came to $4 billion annually. Private long-term capital outflows raised this total to $6 billion, a figure raised to $11 billion with the trade deficit. So, U.S. Treasury officials took the $11 billion and added a cushion of $2 billion to arrive at their estimate of a $13 billion improvement as necessary for the U.S. balance of payments.

Pierre-Paul Schweitzer, managing director of IMF, proposed that the crisis be solved in steps. First, nations should realign currencies and return to fixed parities. The U.S. would eliminate its surcharge at the same time. Then, short-term trade and burden-sharing concessions would be made to help the U.S. longer-term trade problems would be attacked after that, along with a major reform of the monetary system.

The time wasn't ripe for adoption of this package. While the U.S. had dragged its feet on the gold question, attitudes of other nations had hardened toward concessions to the U.S. The meeting broke up with talk about "clarification of positions." There was nothing visible in the way of accomplishments.

The forum shifted to the annual meeting of IMF starting September 27 in Washington, a meeting preceded on September 26 by another fruitless G-10 meeting. Treasury Secretary Connally was elected chairman of G-10, which made him eligible to call the next meeting.

There were forty speeches made by various members of the one hundred eighteen-nation IMF that week in Washington. Many of them helped to "clarify positions." None of them went far toward solving the problem. The U.S. kept insisting that it could go on indefinitely with other nations floating their currencies against the dollar.

IMF Managing Director Schweitzer warned, however, that this might be dangerous. He said:

> Let me stress the importance of moving to an agreed solution to this crisis without delay. For various reasons, the continued floating of major currencies would not provide a satisfactory basis for realignment. Besides the distorting effects of the import surcharge, there is the fact that exchange rates are not being left to market forces but are

being influenced by official intervention and by expedients and restrictions that are growing daily. The protective measures that are being taken may become progressively harder to dismantle, thereby adding a new and growing barrier to a satisfactory solution on the question of realignment. In the meantime, these measures and the uncertainty about present and future currency relationships are hurting international trade and investment planning, and in smaller countries, the domestic economies as well.

In Zurich, Dr. Eberhard Reinhardt, chief general manager, Swiss Credit Bank, also outlined the same dangers which were becoming evident in Switzerland: "In highly developed industrial countries, flexible exchange rates degenerate almost by necessity into government manipulated rates, and these manipulated rates compel one intervention after another, in the dense tangle of which free world trade, so beneficial to prosperity, finally is strangled."

In Bonn, Schiller complained of the "dirty floats" which were being maintained by other countries, without naming the countries. Meanwhile, a growing tangle of controls and regulations against dollar flows appeared to be developing.

Central banks were in a bind. Governments didn't want their currencies to rise much higher in relationship to the dollar. That would have upped export prices and might have contributed to recessions.

On the one hand there was an impetus for a central bank to buy incoming dollars in order to prevent such rises in the value of the domestic currency. On the other, there was a desire to avoid taking a single extra dollar. When convertibility of the dollar had been suspended, over $50 billion was left in the hands of central banks. Nobody knew what the dollar was going to be worth. So central banks accepted more dollars only with reluctance.

Controls to bar dollars seemed to be the answer. Yet, controls hamper trade, for the same controls which hurt dollar speculators would also hit foreign traders. Sometimes the foreign trader and the speculator are the same party. When a company like Mobiloil Corporation transfers funds to Germany

because of monetary unease, it may be termed a "speculator."
If that same company transferred funds to Germany to finance
North Sea oil explorations, then that transfer no longer is "hot
money" but a capital movement. Where should the lines be
drawn with any currency controls? Who would be the impartial
judge to determine those lines?

While nothing much seemed to be happening toward solving the crisis, much statistical work was underway. At OECD
headquarters in Paris, in a converted chateau which once belonged to the Rothschild family and in neighboring buildings,
trade and monetary experts of OECD's Working Party III studied export-import totals, foreign exchange data, and capital
movements. Slowly, painfully, the statistical picture emerged.
Figures showed that Japan did in fact need a substantial revaluation to bring its parity into line.

On Sunday, October 17, Treasury Secretary Connally addressed the President's Business Advisory Council in Hot
Springs, Virginia. In a blunt warning to Europe and Japan, he
declared that the U.S. was under no compulsion to solve the
monetary crisis "this moment or this year." The U.S. had the
world's largest home market and would suffer less from any
trade war than would others.

Two days later, Denmark established a 10 percent surcharge
on its imports. There were veiled threats in Europe that other
nations might retaliate, too, against the U.S. A series of important OECD meetings was scheduled in Paris in late October.

Arguments soon developed in Paris concerning the $13 bil-
lion swing in its balance of payments being demanded by the
U.S. OECD experts claimed this was unrealistic. During a break
in one meeting, a participant took a walk in the nearby Bois de
Boulogne. A brisk wind whipped leaves off the trees in the park
and ruffled the surface of Lac Supérieur. Sitting on a park bench
for a rest near the cascades between the upper and lower lake,
he traced positions at the series of meetings underway.

"Thirteen billion dollars. Preposterous," he said. "The
OECD experts say that eight or nine billion dollars is much
more realistic."

"What sort of revaluations have been mentioned?" he was
asked.

"Nobody wants to commit himself before the United States removes the surcharge. Moreover, the amount of the U.S. gold revaluation must first be known, and the U.S. still is foolishly insisting that it has no intention of changing the price."

"So, no progress is being made?"

"I wouldn't say that." The official shook his head. "We are" —a smile lit his features—"doing what diplomats call clarifying our positions."

"In what way?"

"Well, nobody is saying so publicly. But I'm sure that all of us now realize that parity realignments must result in revaluations of 15 to 18 percent for Japan, 12 to 14 percent for Germany, about 10 percent for the Netherlands, and 5 to 7 percent for Britain, France, and Italy."

"And Switzerland?"

"Switzerland is free to do as she pleases. But she will have to set her franc close to the Germans, or she will find herself with more foreign currency than she knows how to handle. I'm sure that Dr. Stopper realizes this."

But nothing tangible emerged from the series of meetings. And the U.S. emissary, Paul Volcker, had a serene countenance when he told an OECD meeting that the U.S. could live happily with floating exchange rates for an indefinite period.

November arrived. Everybody realized that only the Group of Ten was in position to tackle currency realignments. A mid-November meeting of that body seemed set. Connally had doubts. He still was bitter about the way the Common Market took refuge as a group, yet seemed unable to arrive at a joint position which the U.S. would accept.

"The six is neither fish nor fowl," one Connally aide said, contemptuously, in Washington of EC. "They act as if they are a group. Yet when you come to negotiate, there is no head to talk for that group."

So, the mid-November meeting went by the boards. Editorials in European newspapers pleaded for action to settle the crisis before Christmas. In Washington, Congressman Reuss urged President Nixon to replace Connally with Arthur Burns as Washington's chief international monetary negotiator. The *Financial Times* in London liked this idea so much that one of its columnists wrote a piece with the headline: "Why U.S. Needs New Financial Leadership."

Switzerland is not a nation which does any leading whenever political decisions are involved. Yet, banker after banker in Zurich, Geneva, and Basle insisted that a solution had to be found before the world degenerated into competitive trade blocs. Swiss contended that a gold price increase would be the easiest way to bring about that currency realignment.

In Basle, Dr. Milton Gilbert, the astute researcher with BIS, said: "I'll believe in SDR's when my wife asks me for an SDR bracelet."

It wasn't until the last day of November that another Group of Ten meeting finally got underway, at the palatial eighteenth-century Palazzo Corsini in the Trastevere section of Rome. In this palace, Napoleon installed his mother in 1800, and here one of Rome's most learned libraries has been housed for generations. The palace sits in a decrepit part of the city along the Tiber, a section which does have the saving grace of possessing several fine restaurants. Newsmen and G-10 delegates found the Corsetti and the Romolo on a par with Rome's better known and more expensive eating places.

Participants were almost the same as the group which had assembled in London at Lancaster House in September. But now Connally occupied the chairman's seat. He brought along an especially strong team. Burns and Volcker, of course, were in the delegation. Also included were Dewey Daane, the Federal Reserve's chief man in international affairs, Nathaniel Samuels, deputy undersecretary for economic affairs in the State Department, and Walter Eberle, President Nixon's special representative for trade affairs.

The same ten countries were represented, with Switzerland as the eleventh member of the group in everything but in official title. Nobody wanted to comment on the Swiss side: "We aren't here for speechmaking, or for commenting," said one of the Swiss representatives in a hall of the palace before the meeting started.

Speechmaking wasn't too popular. Anthony Barber, Britain's Chancellor of the Exchequer, presented one of the first addresses to the assembled monetary experts who represented most of the world's holdings of gold and foreign exchange. Britain's position already was on the record for everybody to see, he said. He believed that the time for speechmaking was past. Now the time had arrived for participants to get down to the difficult task of negotiating the parity realignments which everybody considered necessary.

Other delegates agreed. The meeting went into executive session, meaning that delegations assigned aides to technical matters while confining hard negotiations to a closed session. It didn't take long to convince Europeans and Japan that America's surcharge would be lifted as soon as new parities could be decided. Other nations also wanted to know what America would do about gold. Several people talked as if they already knew that a gold price hike of about 5 percent would be America's limit.

Connally, a big, bold man thoroughly in charge of the meeting, halted such discussion in its tracks. "What about 10 percent?" he coolly asked.

Stunned silence greeted him. Seconds ticked away. Delegates exchanged glances, each unwilling to commit himself by making the first rejoinder. Connally looked around the table, a thin smile on his lips. For weeks, Europeans had been complaining that America was stalling by not agreeing to a gold price increase. Now, Europeans and Japanese representatives were confronted by the possibility of a hike much greater than they wanted. One participant in this meeting later said: "That period of silence was the longest I have ever encountered in an important session of this kind."

France, Italy, and Britain had entered this meeting with an informal agreement to align their parities together in any revaluation against the dollar. This understanding had set 5 percent as the upper limit for any such change.

Now, several voices together lamely contended that 10 percent was too much. If the United States raised the price of gold by that amount, then France, Italy, and Britain would have to devalue slightly in the currency reshuffle, too. Connally's thin smile remained. In one bold statement, he had broken the back of any possible gold lobby attempt to use the gold price increase again as a device to fight American positions.

In so doing, however, he also was backing down from the long-held U.S. position against gold. This raises the question of why the U.S. had held out for so long.

"We had to wait until the climate was right to spring this hole card," one American government source said later, speaking in the poker terms which Connally's team seemed to like.

At a press conference, Connally emphasized to the press that the gold question was out of the way. He told newsmen that the first day's sessions had covered "what I call the nuts and bolts."

"Did some of the nuts and bolts include gold?" he was asked.

"Yes," he said.

The second day of the meeting brought delegates even deeper into the nuts and bolts, as they argued over comparative parities. By now, each nation had an idea of the comparative range in which others expected it to establish its currency. Each nation also had its own ideas about that. These positions seldom agreed.

Difficulties were compounded because multi- rather than bilateral negotiations were involved. Germany could accept a rise of 12 to 14 percent in the value of its currency against the dollar. It could not accept the same increase against the French franc. So it went with third, fourth, and fifth countries involved in the cross-trading and bargaining.

No final agreement was reached in Rome. In a statement, Connally said that this was due to the "complexity and sensitivity" of the issues. Another G-10 meeting was scheduled for December 17–18 in Washington in the knowledge that this would be just after a meeting President Nixon and France's President Pompidou had scheduled for the Azores, December 13–14.

As the Rome meeting broke up, there was a feeling that at last pieces of the monetary jigsaw were falling into place. Hope rose for a parity realignment before Christmas. Speculators and foreign exchange traders shared that hope. Immediately after the Rome sessions money markets began to adjust rates in the direction which traders figured would be negotiated in Washington, on December 18.

The free market price of gold, which had held around $42.50 for weeks, jumped to $43.69. The dollar weakened against the

mark, the Swiss franc, the British pound, the Dutch guilder, the
Italian lira, the Japanese yen, and against other currencies
which seemed headed for revaluation.

On December 6 President Pompidou, a former Rothschild
banker, received Togolese president Etienne Eyadema at the
Elysée Palace in Paris. In the greeting, he said: "The international monetary crisis is profoundly disrupting world trade. Its
uncertainties weigh heavily on the value of currencies, slow
down trade transactions, and depress the prices of raw materi-
als."

That statement showed that monetary matters were high
on the agenda of the Pompidou-Nixon meeting of the following
week in the Azores. In Washington, speculation said the summit
would involve East-West matters, the Common Market, and
such. In Paris, they knew better. It was evident that the dollar
was the key topic when Pompidou departed from Paris accompanied by Giscard d'Estaing and a financial retinue. President
Nixon had an equally impressive team with him.

The site for this meeting hardly could have been more
remote. The island of Terceira sits in mid-Atlantic, its villages
of plaster houses dominated by steepled churches. Both presidents landed at the huge Lajes Airbase near Praia da Vitoria, a
fishing village on a picturesque bay. The manueline-styled
church is its main tourist attraction. There isn't even a fourth-
rate hotel for overnight guests. The Portuguese government
hastily arranged for a passenger ship to anchor at Praia da Vitoria to accommodate newsmen who descended on the town with
the two presidents.

Pompidou and Nixon understood each other. They had
come here to settle the monetary crisis. They meant to finish the
job with dispatch. France had been the most insistent that the
U.S. must raise its gold price in any settlement. With almost
everybody in France a gold hoarder of sorts, a French politician
can always win votes by plumping for an increase in the price
of the yellow metal, even if the increase is mainly symbolic.

Tuesday, December 14, news of an agreement broke. It was
Jack Aboaf, the short-of-build, energetic Paris man for Associated Press-Dow Jones Economic News Service who beat the
competition with the story. The news, phoned to London, reported over AP-DJ wires that America would devalue its dollar.

Newsmen on the plane back to Washington were told in a leak that the price of gold would be increased by 8 percent. Actual details would have to be negotiated at the December 17–18 Group of Ten meeting in Washington.

'In some ways, the G-10 meeting at the Smithsonian Institution's red-brick building in Washington was anti-climactic. Ministers reached agreement on Saturday, December 18. President Nixon announced the deal before a battery of microphones in the hall. Chancellor Barber stood by his right hand, and Economics Minister Schiller on his left. Treasury Secretary Connally, looking unaccustomedly tired for a man of his energy, stood further to the president's left, this particular assignment done, and done well.

With perhaps a bit more hyperbole than was justified, President Nixon called the agreement "the most significant monetary agreement in the history of the world."

As usual, Swiss National Bank President Stopper was in the background. But he had been in communication with Berne. Announcement of the Swiss change in its parity was to come from Berne, not Washington.

The agreement provided for broadening of currency bands to 2 1/4 percent on each side of the central rate. The U.S. agreed to ask Congress for an increase in the monetary price of gold from $35 to $38 an ounce. America agreed to cancel its import surcharge, immediately. All parties agreed to undertake discussions to revise the world monetary system.

Terms of the realignment balanced the 8.57 percent revaluation of gold and various currency revaluations to effect the following percentage parity changes in terms of U.S. dollars computing from May 1, 1971:

Japanese yen	+ 16.88%
German mark	+ 13.58%
Swiss franc	+ 13.90%
Dutch guilder	+ 11.57%
Belgian franc	+ 11.57%
British pound	+ 8.57%
French franc	+ 8.57%
Swedish krona	+ 7.49%
Italian lira	+ 7.48%

For Switzerland, the realignment meant a new central rate of 3.84 francs to the dollar. As a result, the Swiss franc's parity vis-à-vis the dollar after the realignment was 13.9 percent above the level of May 9, 1971. On that date, the Federal Council had revalued the franc by 7 percent, a figure that is included in the 13.9 percent realignment.

So ended the money crisis of 1971, a crisis which destroyed the Bretton Woods monetary system. The agreement temporarily helped the dollar. Currency runs occurred again in the first half of 1972. Then, the dollar steadied awhile.

In January, 1973, President Nixon relaxed American wage-price controls. This raised fresh inflation worries. News of a huge trade deficit fanned fears. Confidence in the dollar faded. When Italy floated its weak lira in late January, Switzerland immediately floated its franc to prevent being overwhelmed by speculators. This set the stage for a panic.

Speculators thought Swiss bankers knew something special. They rushed $7 billion into West Germany in early February to paralyze money markets. Only stringent Japanese currency controls kept that nation from being inundated, too. But the United States was tired of a Japan which had a much overvalued currency yet refused to do anything about it.

At 11 P.M. on February 12, U.S. Treasury Secretary George Shultz announced in Washington that America was devaluating the dollar by 10 percent, the second devalaution in fourteen months. This established a new monetary gold price of $42.22 an ounce, well below the free price. Free gold soared to over $75 an ounce in Europe.

Japan floated and its yen jumped 18 percent. That first week the floating Swiss franc soared by 13 percent. The new German mark parity of 2.9003 and the French franc parity of 4.60414 seemed adequate. Britain, Italy, and Canada continued floats with no sensational changes. Israel and others devalued with the dollar; some nations left currencies unchanged, or devalued less than 10 percent.

This eased the dollar's problems. It did not reform the international monetary system, for larger problems were left for later in 1973 and beyond.

PART II

CHAPTER XI

BEHIND BANK SECRECY

Nothing irritates a reputable Swiss banker more than any refer-
ence to the hanky-panky which sometimes occurs behind bank
secrecy. Alfred E. Sarasin, president of the Swiss Bankers' Association and a partner in the bank bearing his name, often is the
official voice of Switzerland when it comes to rebutting any
accusations concerning Swiss banks. He works hard at his job.
"I repudiate with emphasis," he said recently in his Basle office,
"the continually repeated allegation that the Swiss banks might
be less punctilious in the business ethics and sense of political
responsibility than banks of repute in other countries. The best
way of refuting this criticism is to point to the high esteem
which Swiss banking has won all over the world, primarily by

reason of its generally acknowledged trustworthiness and relia-
bility."

All true. Still, Swiss banking hospitality is abused time and
again by people who hide actions behind the screen of bank
secrecy. The past decade has produced the United California
Bank in Basle failure, the I.O.S. Ltd. crisis, the Howard R.
Hughes faked autobiography, plus numerous fraud and stock
manipulation cases involving Americans.

Swiss claim that such stories often are sensationalized. Perhaps. Yet Swiss often seem to prefer no publicity at all, even in
cases where outsiders might feel that public interest is involved.
Sometimes it seems as if more attention is devoted to sweeping
a scandal under a convenient carpet than in airing the subject
to prevent repetitions.

It is not generally known, but Switzerland has an industrial
espionage law which has much broader application than has its
widely publicized bank secrecy regulation. Article 273 of the
Swiss Penal Code makes it a crime to "elicit a manufacturing or
business secret in order to make it available to any foreign official agency or to a foreign organization or private enterprise"
either directly or through an agent, and to make such secrets
available to such foreign authorities or organizations.

Strictly applied, this law could be used against anybody
who dug too deeply into the affairs of a Swiss bank. It certainly
discourages investigative reporting in Switzerland.

One can understand why Swiss are concerned about preserving their reputation for banking integrity. Most Americans,
however, are used to focusing the hard light of publicity upon
scandals. Most believe that such publicity is good for society in
the long run.

Swiss secrecy emerges from Swiss character, the intense
belief that privacy and individual independence take precedence
over whims of any central government. Swiss defend the Aristotelian concept of distributing profits according to the work of
the individual and not by the dictates of the state. They feel it
is no business of the state how those profits are handled, with
only certain minimum limitations. Aristotle's dislike for the
man of finance certainly would not appeal to the modern Swiss.

Today the central government and the "common good" are

paramount in most nations. The "common good" usually is whatever the party in power says it is. Switzerland does not accept that view. The "common good" means so little here that Switzerland doesn't even have a strong centralized government to define what that good is.

This little nation is a confederation of cantons, or little city-states. Each jealously guards its freedom against federal encroachment.

Modern Switzerland came into existence in 1848 under a constitution which delegated control of the currency, the post, weights, measures, and customs to the federal government. That government also was made supreme for international affairs, defense, and a few other limited spheres. All other powers were reserved to the cantons.

The federal government consists of a bicameral federal assembly and the federal executive. The latter consists of seven members of the federal assembly who are elected by that body to four-year terms. The executive functions as a government cabinet. Once a year the executive chooses a member to serve as president, and a second to serve as vice president. But neither the president nor the vice president has a bigger vote than any other of the seven when decisions must be made.

Expert advisory committees assist the government A committee of bankers helps when legislation is being prepared in the banking field. Industrialists advise concerning industrial matters. This means, of course, that there isn't the wide gulf between lawmakers and businessmen which sometimes seems to exist in the U.S. Businessmen and bankers are part of the ruling establishment, in government as well as in business.

There are few class distinctions in middle-class Switzerland. So this situation is accepted. Nearly everyone believes that the banker is the best person to make recommendations for bank legislation, the industrialist the most informed about industry. And if voluntary codes can be drawn, few see the need for legislation.

If credit standards must be tightened, Big Three banks cooperate to set them. If restrictions are deemed necessary anywhere in banking, major banks decide upon the action. Nobody threatens. No financial policemen scrutinize the voluntary agreements. But codes are followed by bankers with that "old boy" spirit sometimes found among fraternity brothers.

In 1972, the system was strained by the flood of money which poured into the country. For the first time, the government introduced controls to tighten the money flow, including establishment of an 8 percent annual charge on foreign money transferred into Swiss francs. (Accounts of 100,000 francs, or about $26,000 and under, were exempt.) Everybody emphasized measures were temporary. Voluntary agreements are far preferred, except where bank secrecy is concerned.

"One of the institutions most worth preserving is our banking secrecy," said Union Bank's Dr. Schaefer. "It is neither merely based on a business contract with our customers designed to protect their personal rights, nor is it a Swiss invention. It simply corresponds to a general, legal principle backed up by our legislation and is in fact applied in a similar manner in other countries as well."

That secrecy is a matter of law, defended by nearly everybody in the country. One banker in Geneva said: "No government in Berne would dare to change our bank secrecy law, because the people wouldn't stand for it."

Outsiders like it, too. There are Spaniards in Franco's Spain who have been smuggling pesos from the country into Switzerland for years. Some Communist politicians in East Europe have Swiss bank accounts. British citizens have outmaneuvered United Kingdom foreign exchange controls with accounts in Zurich, Basle, Geneva, and elsewhere. Many Frenchmen trust the Swiss franc more than their own. In Lugano, over a score of banks and branches line streets, located there to cater to Italians who smuggle currency out of troubled Italy.

A currency-violation tale came, recently, from a Swedish industrialist vacationing at the Santa Catalina Hotel in Las Palmas, Canary Islands. The Canarys are a favorite nesting spot in winter months for Swedes who have taken flight from the cold aviaries of the north. Sometimes they come with their chicks by plane. Sometimes they arrive in cruise ships in great flocks, blanketing beaches on sunny days or filling all seats at folk dancing performances promoted by hotels.

This industrialist had arrived in a private plane, with

enough baggage to fill all the closets of most houses. He was buying a "little place" of fifteen rooms as a retirement cottage, he confided as waiters in the dining room cleared dishes. He lit a cigar, a big, gray-haired man who might have been good material for a football line before he started indulging himself at the table.

"How did I get my money out of Sweden?" He asked a question which his companion had voiced earlier. He smiled, pleased with himself. He already had mentioned that he was retiring. He no longer had a stake in Sweden. As long as he remained nameless, he had no fear of talking to a long-time friend.

"The double-invoice system is a wonderful invention for the businessman who finds that his government's tax system is confiscatory," said he.

"Double invoice? You mean like the double-books system. One for the tax collector and one for you?"

He nodded. "It can only work in a country like Switzerland which has bank secrecy."

He stirred his coffee, then added: "My company in Sweden sold its products in six continental countries. I double-invoiced my customers. Not all the time. But when I knew I could trust a man. There would be two invoices, one for the legitimate charge, the other for a lower figure. The lower figure was paid directly to my company in Sweden, where the books were open to tax collectors. The difference between that and the higher, true figure was sent with the second invoice to a bank in Zurich. The money went into my secret numbered account."

His smile broadened. Outside, an orchestra on the patio near the souvenir shop was tuning instruments for start of the folk dancing. Several of the diners took that as a cue to scurry toward the sound of music in the frantic manner of tourists who must crowd twenty-six hours into twenty-four because that is the way the tour has been laid out.

"I did well," he said, "and I have no feeling of guilt, because I earned every krona of that money myself."

He stood up, held out his hand. "But I wish to take some pictures of those folk dancers. Until tomorrow, maybe."

He ambled away, an aristocrat from a socialist country who had benefited greatly from Switzerland's bank secrecy.

Another evening, another time in Egypt, the lights of Cairo blinked beneath a velvet sky as war clouds gathered over the Mideast. Time: early 1967. Place: the rooftop garden of the Semiramis Hotel overlooking the Nile.

Colored lights strung among the tables provided shadowy illumination. Across the Nile, cars moved like disembodied pairs of eyes on Gezira Island. A felucca lay in midstream, its triangular sail dipped, the glow of a cooking brazier coming from amidship.

At a table, one Cairo businessman spoke dolefully of the way the Nasser government was destroying free enterprise. He was a cultured, French-educated manufacturer who owned a network of businesses which were being throttled by government regulation. Already, most of his properties had been nationalized. It was only his expertise which kept him from being completely divorced from his holdings.

As the evening wore on and a third bottle of Omar Khayyam wine was brought by a white-gowned Nubian waiter, the man became more voluble. He confided that he didn't intend remaining much longer in the country.

"But when I depart, they will search through my baggage as if I were a hashish peddler," he said. He took a manila envelope from an attaché case. "Could you mail this letter for me when you are back in Europe?"

He tried to be casual, but showed nervousness. The letter was addressed to a Swiss bank in Zurich.

His companion shook his head. "Sorry. As a newspaperman, I have my job to think about."

"Just to mail a letter?"

"I really do wish I could oblige." The newspaperman shook his head. "But I survive by conforming to whatever laws I happen to be under."

"I could make it worth your while," the businessman persisted.

"It's not a question of money," the newspaperman responded.

"N'importe!" the businessman said. He dropped the envelope into the attaché case, snapped the bag shut. Then, defensively, he said: "What else should a man do with what little money he has left when the government is confiscating the work of a lifetime?"

The Swiss have their own ideas about taxes and tax legislation. Swiss do pay taxes, contrary to what you may hear. They pay with a nonchalance which might drive any U.S. Internal Revenue man to pot were he to encounter the same situation in America.

The Swiss fiscal system is based on the principle of self-declaration. The taxpayer himself provides to authorities information about his income. Few people like to pay taxes and Swiss are no exception. But the system isn't as slipshod as might appear. Dividend taxes are withheld at the source by banks and companies, with money remitted to the government. When income taxes are settled, the taxpayer must provide a salary-and-wage declaration signed by the employer.

This isn't much different from the American system, so far. Systems diverge when the taxpayer tries to avoid taxes. Tax evasion is not a crime in Switzerland. It is in the U.S. Moreover, fiscal authorities obtain no help from banks in Switzerland in evasion cases. In the U.S., of course, banks cooperate willingly with federal and state authorities.

"If the government came to us and asked us for information about a tax evader who had an account with us, we would say 'it's none of your business,'" an official of Swiss Bank Corp. said.

Swiss fiscal authorities may appear to be disarmed. Not necessarily. Where fraud can be proven, a court order may be obtained to open the bank account for inspection. Where simple evasion is the issue, no such order can be obtained. But here the doctrine of presumption applies. The tax collector *presumes* that a certain income may have been earned by the taxpayer. Taxes are assessed. The taxpayer is presented with a bill for payment.

Now it is up to the taxpayer to either pay the amount or to bring all his financial records to the tax man to prove that the presumption was wrong. Sometimes the taxpayer decides that bank secrecy is not worth the price.

Since Swiss banks won't open books for their own tax authorities, it is evident that they are even less likely to do so for foreign authorities. This results in some ill will between the U.S. Treasury and Department of Justice authorities on the one hand, and Swiss banks on the other. Most Americans, of course, believe that few barriers should exist to hamstring authorities. They often believe, too, that any problem can be solved by passing more legislation, or by giving more power to the federal government.

The Swiss believe that even should their bank secrecy laws be remodeled to please other nations, there would always be crooks who would find fresh loopholes in the laws of those nations. So, Swiss do not want to change. If the United States and other nations want to cure certain ills, then it is up to the U.S. and other nations to do so at home.

"I'm not my brother's keeper," one Zurich banker bluntly said. "Our banking system is much too valuable to throw away. It isn't the system that is imperfect; it is human nature, and we will never be able to change that no matter what sort of legislation we have."

This is a philosophy which invites some abuses of the system. All too frequently, Americans have been involved in some of the more lurid instances of such abuse.

CHAPTER XII

UGLY AMERICANS

One day, a while ago, a well-dressed but paunchy courier boarded Swiss Airlines Flight III at New York's Kennedy Airport bound for Zurich. He clutched an attaché case under his arm as if his life were worth the papers inside.

It was. That attaché case contained $200,000 of the "skimmed" loot from a Nevada gambling club. Money had been surreptitiously withheld from daily takes to avoid United States income taxes. If that courier "lost" that money, certain characters in his particular Mob, undoubtedly, would have been on his trail shortly, for a bloody accounting.

On arrival at Zurich's airport, he wasted no time looking for a hotel, though it was only a little after 8 A.M. Fortunately for him, the security check had been light in New York. The Swiss customs inspection consisted only of the simple question: "Have you anything to declare?"

The courier shook his head. There's no law against bringing money into Switzerland, whether in the form of bills, gold bars, securities, or anything else, as long as it isn't stolen. The large amount of cash might have invited embarrassing questions, though.

A twenty-minute taxi ride brought that courier to a small bank in the heart of Zurich's financial district. Swiss banks open at 8:30 A.M. Executives are apt to be at desks well before that time. Switzerland is a great country for setting examples having to do with hard work and dedication to a desk at early hours.

The money changed hands in one of the bank's sterile customer receiving rooms. In minutes, the courier received a receipt. He slid signed papers across the desk. These requested a $200,000 loan for certain parties in Nevada. In another few minutes, the necessary papers were completed. The loan would be extended through legitimate channels in New York to the "borrowers." Then the courier departed for a hotel and some rest before returning to the States.

The money had been "purified," a term concocted by American organized crime fighters. Had the cash remained in the U.S., its owners might have had difficulty putting it to use without attracting attention.

The beauty of this transaction is evident. Not only were taxes evaded on $200,000, but interest on "loan repayments" to the Swiss bank could be deducted in regular tax accountings. And the "loan repayments" provided an avenue for shifting more money to the Swiss bank. Naturally when the "loan repayments" arrived in Switzerland, they would be treated as deposits.

Swiss bank secrecy is so tight that perhaps it was inevitable that Switzerland should attract the tax cheat, the fraudulent businessman, and the gangster. It is not to America's credit that Americans are among the most unscrupulous when it comes to abusing Swiss bank secrecy.

Shysters, who gypped the U.S. of huge sums of foreign aid through "kickback" devices, used Swiss bank accounts to mask their activity. International dope peddlers sometimes have Swiss bank accounts. Arzi Bank, Zurich, pleaded guilty in U.S. court to violations of U.S. security regulations. Swiss bank accounts helped rig U.S. stock prices in several cases. A U.S. military PX swindle involved several numbered Swiss bank accounts which became treasuries.

Most Swiss bankers are unhappy about this situation. It was Daniel Defoe who said: "A rich man is an honest man, no thanks to him, for he would be a double knave to cheat mankind when he had no need of it."

Established Swiss banks are rich, and they pay their key people well. The head of one bank was earning $360,000 a year when he filed certain information to this effect with Swiss authorities. His declared net worth of $6.7 million indicated he wasn't suffering financially.

His peers are well paid. Fringe benefits might make the average American executive envious. The picture of many greedy Swiss bankers waiting at the door for gangster money not only is an exaggeration, it is false.

But, and there often is a very big "but" in the Swiss bank picture, Swiss bank secrecy is just as strict within the country vis-à-vis one bank and another as it is between an outsider and a bank. A reputable bank does not pry into the business of a neighbor, and there are no credit bureaus to establish the character of a potential client. Such prying is not only contrary to human nature in Switzerland; it is illegal should questions tread on sanctified bank secrecy.

A Swiss banker must even be careful of innocuous questions he might ask of another banker. In Geneva, where a dozen or so private banks flourish in almost complete anonymity except for customers, one banker recently told how he inadvertently asked a competitor how his business was doing that particular year. Both were attending a civic function. The question was one of those queries meant to fill a gap in a dull conversation.

"He looked at me as if I had asked him a question about his personal sex life. Then he turned and walked away without saying a word. That was a couple of years ago. He hasn't talked to me since," said this banker.

That very secrecy which protects clients against outsiders makes it difficult for reputable banks to keep tabs of every customer. References are normally required when new accounts are opened. Anyone with crookery in mind easily may forge necessary papers and records.

Moreover, in Switzerland, there is a tendency to believe that a man is innocent until proven guilty, provided that he happens to be a potential depositor with a nice chunk of cash to deposit. Conversely, however, he may be considered guilty until proven innocent should suspicions arise concerning an irregularity.

The situation is complicated by that already mentioned fact that security violations and tax evasions punishable in the U.S. aren't crimes in Switzerland. If a Swiss bank asks such a violator to take his account elsewhere, it may not be because the bank thinks he is a crook, but because the bank doesn't want any adverse publicity.

Until recently anybody could start a bank of his own in Switzerland too, if he found established bankers a little haughty in manner. What's more, if there is any difficulty, a truly determined party with money may buy one of the many small Swiss banks doing business in the country. When Rafael Trujillo was dictator of the Dominican Republic, he tried futilely to open bank accounts in Switzerland.

"He was turned down everywhere he went," said Dr. Edgar H. Brunner, partner in Armand von Ernst & Cie, Bern. "So he bought a bank and used it as his safety deposit box."

Few Americans are in position to buy a Swiss bank, even on very lenient installment terms. They do manage to do business in Switzerland, though, usually legitimately, sometimes in devious ways.

Perhaps de Tocqueville had it right when he said: "I have never been more struck by the good sense and practical judgment of the Americans than in the manner in which they elude the numberless difficulties resulting from their Federal Constitution."

It is not known whether or not Francis Rosenbaum, a Washington lawyer, and Andrew Stone, a St. Louis businessman, ever read de Tocqueville before becoming involved in overcharging the U.S. Navy by $3.3 million in a supply contract.

The money was channeled into a Swiss bank secret account. The Federal Constitution's difficulties appeared to be eluded, or so they thought. These are only two of many who have banked in Switzerland with that same thought in mind. They, however, were among the unlucky ones.

Their misjudgment concerned U.S. Navy contracts handled in the 1962–67 period by Chromcraft Corp., St. Louis, and its successor, Alsco, Inc. Contracts totaled some $47 million for purchase of 2.75-inch rocket launchers.

Investigation showed that a number of Swiss bank accounts had been opened. Fictitious subcontracts were given to dummy companies concealed by the bank accounts.

In April, 1968, a special grand jury of the U.S. District Court for the District of Columbia returned a criminal indictment against Chromcraft, its successor, and four individuals, charging fraud. Subsequently, Rosenbaum and Stone pleaded guilty.

Perhaps the unusual aspect of this case was that the Department of Justice marshaled an ironclad case against the defendants. The government seldom has been able to do that with cases involving Swiss bank accounts, though its batting average is improving.

It was Robert Morgenthau, diligent one-time U.S. attorney for the Southern District of New York, who focused attention on the way Swiss bank accounts were being used to defraud the U.S. Morgenthau has since resigned in what friends term a political vendetta. In office, he sometimes operated as if he had a personal vendetta against Swiss banks.

Some Swiss bankers, remembering Morgenthau's father, Henry, still contend that Robert Morgenthau was sustaining a feud launched by his father. As Secretary of the Treasury under Franklin D. Roosevelt, Henry Morgenthau determinedly tried to seize all German assets held in Switzerland. To do so he attempted, futilely, to break Switzerland's bank secrecy laws. He seemed totally unforgiving when he failed. Swiss-American relations probably never have been as low as they were in 1945, thanks to the efforts of the elder Morgenthau.

Those who know Robert Morgenthau contend he never

allowed personal considerations to influence him. In any case, he is remembered without much love in Switzerland.

At one congressional hearing in early 1970, Morgenthau said: "We have reason to believe that there are thousands of cases of criminal conduct cloaked by secret foreign accounts which have not been touched by our investigation."

He estimated that deposits in secret foreign bank accounts held for illegal purposes have a value in the hundreds of millions of dollars. Those illegal purposes include tax fraud, manipulation of securities, rigging prices of shares traded in the United States, and other shenanigans.

Estimates of that illegal total are just guesses. Some sources have placed it as high as $5 billion. However, certain other figures indicate this is a wild guess.

Switzerland withholds 30 percent in taxes on all dividends and interest payments made to Americans who have Swiss bank or portfolio accounts. This money is collected, then remitted without details to the U.S. government under the double taxation treaty of 1951. Americans who want rebates on these taxes get them when filing normal income taxes in the U.S. Any American who is gypping on taxes wouldn't make any claims to the U.S. about money withheld in Switzerland. So the unclaimed amount does provide clues to tax evasion totals.

One U.S. government source said recently: "These statistics would seem to indicate that the $5 billion figure is only a wildly inflated guess." Having said that, he admitted that tax evasion through Swiss bank accounts is a problem for the U.S.

There are many legitimate reasons for Americans to have bank accounts in Switzerland. Nevertheless, there is enough crookery to cause concern.

Wright Patman, the wily Texan and long-time chairman of the House Committee on Banking and Currency, said: "Secret foreign bank accounts are the underpinning of organized crime in this country. They are a haven for the unreported income of Americans. They can be used to buy gold in violation of American law. They can be used to buy stock in our market or in the acquisition of substantial interests in American corporations by unidentified persons under sinister circumstances."

Swiss bank secrecy was dramatized in the Interhandel case,

one of the offshoots of World War II which plagued Swiss-American relations for eighteen years. Interhandel's predecessor had been established in Switzerland by I. G. Farben, then the world's largest chemical company and a Hitler regime supporter in Germany. Interhandel became a holding company for Farben interests abroad, including the German company's subsidiary in America, General Aniline and Film Corp.

When World War II started, the U.S. government seized General Aniline. In 1948, Interhandel sued the U.S. government to regain the property, contending that the parent was Swiss. The U.S. argued ownership really belonged to Farben, a Germany company.

An American court ordered Interhandel to produce its records and those of its house bank, the Sturzenegger Bank, Basle. Interhandel refused, claiming that Swiss bank secrecy applied.

Years of litigation followed. Eventually, the American government won a stipulation for a limited inspection of the bank's books. A team of Justice Department lawyers traveled to Basle, where, in 1962, they were permitted to examine and photostat those pages of the bank records *which the bank was willing to show.*

Finally, the case was settled in 1963. Proceeds of the sale of General Aniline shares were divided under a formula which gave the U.S. government over $218 million and Interhandel $121 million. Some American sources contend that Interhandel received $121 million more than it would have gotten if all bank records had been opened.

"Bank secrecy in Switzerland technically can be lifted by the government of Switzerland when the bank is being used to harbor stolen funds," said Pierre Leval, former chief attorney in the appellate division, southern district of New York, in one congressional hearing. "But, that is easier to say than to do. If a prosecutor needs the proof that the stolen funds are in the account there in order to get the bank secrecy lifted, and if he can get that proof only by seeing the account records, then he has succeeded only in chasing his tail. The secrecy will not be lifted and he will not have the proof of the crime."

Sometimes crooks combine "boiler room" operations and facilities of one or more Swiss banks to maneuver stock coups. A "boiler room" is market terminology for a high-pressure tele-

phone sales equities peddler. Stock is likely to be worthless, or
worth only a fraction of the price. Persuasive salesmen call
potential customers, using lists purchased from direct mail companies. Sales pitches stress that particular stock prices shortly
will be shooting toward the moon.

To prevent its sales from depressing the market, the boiler
room may buy shares as it sells. Only a few hundred purchased
shares may support sales of several thousand shares. Telephone
buyers usually are unsophisticated equity purchasers not in
daily contact with brokers. It takes a while for the telephone
sales to catch market attention and so affect prices. Meanwhile,
market purchases of the operators make it appear as if a strong
demand is developing for the stock.

With a portfolio Swiss account, the boiler room places orders through the bank, which handles them in its own name.
Nobody in the market has any way of knowing a boiler room
operator is around. Even the Swiss bank may regard transactions as normal business. Thus, the price of a stock may be
manipulated, while thousands of shares are unloaded by the
fast-buck operator.

The Gulfcoast Leaseholds affair shows how something like
this works. In this case, four Liechtenstein trusts were established by American promoters. Trusts opened Swiss bank accounts. One of the promoters had been enjoined from trading
stock in the U.S. in his own name. In Europe, he purchased
750,000 shares of Gulfcoast Leaseholds for almost nothing. Fact
is he completed the purchase in the name of one of his Liechtenstein trusts which had assets of just $20.80 at the time.

He then opened a boiler shop in the U.S. to sell the stock
to American brokerage firms. As part of his operation, he had
a market advisory letter established to tout Gulfcoast Leasehold
as the buy of the century. In this case, promoters didn't have to
purchase shares to support the market. Brokers fell over their
Dow Jones tickers scrambling for shares of this new hot-shot
share. The demand kept prices climbing. The boiler room kept
unloading. The price of the stock soared to $16 a share. By the
time buyers realized little was behind shares, promoters had
unloaded their holdings. The stock then dropped to under a
dollar a share.

Promoters realized profits of more than $4 million on the original investment of $20.80. They might have faded into the tall grass if there hadn't been dissension among underlings. One of the participants divulged the entire scheme to U.S. authorities. The Department of Justice moved in.

The Liechtenstein trusts mentioned in this case represent another ingenious device used with Swiss bank accounts to thwart U.S. investigators. Liechtenstein is a tiny principality nestled between Switzerland and Austria. It supports itself by selling postage stamps to collectors and by permitting a near limitless number of dummy corporations. These dummy companies become check and letter drops for money going into Swiss bank accounts. Should an investigator acquire some evidence of a dubious operation, he still is frustrated. The Liechtenstein corporation will be listed as the owner of that particular account, and the investigator may have no way of discovering who is behind the trust.

Batteries of Liechtenstein lawyers support their families in bucolic style in Vaduz, the rural capital of the principality, by establishing these corporations for a fee. The owner of the trust may establish his corporation long distance with the help of lawyers in London, Zurich, or New York, without ever setting foot in Vaduz. And he would not miss much.

One lawyer in Vaduz is president of four hundred of these dummy corporations. It's a title which means nothing and which may return only a small fee payable for serving as a letter drop for each corporation. There are so many corporation names on the wall of his entrance hall that it looks like a blown-up page of a stock market report.

From time to time, the Securities and Exchange Commission in the U.S. notes odd reactions by listed stocks. In one case, a listed stock rose more than 20 percent in a month from $14 to $17 on a volume of 102,300 shares. Almost 90 percent of those shares were purchased for the accounts of a Swiss bank and an affiliated Luxembourg bank. Parties behind the transaction were protected by Swiss bank secrecy.

In a thirty-day period, an over-the-counter share jumped from 9½ to 19½. While the shares were going up, 10,520 shares were sold, half of them at prices of $15 and up, for European accounts, including Swiss and German banks, and a Swiss investment company. Such transactions could represent insider activity by some parties operating from behind secret accounts.

U.S. Federal Reserve Board regulations concerning margin trading sometimes are broken by Americans trading through Swiss banks, too. Arzi Bank, Zurich, encountered trouble when evidence of this fell into the hands of the U.S. Department of Justice. The bank actively solicited American clients, then allowed them to trade in the U.S. stock market with as little as a 10 percent margin. The bank acted as the purchaser, shielding American clients behind bank secrecy, which proved not so secret.

A criminal complaint was filed in New York Federal District Court against Arzi. A grand jury returned an indictment, and the bank pleaded guilty. At the time of the indictment, U.S. marshals seized securities held at three New York brokerage houses in the account of the Arzi Bank. The maximum penalty for a violation of margin regulations is two years in prison and a $10,000 fine.

One of the brokerage firms through which Arzi Bank dealt in the U.S. was Coggeshall & Hicks, a member firm of the New York and American Stock Exchanges. Evidence showed that Coggeshall and some of its partners and employees had knowingly engaged in margin violations along with Arzi. In fact, some of the brokers at Coggeshall had accounts of their own.

Over $20 million in securities were illegally traded in this manner for which trades Coggeshall received $225,000 in commissions. A grand jury subsequently returned indictments against Coggeshall & Hicks, its senior partner, the Swiss manager of its Geneva office, and three former registered representatives. All the defendants pleaded guilty and fines amounting to over $100,000 were imposed.

In several instances, Swiss bank accounts have been used in proxy battles by one side or the other. The ability to purchase shares on as low as a 10 percent margin provided some corporate raiders with tremendous leverage for stretching finances far beyond resources were U.S. laws strictly obeyed.

The S.E.C. has authority to require disclosure of any stock purchase involving over 10 percent of a corporation's stock. This provides the government with some clues as to the identity of participants in any proxy fight and of foreign financing involved. Records show that when proxy fights were waged for Metro Goldwyn Mayer, UMC Industries, Roosevelt Raceway, Bath Industries, and several other companies, foreign financing played a role in the takeover bids.

In the M.G.M. case, two foreign loans of $32 million and $30 million were acquired from foreign sources, on collateral of only 150 percent of the loan in stock. A U.S. lender under margin requirements would have asked for 500 percent of the loan's value in stock as collateral.

In proxy fights of this kind, Swiss accounts are handy should parties wish to hide identities. Even when disclosure is made through a report to the S.E.C., it may not list details about who is behind the Swiss banks. Thus, S.E.C. may have great difficulty in determining if regulations are being violated.

Swiss bank secrecy was never established to provide protection in deals such as these. Dr. Samuel Schweizer, retired chairman of Swiss Bank Corp., emphasized recently that only in a very few cases has there been any evidence that a Swiss bank knowingly participated in any of these crooked schemes.

"In the vast majority of cases," he said, "it has been a matter of accounts opened for persons who *a priori* were respectable and of whom it came to light only later that they were undergoing criminal investigation in the United States."

Swiss banks have not been alone in finding themselves swept unwillingly into sordid cases. American banks were cited in several congressional hearings involving Swiss secrecy. Yet there was no implication that these banks had anything to do directly with the illegal activities.

Chase Manhattan Bank happened to be unlucky enough in the 1960's to be the conduit for General Development Corp., a publicly-owned real estate company which got into trouble. In this case, an account of Union Bank of Switzerland's at Chase Manhattan in New York provided the avenue for certain violations of S.E.C. disclosure laws by General Development's treasurer.

First National City Bank, New York City, was mentioned as a conduit in a case involving a company with the quaint name,

"Me Too Corporation." The latter was a Panamanian company with offices in Geneva. The U.S. Department of Justice won convictions against two defendants who were trafficking in heroin. The drug was smuggled into the U. S. in the cans of a European food exporter. Payoffs went to the Me Too Corp.'s account at a Swiss bank. One $150,000 currency settlement passed through First National City, unwittingly, of course.

The minutes of one congressional hearing says: "There was no evidence in either of these cases that the New York bank or the Swiss bank had any knowledge of the underlying narcotics transaction. But the vital part they played in the heroin traffic is unmistakable."

Further testimony in congressional records indicates how legitimate banks may be caught in the financial webs spun by some of the world's international crooks.

The record reads:

CONG. JOSEPH G. MINISH (N.J.): Mr. Morgenthau, on the bottom of page four of your testimony you said that the facilities of a California bank and a midwestern bank were used under circumstances that should have aroused suspicion, to transfer funds from an American company to a Swiss bank that were used to pay kickbacks to employees of noncommissioned officers' clubs. Are you in position to go into more detail on that?

MR. MORGENTHAU: Well, I can give a few more details on that. That involved the Bank of America International, the Marine National Exchange Bank of Milwaukee, and three companies, American Vending Service Co., American Industrial Services Ltd., and American Service Sales, all of which were doing business with noncommissioned officers' clubs and enlisted men's clubs in Vietnam. And they were using Marine National Exchange Bank and Bank of America to transmit moneys to Swiss banks to pay kickbacks to army personnel and to American personnel working in official positions in Vietnam.

Obviously, even the most careful bank or corporation can be hoodwinked by the sophisticated, modern-day financial crook who uses fake certificates of deposit, unmarketable company securities, or forged warehouse receipts as his stock in trade. In the international arena the dangers are magnified. There is no S.E.C., backed by scores of laws and regulations, to protect the investor and legitimate businessman. Switzerland's free enterprise, freely convertible money market is one of the most efficient in the world for the completion of most business transactions.

That very freedom allows the fast-buck operator to jump onto the money train. Few of the fast-buck operators got quite the ride that did Bernard Cornfeld's I.O.S. Ltd., on Switzerland's money-go-round train.

CHAPTER XIII

I.O.S. AND THE PIANO PLAYER IN THE WHOREHOUSE

It was Russ Boner, then an enterprising reporter with the *Wall Street Journal*'s London Bureau, who first uncovered the story of what subsequently came to be known as the I.O.S. Arctic Land Deal. The story concerned an intriguing and complex financial transaction through which Investors Overseas Services, Geneva, gave itself an alleged profit of $9.7 million. Yet developments showed that little had really changed, only figures on an accounting sheet.

The story didn't draw much attention at first, except in offices of German and Swiss banks which had been holding I.O.S. shares in their portfolios. They quietly started dumping them. This activity played a part in the subsequent rapid down-slide of Swiss-based I.O.S., adding one more problem to many. The company already was sick, though even top executives didn't seem to know it. Switzerland also was quite sick of I.O.S., but didn't know what to do about it.

I.O.S., of course, is the big mutual fund and financial services group which was founded, nourished, and lost by Bernard Cornfeld, a Brooklyn-raised sales genius who was going to make everybody rich.

IOS FUNDS RECEIVE
LATE YULE PRESENT
FROM POLAR REGIONS

That was the head on the story published December 30, 1969, in the *Wall Street Journal*. The story appeared even before the company had completed the intricate dealings connected with this particular transaction. Later, one I.O.S. director reported that his first knowledge of the transaction came from reading the *Wall Street Journal*.

The story related how Fund of Funds and I.O.S. Growth Fund, two in the I.O.S. stable, increased net asset valuations markedly through sale of part of their holdings in Canadian Arctic gas and oil exploration permits. Ten percent of the I.O.S. holdings were sold to a company closely connected with I.O.S. On the basis of the "profit" on that sale, the remaining 90 percent of the retained rights were valued upward sharply, though nobody really could say what they were worth.

Imagine a situation whereby a man holds 100,000 acres of frozen tundra. It could be worth a few cents or many dollars an acre. Nobody would know until a buyer made an offer. The owner arranges to have a friend buy a small piece of the frozen wasteland for $100 an acre. On that basis, a valuation of $100 an acre is set for the entire bloc of real estate. Overnight, the whole chunk is valued at $10 million, though it is the same raw wasteland which had had no price tag at all earlier.

This particular deal increased the value of I.O.S. Arctic holdings from $17 million to $119 million, on paper. The parent company then collected a management fee of $9.7 million from Fund of Funds for creating all of this new "wealth."

Mutual funds take investors' money and reinvest it in diversified stocks or other holdings. They are managed by parent companies which have shares of their own, which usually belong to a small group of managers. Parent companies collect fees for their management skills. If the management makes profitable investments, the mutual fund shareholders are paid dividends and the value of shares appreciate. Most mutual funds continuously sell fund shares to the public. Good ones are ready to redeem fund shares at any time at their net asset value.

Asset valuation of a fund is a key progress indicator. Salesmen use these figures for their sales pitches. A rise allegedly shows good management, increasing sales appeal of the shares. Up to time of the Arctic Land Deal, Fund of Funds faced a bleak prospect. Net assets for the year-end were down sharply from a year earlier.

That complex land deal enabled Fund of Funds to hike its asset value per share from $20.57 to $23.29. This didn't quite match the previous year-end figure of $26.93. It did look much more respectable on a balance sheet, or in a salesman's selling kit. As for I.O.S. itself, that $9.7 million of earnings later proved to be most of the total profit of the parent in 1969.

That profit didn't fool hardnosed German and Swiss bankers who also function as brokers in equity markets. The *Wall Street Journal* story, which was also carried via the Associated Press–Dow Jones Business News Service, warned astute money men that I.O.S. was stretching hard to improve asset valuation of its most important fund.

One Basle banker later explained: "Whenever the value of any share, or a company's reported profit, moves sharply upward or downward, we study the factors behind it. If the upward push is based on sound conclusions, we want to participate in that rise. If the upward push is based on unproved factors, then we would like to know if a company is propping its shares or padding its profits. Perhaps we should be lightening our holdings in that company."

That is a good policy for any shareholder to follow, of course. Trouble is most small investors do not have access to the inside information on which such decisions are made. They might not have enough understanding of what is published, either, to comprehend that a story like that of the belated Yule present should have been read as a warning of I.O.S. troubles rather than as a bullish factor for the company.

The Arctic Land Deal did flash a "sell" signal to knowledgeable money men in Switzerland and elsewhere. For most Swiss money men, it was a welcome signal. Cornfeld had few friends in the Swiss banking fraternity. I.O.S. had engineered numerous clever deals during its rambunctious and often controversial life. Many of them upset traditional Swiss bankers, either by taking business from them, or by forcing them to meet the competition. Moreover, some Swiss thought I.O.S. was giving Switzerland a bad name.

I.O.S. did have a freewheeling, buccaneering record more akin to capitalism of the nineteenth century than to the banking practices of Switzerland in the twentieth century. I.O.S. salesmen were tossed out of Brazil on suspicion of violating that country's currency laws. Greek police raided and closed I.O.S.'s offices in Greece. The United States Securities and Exchange Commission barred I.O.S. from doing business in the United States.

"If you want to make money, don't horse around with steel or lightbulbs. Go where the money is—in the money business," Cornfeld once told a *Wall Street Journal* reporter. This he certainly did.

I.O.S. operated to gain maximum benefit from tax havens and easy currency laws around the globe. Originally, Cornfeld settled in Paris. In 1958, when France's currency controls restricted his activities, he loaded his records into his 1947 Chrysler convertible and drove to Geneva. There, he opened shop in an apartment building behind an Esso Service Station at 119 rue Lausanne, along Geneva's lakefront. In 1960, he incorporated Investors Overseas Services as the parent for what was to become a complex organization with subsidiaries in the Bahamas, Luxembourg, and anywhere else where taxes and governmental interference could be minimized.

Why Switzerland for an operating base? No other nation in the world had comparable currency freedom. No other nation allowed a free-wheeling mutual fund to operate with as few controls. Banks were easy to establish, and I.O.S. needed its own bank to expand.

Switzerland did pass a law outlawing door-to-door selling by mutual fund salesmen. This didn't bother Cornfeld. Door-to-door selling was a favored gimmick with his crew. But Cornfeld's operations were designed to use Switzerland as a receptacle for funds from all over the world, not as a sales arena.

And what did Swiss bankers think of the new arrival? Not much. Cornfeld's personality didn't help. A favorite conversational opener with him was: "Listen, you schmucks." The greeting is not mentioned in usual listings of correct forms of address.

Moreover, his nightlife exploits, sometimes recounted with embellishments in Europe's more lurid journals, didn't agree at all with European banking ideas about how a money manager should conduct himself. The typical Swiss money manager operates on an 8 A.M. to 6 P.M. hard business day for six days a week, then spends Sunday reading company reports and balance sheets. He may have his surreptitious pleasures. They aren't centered around night clubs, not in Switzerland, anyway.

"But I.O.S. was operating legally in Switzerland, paying regard to our laws. There was little we could do just because we did not like Cornfeld," one Zurich banker explained recently. Later, of course, Switzerland was to tighten its mutual fund laws, which indicates that they could have done so earlier, too, was not *laissez-faire* such a fixed notion in Swiss minds.

In international business today, there is a vast gray area where national laws end, with no international laws applying against certain sharp business practices. The United States S.E.C. does try to regulate American financial corporations abroad, at least insofar as their activities have a bearing on internal U.S.A. matters. Cornfeld insisted from the first that the S.E.C. had no business trying to run his operation. I.O.S. managed to escape such control through most of its existence, though S.E.C. did enjoin the company from doing business in the U.S.A. or from selling mutual fund shares to Americans anywhere.

"If Switzerland had an S.E.C., I.O.S. would have been out of business long ago," one U.S. government man griped in

Washington recently. But Switzerland has no such agency. Swiss bankers don't want any. I.O.S. was one of the trials the Swiss banking industry had to bear for the financial tolerance which has been built into the country's system.

Edward M. Cowett, the legal genius of the Cornfeld operation, has one of the keenest legal minds to be found anywhere. He is a tough, quick-moving man of medium build who cuts incisively to the heart of a problem almost immediately after hearing a few details. Once he told a reporter: "We operate within the law . . . just within."

Perhaps it was an unfortunate quote, for it is cited often when I.O.S. is mentioned. Subsequently, the U.S. government charged I.O.S. with going beyond the law with illegal dealings in gold. There are pending lawsuits galore. Nobody yet has gone to jail. But S.E.C. charges that $224 million of I.O.S. funds have disappeared, though Cornfeld and Cowett are not blamed for that.

S.E.C. never stopped trying to assert its control over I.O.S. I.O.S. consistently used Swiss bank secrecy as its shield, arguing that cooperation with S.E.C. would violate Swiss law.

One S.E.C. document presented to a congressional hearing in Washington showed that S.E.C. officials, too, were among those who read that *Wall Street Journal* story about the Arctic Land Deal. Said one official: "We have twice requested that I.O.S. supply us with details of that transaction, but to date we have received no information from them."

That same hearing suggested that I.O.S. might have violated its own agreement with S.E.C. to avoid selling funds to Americans. This dialogue occurred between Robert R. Parker, former attaché at the U.S. Embassy in Saigon and Congressman Henry S. Reuss (Wis.-D.).

REUSS. Now, you were saying that when you were in Vietnam you had some insight into the activities of Investors Overseas Services.
PARKER. Yes. In 1967 and 1968.
REUSS. And would you tell what activities you observed.
PARKER. Within the AID mission a number of different mutual fund solicitors had come into the offices and were attempting to sell various mutual fund plans. I.O.S. was

one of those about which one of the people on the staff complained.

REUSS. When was this attempted solicitation by I.O.S. to make sales of their mutual fund to U.S. civilian and military personnel in Vietnam?

PARKER. To the best of my knowledge and recollection, sir, in the spring or early summer, 1968.

Through much of its existence, the I.O.S. story has been the story of its founder, Cornfeld, a man who was always "Bernie" to everybody.

Cornfeld, forty-six in 1972, is an Istanbul-born, Brooklyn-raised American who combines left-wing social philosophies, Boy Scout dogmas, and sharp salesmanship into a short, slender frame. He is a womanizer who believes in that Boy Scout motto: "Be prepared." When traveling, he sometimes takes female companions along in groups, four, five at a time. Usually, they're all good looking, all young, all looking like live center-spreads from *Playboy*, but with clothes.

During the early days of his empire building, Cornfeld became so overweight that he looked like a beer-drinking truck driver between road hauls. (Actually, he doesn't drink at all.) Then, he dieted and raised a beard, even as he was losing some of the hair on his head and some of the control of his financial empire.

That beard blossomed shortly after Cornfeld met Pope Paul at a private audience in Rome. It is not known whether there is any relationship between these two developments. The beard certainly made Bernie look like the apostle of a cause, which was how he saw himself. Not many people can see the relationship between social welfare and mutual funds. Bernie could.

"If we help some jerk to straighten out his finances through one of our fund programs, aren't we helping him to improve his social condition, too?" Bernie asked one day when he still controlled I.O.S.

As a student at Brooklyn College in New York City, he formed the largest Socialist club on any campus in the United States. He served as president of the nation's largest chapter of the Congress of Racial Equality. In 1948, he collected more signatures on Norman Thomas-for-President petitions than anybody else in the country. His hero at that time was Aneurin Bevan, the British socialist, who delighted in baiting Britain's Establishment.

Cornfeld's liberal views led him into social welfare work in Philadelphia. The job paid so little he turned to selling mutual funds on the side. Said he: "I found I had an affinity for selling."

Others describe it as a "genius for selling." This Billy Graham of mutual funds saw himself as a missionary of "people's capitalism" sowing the seeds of security by helping people to save money in his mutual funds. Shortly, he was in Europe spreading the gospel among "heathens" who hardly knew what a mutual fund was. And he prospered, initially, anyway.

The Cornfeld beard ideally fitted the sanitized hippie role which Bernie liked to play. He regarded himself as a social rebel stoutly aligned against some of society's hypocritical mores, and many of the restrictive mandates of government, especially those having to do with high taxes on corporate profits, or S.E.C. regulation.

The I.O.S. headquarters staff in Geneva had a predilection for facial hair and jolly rebel attire in the expensive mold. Two of Cornfeld's chief aids sported facial hair in the glory days of the I.O.S. empire. Allen R. Cantor, long Cornfeld's sales chief, featured a bristling, "scots terrier" beard. Ed Cowett, executive vice president and briefly the president, had the sideburns and chin hair of a Victorian dandy until the mental tensions of I.O.S.' troubles raised a rash on his chin. The itchiness increased as troubles mounted after the Arctic Land Deal became public knowledge. Finally, Cowett shaved.

Most titans of finance, today, aren't bearded. Swiss bankers like mustaches, but a beard is regarded as rather gauche, either a stamp of immaturity or an admission that one can't afford razor blades. Neither the stamp nor the admission coincides with the Swiss banker's picture of himself.

The S.E.C., long a major Cornfeld opponent, was viewed, not as part of the Establishment, but as a tool of it. I.O.S. was not against hiring S.E.C. officials when they left government. In one crucial legal tussle with S.E.C., Cornfeld had eight lawyers defending his interests. Four of them were ex-S.E.C. officials who had been lured onto the Cornfeld payroll.

Cornfeld delighted in the shock effect he created. Once, in Geneva, he was invited to address a staid group of local bankers. They waited for him in a nineteenth-century hall with cut glass chandeliers, everybody dressed in funereal black or dark blue suits, everybody so serious that even the pre-dinner sherries and glasses of fendant failed to enliven the atmosphere. Cornfeld arrived when everyone was sitting down. He wore a colorful Pierre Cardin jacket, a flowing tie, and that studied carelessness which is a feature of this generation's sartorial splendor. A ravishing blonde clung to his arm, apparently oblivious to the stony stares she attracted. Cornfeld's only concession was that he did not open his address by saying: "Listen, you schmucks."

Another time, Erich Mende, a prominent German politician and I.O.S. top man in Germany, invited Cornfeld and Director James Roosevelt to an I.O.S. meeting in Bonn with German bankers. Star speaker was to be Karl Schiller, then economics minister.

Bernie arrived accompanied by his company spokesman, Harold Kaplan, and a striking brunette who didn't appear to be out of her teens, but did appear to know how to handle herself. Kaplan served with the U.S. Information Service for years, performing capably as the American spokesman during the Kennedy Round of tariff negotiations in Geneva. He switched to I.O.S. in time to become the overworked, harassed spokesman during its troubles.

The trio arrived at the plush dining hall on a hilltop retreat overlooking the Rhine. Economics Minister Schiller and a battery of German bankers already had arrived. Everybody was garbed in almost identical black suits, everybody maintaining that dignified air of controlled well-being which bankers usually exude at parties.

Then, a Mende assistant sighted the girl. He hurried forward, red faced, grabbed Kaplan by the arm, pulled him aside.

"What do I do with the girl?" he hissed.

"I would suggest that you feed her," Kaplan coolly responded. A typical response from a confirmed Cornfeld man.

It is easy to say that Cornfeld's money helped to charge the magnetism which flowed from him when he elected to switch on his charm. Actually, Cornfeld, beneath that brash, aggressive façade, can be a kind and friendly man who has no trouble projecting these qualities when caught in female company, or when in any company for that matter. He does like to have his own way. He does like to dominate the conversational floor, even when he has nothing to say. His span of interest can be very short, along with his temper. Yet he found it almost impossible to fire anybody who once joined his team.

Above everything else, Cornfeld always was a salesman, even when he had a two-billion-dollar company at his fingertips. "I'm a lousy administrator," he once confided to a friend. Certainly he was, as events proved.

Nobody could fault his salesmanship, though. I.O.S. honored the sales producer, discouraged the selling drone. It paid salesmen only on a commission basis, but paid them well when the sales were completed. When one early I.O.S. salesman was hospitalized with bronchial pneumonia, he solicited doctors for potential mutual fund sales, hired a chauffeured limousine to transport outside prospects to his bedside, and transformed his hospital room into an office. Before release from the hospital, he sold $298,000 worth of investment plans.

That was Cornfeld's type of man.

Another alert salesman noted the long stream of patients at a doctor's office. He reasoned that any doctor with that amount of business must be doing well financially, but probably had little time to devote to his financial affairs. So the salesman took a seat in the waiting room, apparently, a patient. Once inside, he launched into his sales presentation and sold the doctor $50,000 worth of mutual fund shares.

I.O.S. salesmen descended into mine shafts to contact engineers, paddled canoes up jungle rivers to reach plantation managers, and rode in sand buggies across deserts to meet oil rich sheikhs. In Ghana, just before the collapse of Kwame Nkrumah's dictatorship, an alert I.O.S. salesman was selling investment plans to jittery government officials who didn't know where their next graft payment would be coming from.

Money poured into I.O.S. headquarters in Geneva to be invested by a team headed by C. Henry Buhl III, the affable scion of a prominent and wealthy Detroit family. Henry and his team did all right in the initial years. I.O.S. went off the track when its funds invested in things far removed from Wall Street, such as potential oil lands in Canada's frozen North. And even the Wall Street investments seemed to be concentrated in high flyers like Commonwealth United, Giffin Industries, and Unexcelled, Inc., which flew well in the hot air atmosphere of a 1968 bull market. They didn't fly at all when the bear market of 1969 and 1970 dissipated the hot air.

On almost any spring or summer day you can sit along the green lake shore in Geneva, close to beds of tulips, and watch the Jet d'Eau fountain, world's highest, throw a jet of water four hundred and fifty feet into the air. The water rises in a lovely plume, spreads into white spray at its zenith like an exploding rocket, then falls downward in a misty cascade. The I.O.S. empire shot into the world's financial sky just as dramatically to $119.7 million in assets in 1964, to $522.8 million in 1966, to $1.5 billion in 1968, and to a peak of $2.3 billion in assets at the end of 1969.

Today, there are Swiss bankers who insist they always knew Cornfeld would fall flat on his Cardin-tailored pants. There are veiled references to Ponzi, Samuel Insul, Kruger, the Swedish match king, and various other money men who lost their magic and their money in spectacular style. Actually, when Cornfeld rode high many of the Swiss bankers were seeking whatever business they could obtain from this company which could generate money faster than some mints. For a time, Swiss Credit Bank was a depository for I.O.S. Union Bank and Swiss Bank Corp. overhauled some of their stodgy mutual funds after feeling the competition of I.O.S.

Cornfeld sought to guarantee the loyalty of his key people through lavish stock bonuses. These accumulated over the years, for there was no market for the stock except through resale to the company. That situation was corrected in September, 1969. About a fifth of the equity, 10,992,000 shares, was sold to the public in three stock offerings, including some private holdings, at an initial price of $10 a share. Shortly, the over-the-counter price zoomed to $19.

Net proceeds of $52.1 million should have been more than

enough to carry the company through a trying period. But nobody in management even suspected the trouble ahead. As the Arctic Land Deal was being arranged, Ed Cowett was borrowing $2,843,000 from an I.O.S. bank to buy more I.O.S. shares for his family. I.O.S. earnings for 1969 were expected to amount to about $28 million, according to the faulty reasoning of top executives. There was talk of I.O.S. shares hitting $50 a share in 1970.

In February, 1970, the company held a sales meeting at Royal Albert Hall in London for several thousand salesmen. Cornfeld thought it would be classy to have a minister open the affair. Martin Sullivan, dean of the prestigious St. Paul's Cathedral in London, undertook the job. Invocation theme was: "There is good in every situation, no matter how bad it may appear."

No irony was intended. But, I.O.S. already was in a bad way. Company executives were becoming aware that the golden money tap was slowing to a trickle. Not only were sales declining, but people were redeeming shares. In the second quarter of 1969, the average monthly inflow had been $105.9 million. This declined to $61.9 million in the third quarter, $46.1 million in the fourth quarter and to $33.9 million a month in the first quarter of 1970. Meanwhile, the price of I.O.S shares eroded under the selling pressure of European banks.

It seemed as if the only people who were buying shares were I.O.S. salesmen and executives. They had great faith in the company. Salesmen must be optimistic if they are to ring doorbells. Now they were borrowing money to buy still more shares of the company.

This was only a temporary slowdown, claimed executives at rue Lausanne, if they even knew a downturn was underway. So muddled was the administrative organization that executives didn't really know what profit, if any, was being generated from that high pressure sales staff in the field.

Prayer, indeed, was in order at that sales meeting in London, prayer plus good works on the job. Events subsequently showed that for some time numerous company executives, directors, and salesmen were following a religious slogan of their own: The Lord Helps Those Who Help Themselves. They were helping themselves to some of the company cash in the form of nearly $50 million in loans, guarantees, and advances.

George von Peterffy, tall, earnest associate professor at the Harvard Business School and an I.O.S. director, focused attention on that situation. Von Peterffy was one of Cornfeld's selections. Bernie figured that his company needed a long-range planner. He reached for the best available in von Peterffy, thinking that the Harvard Business School connection would add prestige to an organization woefully weak in management talent.

So, enter von Peterffy, first as a consultant, then as an outside director, and through the crisis of 1970, as an insider. The difference between von Peterffy and some of the other executives in the I.O.S. suite was that George could analyze balance sheets, evaluate costs and profits, and summarize conclusions. The talents of other executives leaned toward selling.

"Those guys can sell the pants off of you, but they aren't organized to make decisions, even the little ones. They just can't manage," von Peterffy exploded in exasperation one day to *Wall Street Journal* reporter Neil Ulman.

For months, von Peterffy worked in the Geneva offices, making administrative suggestions which were ignored, recommending creation of management controls, which nobody wanted imposed. It was a frustrating task for a management expert. Still, he dug hard into company records, trying to do the job for which he had been hired.

In March, 1970, von Peterffy's digging revealed that the company had less than $10 million in working capital. Yet it had raised $52.1 million in that public offering. Where did the money go?

Investigation revealed that executive after executive had obtained loans or loan guarantees for individual deals, or for stock purchases. Five million dollars of I.O.S. funds had been deposited with Wells Fargo Bank, San Francisco, to guarantee loans to I.O.S. directors and officials. A like amount was deposited with a European bank for the same purpose. Richard Gangel, a semi-retired I.O.S. official, had $830,505 in loans outstanding at end of 1969. Bernie Cornfeld had $530,820. In addition, the company had guaranteed a $4.4 million loan owed to British

Aircraft Corp., for Bernie's private plane. Cowett had borrowed $2.8 million to buy shares of the company through Atlas Trust Co., a family trust. George Tregea had borrowed $330,800.

So it went, for loan after loan. Loans outstanding to officers and directors totaled $30.7 million at the end of 1969. The total at peak was around $41 million. Loans, guarantees, blocked accounts, and commitments had depleted the treasury and tied up most of the cash remaining.

The tale appalled von Peterffy. As a director, he felt a responsibility to stockholders, as well as to the management which had hired him. He immediately contacted two other directors who also were becoming concerned, Buhl and Sir Eric Wyndham White. Sir Eric, a one-time British civil servant, had headed the General Agreement on Tariffs and Trade in Geneva from its creation in 1947 through completion of the Kennedy Round of worldwide tariff cuts. He is a stubby, bulldog of a man who was a persuasive negotiator during the three years of the Kennedy Round.

He had been hired for his name. Bernie always did like to add prominent people to his team to give it class. Count Carl Johan Bernadotte of the Swedish royal family was a director. So was Erich Mende, one-time deputy chancellor of Germany. James Roosevelt, son of FDR and a diplomat in his own right, took charge of I.O.S.'s diplomatic relations.

Von Peterffy demanded that a board meeting be called to analyze the company's financial situation. Cowett stalled, say Cowett's enemies. He says he was already aware of the company's precarious position and was seeking outside support. In any case, the meeting was not made a matter of urgency.

But news of financial disasters travels fast through brokerage houses. Now everybody wanted to sell I.O.S. shares. In early April, the price sagged below the introductory $10 a share. Cornfeld, as usual, was away from Geneva. He had been spending less and less time in the office, preferring to maintain his contacts on the jet set circuit. He was enjoying himself in Israel with the usual bevy of pretty girls around him, the usual cluster of business deals in the offing. The Tel Aviv Hilton Hotel was up for sale, and Cornfeld expressed an interest in it.

He was playing backgammon at Eilat on the Red Sea when

a come-home-at-once telegram was thrust into his hands. Within hours, Bernie was in the air over the eastern Mediterranean heading for home in Geneva. Well, one of his homes. Cornfeld maintained a flat in London, an apartment in Paris, a house in Geneva, and a castle in the Haut-Savoie in France, a few miles from Geneva. Yet home was just as apt to be the sumptuous cabin of his private BAC-III jet, a plane which some friends say was inspired by the super-swank private jet that *Playboy*'s Hugh Heffner purchased.

Cornfeld did not return as the conquering hero. Everybody now realized that disaster faced the company. Many of the one hundred sixty paper millionaires created by I.O.S. were on the board, or on the management team. This downslide was becoming personal, hitting at the pocketbooks of everybody on the team. Old relationships mean little when paper millionaires see that paper becoming worthless because of mismanagement. Bernie was a good man to blame.

Cornfeld had headed the company almost as a one-man operation. But he seldom was around to tend the store. He rewarded salesmen excessively, and thought accountants only got in his way. When spending money (company money that is), Cornfeld could teach a drunken sailor a few tricks, for no drunken sailor ever had the resources of I.O.S. in his hip pocket. Three thousand bottles of Moet & Chandon champagne flowed at one memorable I.O.S. Christmas party at the Geneva Intercontinental Hotel. Once when a Cornfeld-trained executive vacationed in Italy, he hired one chauffeured limousine for himself, a second for baggage.

Bernie not only liked to spend money; he wanted to be seen spending it. This was part of his success image. Like John Betjeman the British poet, Cornfeld believed that "nothing succeeds like excess."

Sunday, April 12, directors assembled in a room half paneled with red velvet at Belle Vista, the I.O.S. lakeside mansion in Geneva. The place was another Cornfeld extravagance, a mansion which had once belonged to the Colgate family. Bernie thought it would impress salesmen at sales conventions. So he bought it. Now the mansion became the scene of the Cornfeld management's death agonies.

Cornfeld opened the meeting with a few rambling words concerning the solidity of the enterprise. It was the salesman's analysis of a desperate situation when future commissions depend on convincing people that things aren't so desperate after all. His remarks fell flat.

"I didn't come here to listen to crap," an impatient director cried out.

Another demanded: "Tell us what is really going on here."

Cornfeld had lost caste.

Melvin Lechner, the company's treasurer, was called to report data about the firm's finances. It was a sad tale, a story of how loans had depleted the treasury. Directors listened, glumly. Then, the wrangle started, with everyone blaming everyone else. Greed had helped create the crisis. Nobody wanted to admit his own avidity. Confession comes hard when its voice box is a pocketbook. Many of the twenty-one directors present were among I.O.S.'s one hundred sixty paper millionaires. All were seeing their holdings melt away like ice cubes in a summer drink.

Through most of April, the I.O.S. board deliberated day and night. Nobody knew what to do. By now, Cowett was president, with Bernie as chairman and chief executive officer. Both insisted that there was nothing improper about those loans which had milked the treasury. In public, Sir Eric termed those loans "unwise." In private, he termed them "stupid."

The financial community, however, pays nothing for stupidity, since there already is so much of it around. I.O.S. shares dropped down and down. The average mutual fund investor, who probably did not know the difference between I.O.S. shares and the mutual fund shares, grew worried. Redemptions soared. People in Europe talked of a crisis of confidence. I.O.S. had 800,000 customers. Suppose they all panicked and demanded their money? Could this be the start of another 1929 crash?

The company needed money, and a dozen different schemes developed to get it. Rothschild interests in Paris seemed willing; but the $1.25 a share price they set on the stock appeared skimpy to most directors, even though the market price slid steadily in the direction of that price. The Bank of England had to deny that it had any plans to salvage a commercial company like I.O.S.

Then, Cowett thought he had found a savior in John M. King, chief of King Resources Co., Denver, a razzle-dazzle outfit in the oil and financial services field. King is a mountain of a man who thinks big, acts big, and is big, physically. He had a burning ambition to be a billionaire, and he lived the part before reaching his goal. Electronically-controlled doors guarded the entrance to his red-carpeted penthouse office atop the thirty-one-story Security Life Building in Denver.

Much of his time was spent at a palatial ranch in the country, on safari in Africa, or galloping about the world to survey various interests. He had a fetish about elephants, collecting carvings and paintings of them, sometimes regaling friends with tales of elephant shrewdness noted on his safaris. One friend said: "I think he really sees himself as a big bull elephant stomping through the grass."

King wasn't quite big enough to swing a deal to give himself control of I.O.S., though already he had close relations with I.O.S. King had helped engineer that Arctic Land Deal. A King subsidiary acted as the willing buyer for the oil exploration rights sold by Fund of Funds.

As the King-I.O.S. relationship unfolded, it became difficult to determine if King were trying to save I.O.S. or if he were trying to save his own company from repercussions of an I.O.S. collapse. In any case, he was stymied by the S.E.C. King's American companies operated under the S.E.C. blanket. I.O.S. had stubbornly insisted on remaining outside. Now Cornfeld was paying the price for that independence.

King, as a staunch Republican and supporter and friend of President Nixon, must have hoped that his political clout would carry some weight with the S.E.C. It didn't. After a meeting with S.E.C. officials in Washington, King emerged, shaken, to announce withdrawal of his I.O.S. salvage offer.

Meanwhile, Sir Eric had become the interim leader of I.O.S. One clause of the King deal had called for the resignations of Cornfeld and Cowett. Wyndham White was elected chairman for what everybody thought would be a brief period until King took over.

During Wyndham White's early months with the company, Cornfeld could never remember his name. He started calling him "Sir Eric Windmill" among intimates, then used the name as a term of derision when Sir Eric became chairman. Sir Eric proved to be considerably stronger than Cornfeld had reckoned, though he did take it to heart when the *Sunday Telegraph*, a British national newspaper, referred to him as "the piano player in the whorehouse."

It was an unkind remark. Sir Eric took office only with the intention of preserving I.O.S. so that its hundreds of thousands of mutual fund holders would not lose all their money.

At the annual meeting in Toronto, June 30, 1970, Sir Eric successfully marshalled a majority of the shares outstanding behind him. Cornfeld's bid to rally proxy votes failed. He didn't even win a director's seat.

Sir Eric, without Cornfeld, set out to find financial help for the ailing company. The job wasn't easy. None of the big financial institutions wanted to become connected with I.O.S. as long as Cornfeld lingered in the background. His 7,400,000 preferred I.O.S. shares represented 13 percent of the total and made him the largest individual shareholder. He was trying hard for a comeback.

Cornfeld attacked Sir Eric's management. He traveled extensively to contact other big shareholders who had seen their shares fall to $1.50 each in June, 1970, then to as low as twenty-five cents a share as the recriminations mounted.

A new I.O.S. rescuer appeared on the scene, Robert L. Vesco, president and chief executive officer of a medium-sized company located in Fairbanks, New Jersey, called International Controls Corp. At thirty-four, Vesco was a self-made man who had taken a small electrical controls company, reorganized it, and created what he himself described as "a holding company with interests in data processing and automatic controls."

Early in August, 1970, he offered a $5 million loan to I.O.S. plus a $5 million line of credit, with the possibility of more financial assistance in the future. Sir Eric and other I.O.S. directors endorsed the aid, though it meant that I.O.S. was to give I.C.C. certain warrants. Eventually, these warrants totaled 3 million, giving Vesco's company the right to purchase common shares of I.O.S. at $2 per share for each warrant.

Cornfeld fought the package, recognizing that it would put I.O.S. further away from him. He threatened a proxy fight and a lawsuit, then relented when it appeared that any further infighting might kill the company. In early September, the I.O.S. board certified the aid package. Vesco moved in.

Sir Eric worked with the Vesco team to salvage the company. I.O.S. posted a loss of $25.8 million for the first half of 1970, quite a contrast to the $10.5 million profit of the same period a year earlier. And cash still was draining away.

Vesco, a dapper, mustached man in a double-breasted dark blue suit, appeared at a press conference at I.O.S. headquarters to assure everybody that he had no intention of taking management control himself. Later he was to tell the S.E.C. in Washington that he really thought he was fronting for the Bank of America, largest bank in the world. He thought that, after he had overhauled ailing I.O.S., he could deliver it in healthy shape to the bank. Alvin C. Rice, executive vice president, Bank of America, admitted that conversations about I.O.S. had taken place with Vesco. But nothing definite had been arranged, he said.

Sir Eric, confident that he had placed I.O.S. in good hands through his interim managing, resigned. R. E. Slater, former chief of John Hancock Mutual Life Insurance Co., was named president and chief executive officer in October, 1970, with the endorsement of Vesco.

But Cornfeld still remained in the background, a threat to Vesco's growing hold on I.O.S. Then, in January, 1971, I.O.S. announced that Cornfeld had sold his shares to undisclosed sources severing all connections with the company. An era had ended. Vesco had control, and a month later he was named chairman of I.O.S. Later it was revealed that an offshore company affiliated with his interests had purchased 6 million shares held by Cornfeld. Price was undisclosed, but certain sources said it was in the $1 to $1.20 a share range. That wasn't much for stock that might have been worth $120 million at one time. Still, it was more than the market price.

Vesco inherited I.O.S.'s rift with the S.E.C. Soon he was

plunged into a court case against S.E.C. He didn't want the Washington agency to dig into the relationship between International Controls and I.O.S. In the U.S. District Court in Newark, New Jersey, Sherwin J. Markham, attorney for I.C.C., told the court that the company "badly needed protection of the court" against an overzealous government agency.

Robert E. Kushner, assistant general counsel for S.E.C., declared that International Controls had "deliberately sought to shroud" its relationship with I.O.S. "in an atmosphere of secrecy."

In May, 1971, the Newark federal judge dismissed the I.C.C. suit to bar S.E.C. from investigating its affairs. It was the first of several defeats for Vesco. Meanwhile, the S.E.C. scored another victory over Cornfeld. It barred him and Cowett from engaging in the securities business in the United States. The two ex-I.O.S. officials had been found in violation of securities laws in the 1967-69 period.

Vesco successfully opposed a rebellion of dissident I.O.S. stockholders who tried to unseat him at the June 30, 1971, annual meeting in Toronto. The group included Morton I. Schiowitz, one-time chief financial officer of I.O.S., Allen R. Cantor, its ex-sales chief, Hyman Feld, George Landau, Lawrence Rosen, Don Q. Shaprow, George W. Tregea, and Samuel C. Welker.

Through all the bickering and battling over I.O.S., Swiss authorities remained far in the background. Its own securities laws were so liberal that I.O.S. could claim none were being broken. Meanwhile, I.O.S. hid behind Swiss bank secrecy whenever S.E.C. tried to pry into its affairs.

However, that 1971 proxy battle resulted in a situation which aroused Swiss ire. A bloc of I.O.S. shares had been reposing in vaults of its Geneva subsidiary, Overseas Development Bank. These shares were withdrawn allegedly without proper authorization to vote for the Vesco slate in the close proxy fight. When Vesco appeared in Geneva in December, 1971, to answer this charge, he was tossed into jail for a night before bail was allowed. It was the only direct move by Swiss against I.O.S. during its period of turmoil. Charges against Vesco later were withdrawn by Swiss authorities, without apology.

Subsequently, I.O.S. closed its rue Lausanne office in Geneva and most of its operations faded into a maze of corporations created by Vesco. On January 13, 1972, I.O.S. announced that it was revising downward the valuation of those Arctic oil leases included in the notorious Arctic Land Deal. A simple announcement said properties were being valued "at the acquisition costs of the predecessor."

After two years, events had come full circle. It had been an eventful two years for I.O.S., and for Switzerland, too. Things grew more eventful late in 1972. The S.E.C. in a civil case charged that Vesco and forty associates helped themselves to $224 million of I.O.S.'s remaining assets.

Swiss money men wondered how free-wheeling financial companies such as I.O.S. should be controlled in the future to protect Switzerland's good name as a safe haven for money.

WINNING AND LOSING

On Friday afternoon, July 31, 1970, Paul Erdman, thirty-seven, chief operating executive of the United California Bank in Basle, Switzerland, anxiously studied the accounting sheet on his modernistic, black-finish desk. Worry wasn't normal for him. Power and position had arrived so smoothly that he saw the optimistic side of everything. Usually, he felt as if he could master any business situation.

But this?

He leaned back in his swivel chair, tall frame almost touching the pastel wall of his soft-lighted office. He was a loose-limbed, rangy man, with thinning, blond hair and such a grasp of monetary affairs that reporters from the *New York Times,*

Barron's, and other publications frequently sought his opinions. Now he needed some advice himself, 25 million Swiss francs, or nearly $6 million worth at the 1970 rate of exchange.

A secretary brought more papers into the gray-carpeted office with its air of money well spent. Even the four-foot-high African carved figure in one corner had seemed to settle into comfortable domesticity in these luxurious surroundings which clearly advertised success.

As the fastest growing bank in Switzerland, UCB in Basle had money to spend, or so it seemed. Anton Bec, a youthful and eager Basle architect was in the bank that very day, drawing plans for the addition of an executives dining room, and an expansion of facilities.

Erdman, an aggressive American with a master's degree from Georgetown University and a Ph.D. from the University of Basle, had built this bank from nothing into one which was giving competitive headaches to its staid Swiss neighbors. Only fifteen months before, big United California Bank, Los Angeles, had bought control.

It had been a most harmonious takeover, topped by an extravagant party at the Schuetzenhaus Restaurant in Basle, where the prestigious Bank for International Settlements often holds its social gatherings. At that party, Frank L. King, then chairman of the Los Angeles bank and its much bigger parent, Western Bancorp., had jokingly told a neighbor: "We bought the bank to get Paul Erdman."

Now, as he studied the accounting sheet, Erdman wondered what the Los Angeles bank might say. There was a discrepancy of 25 million Swiss francs in the bank's commodity department. Was this a loss, or a statistical error?

Erdman's frown deepened. His wife, Helly, and the two little girls, waited in the El Dorado Cadillac in the parking lot behind the bank. Suitcases filled the car's trunk. Several bags spilled into the back seat.

The Erdman family was poised to depart for a long anticipated vacation on Spain's Costa del Sol. A suite awaited them at the Marbella Hilton Hotel in Marbella.

Erdman studied the figures again.

"Damn!" He uttered an uncharacteristic oath. He had a

strict Lutheran upbringing with formative years spent at a Lutheran school in Fort Wayne, Indiana. He knew that normally
a man did not have to shout and swear to get things done.

He picked up the phone, dialed the interoffice number of
the commodity department a floor below the executive suite.
"Give me Kummerli," he said to the clerk who responded.

Bernard Kummerli, a thick-spectacled, thirty-seven-year-
old fellow with a computer brain, headed the bank's commodity
and foreign exchange department. He could pair shifting foreign exchange rates of a half dozen currencies in his head where
someone else might need minutes on a calculating machine for
the correct tabulation.

"Mr. Kummerli is in London," a voice responded.

"Damn." Erdman mumbled again. He glanced at his watch,
noted that it was nearly 3 P.M. He had promised Helly that he
definitely would quit the bank by early afternoon to begin that
long drive to the Costa del Sol.

She hadn't wanted him to stop at the bank at all. "Everytime you stop, you find something to do, and you will be there
most of the day," she had said.

Now Erdman realized that he should investigate this matter. Several more millions of dollars might be involved. It might
be necessary to straddle the market to reduce losses. Any bank
in the sensitive, fluctuating cocoa commodity market expects
some losses. The aim is to generate enough profits so that the
profits exceed the losses at the year-end accounting.

But 25 million Swiss francs!

Then, the Costa del Sol loomed into his mind, the sunny
coastline with its miles of indented coves and friendly beaches.
This must be an error, after all, he thought. Impulsively, he
swept the papers on his desk into a drawer.

"I'm on my way," he called to the secretary who had been
with him since he opened the bank in 1965.

He didn't know it then, but the bank was about to fold in
one of the biggest crashes ever to hit Swiss banking. Losses
would surpass $50 million. The catastrophe would sweep away
UCB Basle, put seven bank officials, including Erdman, into the
seventeenth-century revamped monastery which serves as the

Basle jail, and lead to a barrage of lawsuits which may be outstanding in 1978.

"I picked a poor time to go on my vacation," says Erdman, wryly, when recapping incidents of the case. The story is the familiar tale of a bank whose traders encounter market losses, plunge deeper to recoup, lose more money, then speculate even deeper in a desperate and unsuccessful comeback gamble. The bank's story raises questions about Swiss bank regulation, or lack of it.

Erdman didn't settle into a tranquil vacation at the Marbella Hilton. Those figures kept running through his head. Twenty five million Swiss francs! If that were a loss, then the bank was in trouble. But was it a loss? It was a good question. There had been inklings of trouble at UCB Basle for some while. That commodity department had been stumbling along the edge of disaster. Collapse of silver prices in late 1968 and early 1969 had hurt, though a quick salvage operation had minimized losses. There had been several bad cocoa trades. But all this had been straightened out. Or had it?

The third night of the vacation, he sat up in bed, groped for the light switch. "Helly. We're going home," he said abruptly. "I think something is wrong at the bank."

Something was. Back in Basle, muddled records of the commodity department revealed deep trouble. Losses on cocoa trading amounted to millions of dollars. Millions. It had to be a rough estimate because those records were so disordered that only a complete audit could reveal the facts.

"God!" Erdman slumped at his desk. Those earlier cocoa losses hadn't been recovered. They had mounted higher and higher as the commodity department sought to balance earlier losses with ever bigger trades in hope that these would be successful. Ultimately, futures for half the world's cocoa were in the bank's hands. And the market had gone down, instead of up.

Cocoa is a commodity which everybody knows goes into chocolate bars, fudge, and various other confections. It comes from the cocoa tree which grows in Ghana, Brazil, and other equatorial countries. Trees are constantly plagued by black pod disease, certain horticultural insect attacks, and vagaries of weather. The trees are an oddity. Pods grow directly from trunks, looking like yellow gourds that have been fastened on hooks to the trees. Inside pods are the cocoa beans, the substance of the world's cocoa market.

A good cocoa harvest through the October-January pod-picking season sends cocoa prices down. With a bad crop and scarcity, cocoa prices zoom. A smart speculator plays market swings by purchasing cocoa futures.

These futures are promises to deliver cocoa at some future date. The speculator pays the going rate for cocoa when he purchases his futures contract, playing the market either long (for a price rise) or short (for a price fall). If the price rises while he holds a long contract, he can make his delivery and collect at the higher price. If the price per pound drops and he has a long contract, he may be wiped out. Short selling operates in reverse, profits lying with a price fall and disaster with a price rise. It's all done on paper, with speculators never seeing the cocoa on which their fortunes may be riding.

If anybody asks what a bank has to do with such a wildly speculative market, it is a good question. But banks in Switzerland are department stores of finance, remember? They may do anything from dealing in gold to managing portfolios and from speculating in commodities to underwriting a bond issue. UCB Basle wasn't acting illegally. It was only proving that banking in Switzerland isn't necessarily confined to conservative 4.5 percent savings and 7 percent lending operations, where profits are virtually guaranteed for the bank.

Cocoa futures may be purchased with only 10 percent margin. A $100,000 investment thus may be financed with $10,000. If the cocoa price doubles on a long trade, the gross is $200,000 not $20,000. Instead of doubling his money a speculator in such a deal can run his $10,000 to $110,000 (the $200,000 less the $90,000 unpaid investment on the $100,000 contract), less the commission.

Possible profits are balanced by heavy potential losses. If the cocoa price drops by only 10 percent, the speculator is wiped out. And if the speculator is operating with really big stakes in such a decline, the end result is the same, zero, zero, zero. And the loss may be astronomical.

UCB had been playing with big stakes for its own account.

And it had lost. Erdman's long record of successes had come to a sad end. So had UCB Basle. Repercussions were still to come.

The bank's history is so closely interwoven with that of Erdman that its story is like an Erdman biography. He was only thirty-two when he conceived the idea of creating a bank. Already he had had a meteoric record after obtaining his Ph.D. at the University of Basle in 1958. A professor there remembers Erdman as "one of the most brilliant students ever to attend" the school.

Though he was a Canadian-born American, he mastered German so well that he wrote economic textbooks in the language. Economic credentials earned him a job with the European Coal and Steel Community in Luxembourg. Shortly, he caught the attention of Stanford Research Institute, Palo Alto, California. They lured him away from the bureaucracy of the Common Market to a job as the Institute's European economist.

Senator Alben W. Barkley, the crusty Kentucky politician of another day, once described an economist as "a guy with a Phi Beta Kappa key on one end of his watch chain and no watch on the other end." It was a remark made before the "dismal science" remodeled itself into an arm of business. Economists, today, are corporate astrologers bearing highly saleable "management consultant" titles. They not only have watches for their watch chains, pieces are solid gold watches at that.

Erdman's job was to serve as a consultant to large international corporations. He also wrote analytical studies to aid corporations in their long-range planning. After a year in Palo Alto, he shifted his base to Basle.

In 1961, Erdman accepted a vice president's post with Electronics International Capital Ltd., a Bermuda-based closed-end investment company which owned and operated a series of industrial corporations in Western Europe. The group was controlled by one Charles Salik, a wealthy financier from San Diego, California.

Paul Erdman was rising in the world of business. A vice president yet, earning a good salary, at age twenty-nine.

Says Erdman today: "As a result of my experience with the Salik Group, it appeared to me that there was room for the creation of a new type of bank in Central Europe, one which would cater to the needs of American corporations and American individuals."

Salik Bank in Basle AG came into existence in January, 1965. Financial backers were Charles Salik, his father, David Salik, and his brother-in-law, Maurice Rice. Initial capital was 2.5 million Swiss francs, about $600,000. Charles Salik became the absentee chairman. Erdman became vice chairman and chief executive officer.

The bank opened in a two-room office where the most conspicuous piece of furniture was a three-foot-high safe. Early, portfolio accounts became an important part of its business. In 1967, the bank scored a coup for customers. It predicted the British pound sterling devaluation to the correct pence several weeks before it occurred. One customer reports he earned a profit of $80,000 over a weekend by selling pounds for future delivery worth $2.80 and then replacing them after the devaluation with $2.40 pounds. And he was only one of numerous customers who profited from Erdman's counseling.

The bank prospered. Assets totaled $3.1 million at the end of 1966, $9 million at the end of 1967, and $49 million at the end of 1968. By 1968, the value of the portfolios under management totaled about $100 million. Annual net profit was estimated at about $1.6 million.

Meanwhile, Erdman was assembling his team, a team which was to be jailed with him when repercussions of the bank's troubles hit. One of the first to be added was Dr. Beat Schweizer, a veteran banker who already had fifteen years' experience with Swiss Bank Corp. and five years with the Bank for International Settlements. He took charge of Salik's lending operations.

Schweizer, a Bernese, originally had hoped to become a concert violinist. He had become a banker instead. A careful, efficient worker, he had a reputation as a plodder and a man of integrity.

One friend says: "His greatest failing was, perhaps, his inability to recognize flaws in his own capability. He never made mistakes, only his subordinates did. Thus, his relationship with his subordinates was always a highly uncomfortable one."

A chance meeting in the bar of the Euler Hotel in Basle in

the spring of 1967 brought Dr. Alfred Kaltenbach to the Salik Bank. Alfred was between posts and available. He was another veteran banker, a man of forty-three with a cheery disposition, graying hair, and the kindly manner of a concerned bedside physician. You instinctively liked Alfred, unless you were a conservative Swiss banker. They didn't like his swinging attitudes. Kaltenbach had a certain flamboyance which disturbed staid folk. Alfred probably was the first man in Basle to start wearing colored shirts when they came into style. He might have been the first to grow sideburns when hair again became respectable (or at least noncontroversial).

Kaltenbach joined Salik and took charge of client relationships. Helmuth Brutschi, a Kaltenbach friend, joined the bank at the same time. He was a fellow who had started as an office boy in a private bank in Basle. Over a period of twenty years, he slowly worked his way to a position of trust in the securities department of that bank. One friend describes him as "the eternal number two man in a department who was perfectly satisfied with being number two."

The bank's success in the foreign exchange field just before and after the British devaluation convinced Erdman that this area offered great promise for the bank. Erdman himself was a knowledgeable monetary expert. But he knew little about the technical aspects of foreign exchange trading.

Brutschi and Kaltenbach suggested that they knew just the man to head a foreign exchange operation, one Bernard Kummerli. Kummerli then was the foreign exchange trader for Bank Hoffman, a reputable private bank in Basle. Brutschi had gone to school with Kummerli at Rheinfelden, a small town a few miles upriver from Basle. Kummerli had an excellent reputation. His father had been a local bank director in the home town.

The report on Kummerli which now reposes in files of UCB Los Angeles, written in 1969, says:

> B. Kummerli is the head of our foreign exchange, precious metals and commodities trading operations. He has almost all of the typical traits of professional traders in exotic types of markets, nervous, sometimes touchy, jealous of his privileges, extrovertish, and at times not too prudent.

He not only is extremely talented as a trader, but has proven to be able to recruit, organize and maintain the loyalty of an extraordinarily able team of people. He has more talent among his staff of sixteen than any other department of the bank.

The above report was written by Paul Erdman, then at the peak of his banking career.

In 1968, Kummerli joined the bank, bringing his own team of foreign exchange specialists with him. One was Victor Zuhrmuhle, a bright foreign exchange dealer in his mid-twenties who had worked for Kummerli at Bank Hoffman. And already he was showing signs of outshining his brilliant boss, always a touchy situation where business egos are concerned.

A report about Zuhrmuhle, written by Erdman after the troubles of the bank, speaks well of the man. This report reads:

Victor Zuhrmuhle was Kummerli's No. 1 boy at Bank Hoffman. Young, around twenty-five, extremely intelligent, a fellow who enjoyed working twelve hours a day plus weekends out of sheer enjoyment of his job.

He came to the Salik bank about six months ahead of his boss. His track record in terms of activity and especially profits during this period was superb. Then, in mid-1968 with the arrival of Kummerli, his moment of glory passed. But, he apparently now considered himself more of a rival, than a subordinate, of Kummerli. And obviously, Kummerli felt the same. It seems to me that this psychological situation led Kummerli into his first mistakes. He simply had to prove himself a better profit producer than his boy.

Zuhrmuhle was supremely confident of his ability. He was hot tempered, nervous (packs of cigarets each day), a telephone addict like all traders. He left the bank in the autumn of 1969, after he was accused of massive commodity trading, well beyond the limits which had been strictly laid down to him by the entire management. Whether he was framed or not remains to be seen. Who did what, when, is still completely unclear. It is a compliment to Zuhrmuhle that, in spite of what later happened at U.C.B., he still works for a major commodity firm (Altco), and is apparently held in high respect as a professional throughout the trade.

In the fall of 1968, Erdman completed the team with the addition of Louis Thole, a blond, soft-spoken Dutch national of about forty, who had worked for years for a private bank in Amsterdam. Thole had an easy-going, unruffled disposition, and he knew the bond market well. Like Kaltenbach, he had a winning personality, but with a low-key pitch.

With the new team, the bank thrived, or seemed to at first.

Unlike most Swiss bankers who shun the press, Erdman cultivated newsmen. He granted interviews. He outlined complicated monetary matters to reporters. He made public speeches. Clyde Farnsworth, the ace European business reporter of the *New York Times*, called frequently. So did Neil McInnes, *Barron's* capable man in Paris.

Switzerland's Big Three banks sent Erdman a letter suggesting that he curtail his associations with the press. Erdman ignored it.

Erdman had the go-go American flare for salesmanship and promotion. His executives literally rang doorbells outside the country drumming up business. At one time, the bank claimed to be Swiss Airlines' second largest customer in Basle. Erdman alone accounted for 125,000 miles of flying in one year contacting potential customers, addressing groups, promoting the bank. Soon, Salik had 3,200 customers, more than half of them American.

The bank's success attracted the attention of top executives at United California Bank, Los Angeles. United California, like many another American bank in 1968, wanted to establish branch operations abroad. Big, multinational American corporations were expanding around the globe, building factories, assembly plants, and facilities. Banks had to follow their MNC customers abroad, too. Frank L. King, UCB Los Angeles chairman, took a special interest in pushing UCB abroad. He liked the Salik Bank operation from the first, especially with Erdman at the helm.

The fall of 1968 proved memorable for Salik Bank for two reasons. One, the first contact was made between the bank and

UCB Los Angeles. Two, Salik Bank edged into the cocoa market just enough to convince executives that cocoa offered a wonderful opportunity for quick profits. It didn't matter that nobody in the bank really knew anything about cocoa or its market reactions. Erdman hadn't known much about banking, either, before launching the bank in 1965.

Already, demands of customers had interested the bank in commodities. Following the British pound devaluation in November, 1967, worldwide interest of investors and speculators focused on silver as a hedge against currency fluctuations. The dollar was weak. Some people thought the pound might be devalued a second time. Gold and silver seemed to offer refuges against possible collapse of currencies.

"Our clients, particularly our American private clients, wanted to invest in silver and silver 'futures' through our bank. Therefore, we started to accommodate them, although no one had any real expertise in this field," Erdman admits today.

As with other commodities, silver may be purchased on margins of as low as 10 percent. This provides enormous leverage for an investor, since every dollar invested may do the work of ten. But, as with all margin trading, the margin may be wiped out fast if the market swings downward.

In 1968, bank customers built up speculative silver positions in the range of $25 million. This is a sizeable figure for a bank which then claimed total assets of about $50 million.

"Our clients made an awful lot of money in the process, since a tremendous bull market in silver developed which drove the price of $1.29 an ounce to $2.60 an ounce," says Erdman. "Many customers doubled, tripled and quadrupled their money."

But Erdman grew uneasy. On May 28, 1968, he wrote a circular letter to all clients of the bank warning them against any further investments in silver. "A sharp break seems to be around the corner," wrote Erdman.

In the bank, other executives didn't agree. Salik's go-go portfolio managers read some of the silver market letters predicting that silver might zoom to a price of $3.50 an ounce because of worldwide shortages. Seers had overlooked India, and the Dubai smuggling route. Even then, smugglers were preparing the biggest silver traffic movement in history from India through Dubai to those world markets which were supposed to be so short of silver.

In the summer of 1968, Salik portfolio managers engineered what, within the bank, came to be called the "gold-silver switch." They sold gold bullion in accounts of discretionary clients (those clients who permitted the bank to make investment decisions for them). Then, managers bought silver. Where the gold had been 100 percent paid for, they applied the proceeds as 10 percent margin on silver.

Gold had been a disappointment. It was evident by late spring of 1968 that speculators who gambled on a major revaluation of gold were to be disappointed. Salik portfolio managers thought they were doing customers a favor by shifting into silver.

"Our guys went wild buying silver, a lot of it at $2.72 an ounce, not only for our own account, but for accounts of customers as well," Erdman told a *Wall Street Journal* reporter during a jail interview in October, 1970.

Despite Erdman's May, 1968, warning about silver, the plunge into that metal did seem to be a good idea, at first. The silver price edged upward very slowly to $2.75, moving like a tired horse climbing a hill. Like that horse after rounding the hilltop, the price started down in October, 1968, much faster than it had climbed. The price slid to $1.85 in a sharp drop which stunned silver holders, held a few weeks, then slumped to $1.81 before the year ended.

By June, 1969, the price was down to $1.54 an ounce. Because of management's bad judgment, a good number of the bank's clients had lost a lot of money. Now Erdman's May letter proved an embarrassment. He had warned customers to beware of silver. The bank had put them into it for heavy losses.

Erdman may have, then, made the first in a series of mistakes. He said: "I felt that one had to examine the particular circumstances in each one of these accounts, and in those instances where behavior had been reckless, the bank should buy all or part of the silver involved in this switch."

This may seem to be the honorable way. But in banking or stockbrokering, few institutions repay customers for the mistakes of portfolio managers. Institutions claim that customers must accept risks along with profit potential when they invest.

Erdman felt otherwise. Moreover, he was a whiz kid on the rise, confident that he could recoup any loss assumed by the bank. In one interview with a newspaperman about that time, Erdman said: "It's easy to make money in these times. You hardly can avoid it."

It was a confident belief which was to govern his actions almost to the last days of the bank. So, the bank accepted losses where the customers had nothing to say about the gold-silver switch. It wrote off nearly $900,000 in losses in various ways. Writeoffs were made through formal depreciation and by means of compensation through trading profits made by the commodity department. Kummerli had joined the bank in May, 1968, and this department had been placed under his direction along with foreign exchange trading.

As silver prices declined, Kummerli started trading in the cocoa market. Transactions were small. He made a consistent profit on the deals.

In September, 1968, the bank made a new capital issue through a private placement and raised around $4 million. Erdman himself borrowed about $150,000 from a subsidiary of the bank, Handelstrenhard AG, and took 5,000 voting shares of the issue. At this point the bank claimed close to $50 million in assets and $1.6 million in annual profits, despite the unfortunate commodity experience.

Cocoa seemed worth investigating. Disgruntled customers don't stay long with a bank if the bank's track record isn't good. Salik Bank needed some winners to wipe out the image of the silver fiasco.

Kummerli suggested in that fall of 1968 that he should travel to Ghana to study the cocoa business. Here, the script begins to resemble Jerry Goodman's (Adam Smith's) chapter on "The Cocoa Game" in his book *The Money Game*. Ironically, Goodman later was to become one of the stockholders in the bank. His cocoa chapter, however, was written before he ever became acquainted with United California Bank in Basle. This proves that Goodman characters are found in Switzerland as well as on Wall Street, though they might speak German instead of English, and prefer pork and dumplings to corned beef sand-wiches.

Like Goodman's character, Marvin from Brooklyn, Kummerli didn't know a cocoa tree from an elderberry bush. Undeterred, he set out from Zurich Airport without any help from Abercrombie & Fitch. His brief from the bank management was in his head: "Learn everything there is to know about cocoa, paying special attention to how to make money at it."

He was given a week to ten days for the assignment.

Swiss Air has a direct flight to Accra from Zurich. It is a rough, grueling flight which arrives at Accra's humid airport at 4:30 in the morning, no fit time for any cocoa inspector to be about.

But the Mammy Wagons were already on the streets. These are gaudy painted buses which bear such imposing names as "Fit to Kill—You," "Mother's Boy Friend," "Pick Me Up," "Women Like Sweet," "Vat 69," "Oh, God!," "Anytime," and whatever else strikes the fancy of its African chauffeur.

Cocoa plantations commence along the road leading to Kumasi. Kummerli hired a car and driver, and proceeded to make his survey of Ghana's cocoa. A third of the world's cocoa comes from Ghana, and this West African nation usually paces the market. If Ghana has a good crop, the price is apt to be low. If Ghana has troubles with its crop, the price rises. So, the cocoa speculator's task is to guess whether Ghana is going to have a good crop or a bad crop, then play the market accordingly. It is a highly unscientific method of investing which seems deceptively easy, but which can be devastatingly complex.

Every major cocoa house and commodity trader is also trying to guess which way the market may go. Some specialists spend their lives in the trade, listening to scuttlebutt in the hotels of Accra, conversing with plantation owners while standing in their groves of cocoa trees, studying every scrap of paper issued by Ghana's Cocoa Marketing Board. The reports issued by these specialists clutter the cable and telex lines from Accra to London, New York, Zurich, Hershey, Pa., and various other places where interest in cocoa is high. Every commodity firm hopes to obtain that inside information which will enable it to beat the market.

Kummerli took notes. He learned that cocoa pods in Ghana are harvested from October to December, with a much smaller harvest following in the spring. Ghana had produced 415,000 long tons of raw cocoa in the 1967–68 crop year. Now, with the 1968–69 crop coming in, there were rumors that the crop might be a small one.

It looked as if the market in the period ahead would be one to play long, betting on a rise in cocoa prices. Kummerli returned to Basle a self-styled cocoa expert.

One Kummerli friend says: "Bernard's weakness was that he could never admit that he was wrong when he made a bum trade, or that there was something that he didn't know."

He had no trouble, though, in convincing management of his cocoa expertise. With Kummerli's advice, management thought it a good idea to put a limited number of clients into cocoa. Contracts were purchased at prices of around forty-seven to forty-eight cents a pound.

Cocoa prices were supposed to rise by Kummerli's reckoning. Instead, they dropped. Early in 1969, the price hovered around forty-four cents a pound. Customers had lost substantial amounts of money, with the amount depending upon the margin. Again, Erdman thought it wouldn't be fair to stick customers with those losses. He said: "I think for something like around fifteen to twenty clients we took the cocoa on our own account."

In September, 1968, business took Erdman to Los Angeles where he had a fateful encounter with Edward Carter, president of Broadway Hale, a Los Angeles department store, and a director of UCB Los Angeles and Western Bancorp. Over drinks, Carter suggested that Erdman meet UCB officers concerning matters of common interest.

At 9 the next morning, Erdman visited the bank in central Los Angeles. He was greeted by Clifford Tweter, vice chairman of the board, and Victor Rose, head of the bank's international operations. They asked if Salik Bank might be for sale. UCB had decided to expand its overseas operations, and saw the possibility of gaining a foothold in Switzerland without the time-consuming process of launching a bank from scratch.

The bid came at an opportune moment. Bank-owner Salik had gotten into trouble with the S.E.C. over handling of Republic Technology Fund. The S.E.C. suspended him from further activities in the public investment field within the United States. Swiss Bank Corp. gloatingly reported this in its new bulletin, making certain that the European banking community received the story. Some Salik Bank depositors withdrew their deposits. It became harder to attract new depositors.

Though Erdman had no power to sell the bank, he was receptive to a UCB takeover when he met a persistent King at the Hilton Hotel in London in October, 1968. That meeting lasted for eight hours, with King insisting he wanted Salik Bank. Negotiations for purchase opened between Salik and UCB Los Angeles.

At that time, the net worth of the bank was computed at 27 million Swiss francs, or about $6.5 million. A selling price of 215 percent was established, with provision that all Salik interests were to be sold. Shares amounted to control, 52.18 percent of the equity and 68.54 percent of the voting shares. The takeover occurred in late May, 1969. A report of Salik Bank prepared by Neal Moore, UCB Los Angeles senior vice president, shows that the Los Angeles bank was very much aware of the free-wheeling commodity trading then being done by Salik Bank. That report even listed the amount of margin deposits at Salik as totaling 48,211,366 Swiss francs at the end of 1968.

In June, 1969, the name of the bank was changed to United California Bank in Basle AG. Frank King became chairman. He and Victor Rose joined the board from the Los Angeles Headquarters. Erdman remained vice chairman and chief executive officer. Whereas Salik Bank had been a comparatively small operation, UCB Basle now had the $5 billion in assets of its parent behind it. The bank was to need them.

The old management remained virtually intact. About the only difference was that UCB Los Angeles installed a resident man in the Basle subsidiary in September, 1969.

"I would say he was a 'watch dog,' " says Erdman.

There was no question about who was to be in charge.

"You run the bank, Paul," King told Erdman.

King did insist that gold trading be dropped. Subsequently, Norman Barker, president of UCB Los Angeles, was to tell newspapermen in Basle that bank troubles stemmed from "unauthorized trading in commodities." Erdman insists that shortly after the bank takeover, another conversation occurred between him and King concerning commodities.

Says Erdman: "I suggested that while we were at it we might as well drop all activities in the commodity area as this was a high risk field. King's reply was, 'No. This is an investment field like any other. Just don't make the big mistake, Paul.' "

The discrepancies are likely to be clarified in Basle court. In any case, the big mistake may already have been shaping up.

In the first quarter, the bank had showed a profit of 1,700,000 Swiss francs. It closed the first half with a profit of only 1,000,000 francs. Money costs had climbed. This hurt. The credit department failed to watch accounts closely. Margin account collections were lax.

Worse was to come. Erdman was sitting in his office one hot day in July 1969 when Zuhrmuhle, Kummerli's chief trader, entered with disturbing news. Kummerli had been making massive unsuccessful trades in commodities. Those trades had not been registered on books. Zuhrmuhle claimed he had corrected the situation by playing the cocoa market heavily and earning big profits.

Zuhrmuhle repeated the same story to the bank management. Kramer, another trader, supported the story. Kummerli happened to be vacationing at the time.

"How do we stand today?" Erdman asked, quietly.

"After we liquidate our positions, we should be about even," Zuhrmuhle replied.

Erdman breathed easier. Others exchanged relieved glances. Commodity trading isn't a business for anyone with heart trouble. Huge losses may face a speculator one day. Sound nerves and a cool head may correct the situation, quickly. Sometimes a loss can be turned into a nice profit.

But what to do about this particular situation? Kummerli, for all his troubles with commodities, did know foreign exchange. He handled that department so well that Erdman hesitated to make an issue of something which seemed to have been corrected.

Even at that moment, many of the bank's customers were

positioned to make a good profit on the 11.1 percent devaluation of the French franc which was to come within a couple of weeks. On April 28, 1969, when negotiations still were underway for purchase of Salik Bank by UCB Los Angeles, a letter composed by Erdman had gone to customers.

It said: "It now appears highly likely that the French franc will be devalued within a fairly short time. . . . Such a devaluation will probably be in the range of 15 percent."

The estimate wasn't quite as close as the earlier prediction about the pound sterling. It was close enough. That advice prompted many of the bank's customers to short the French franc, for a nice profit.

Moreover, Erdman came from that American management school which contends that when you assign a job to an executive you let him get on with it. You don't lean over his shoulder constantly, dictating how he should operate. In this particular instance, Zuhrmuhle's charges might have been due to his personal differences with Kummerli. By now it was generally known that the two men did not get along. In the commodity trade, Kummerli and Zuhrmuhle were known as "the Lee brothers, Kaylee and Zeelee." Any camaraderie this might have implied was only an illusion.

So, Erdman shelved the idea of recalling Kummerli and ordering an accounting. It was another mistake added to his management blunders. It is all very well to delegate authority, and then to sit back waiting for results. In the final analysis, it is the top executive who may be held responsible for the failures of subordinates. In well-ordered banks, there are checks and cross checks within the administration. Even the brilliant individualist may have to fit his personality into the prescribed mold for his own protection as well as for the bank's.

Checks are especially necessary in the commodities and foreign exchange fields. UCB Basle hadn't yet found a way to make profits consistently in commodities. That April 28 bank memo which had been so prescient about foreign exchange, for instance, contained the following paragraph about silver: "Although silver is no longer a monetary metal, events in the monetary field still influence the market for this precious metal. We feel that the monetary influence during the next months can only be positive, and that last Friday's prices [$1.75½ per ounce spot New York] may represent the lowest silver prices we shall see for quite some time."

Instead of being poised for a rise, the silver price was merely sitting on a ledge, ready for another steep fall. Any silver speculator who followed the bank's advice lost more money.

After returning from his vacation, Kummerli had what seemed to be a plausible explanation for his cocoa trading. This was a field where chances had to be taken if profits were to be made, he explained. He knew what he was doing. Erdman, a man who can be surprisingly candid at times, admits that he didn't know enough about the technicalities of commodity trading to decipher the cocoa deals. Yet, as chief executive office, he should have investigated the situation thoroughly, with outside auditing help if necessary, even he now admits. He didn't. This added another to the list of managerial blunders he was accumulating.

In September, 1969, he and Louis Thole, the quiet, efficient Hollander who had become the number three man in the bank, departed from Basle for a combination business-pleasure trip. Wives came along, and the trip took them to the Caribbean, to Puerto Rico, and to New York. They checked into the Plaza Hotel overlooking Central Park. It was there that Thole received a disturbing telephone call at 6 o'clock one morning from Switzerland. Of course, it already was II A.M. in Basle, and Kaltenbach had been hard at work for several hours.

Kaltenbach in Basle reported that Zuhrmuhle had gone on vacation to the island of Rhodes in the eastern Mediterranean. In his absence, Kummerli had checked the books and discovered that Zuhrmuhle had plunged heavily into cocoa futures without authorization. Dealings were made through dealers in London, New York, and elsewhere. It appeared that seven thousand cocoa contracts were involved.

Thole awakened Erdman and gave him the news. Average price of cocoa contracts was $9,000 each. The bank had purchased $63 million worth of cocoa for future delivery gambling on a rise in the price. Pound price at time of purchase was around forty-five cents.

Erdman phoned to Basle, learned that Kaltenbach had al-

ready launched a crash program to straddle the market. A straddle operates as a hedge in the same manner in which a bookie
may layoff bets if the volume of bets is larger than he can handle.
Thus, a speculator may purchase a thousand long contracts for
delivery in, say, six months' time. Then, he obtains information
which prompts him to think the price six months from now may
be lower than it is now. Quickly, he shifts his tack selling a
thousand contracts short. If the price goes down, he makes
money on the short contracts even as he loses on the long contracts, and vice versa.

Properly handled, a straddle may cancel the possibility of
a big loss, though profit potential may be canceled, too. And, of
course, margin money is tied up for both the long and the short
contracts.

"Most of the contracts are already straddled," Kaltenbach
told Erdman. "I think we'll be all right."

Thus reassured Erdman and Thole proceeded to Dallas for
another business meeting. There they received a second call
stating that the long positions had totaled 11,000 rather than the
7,000 originally mentioned. But the straddling process was continuing.

A cable was dispatched to Zuhrmuhle discharging him.
Subsequently, Zuhrmuhle denied that he was responsible for
the wild trading. Certainly, he made a fine record for himself as
a commodity trader for Altco, a firm in Lausanne, after departing from UCB Basle.

On his return to Basle at the end of September, Erdman
called a management meeting. He was briefed by Kummerli,
Kaltenbach, Schweizer, and Brutschi about the situation. It was
described as "fantastically complex." Involved were a network
of straddles in New York, London, and Dallas in sterling, dollars, and other currencies, on hundreds of different dates.

With long and short contracts, the bank had 17,000 contracts
worth $153 million for delivery at various times over the next
twelve months. Contracts were on margin, of course, with the
bank actually on books for 115 million Swiss francs, or about $25
million. Deals were concluded with Hayden Stone, Merrill
Lynch, Lomcrest (London), and just about every other cocoa
trading firm.

Margin figures must be listed somewhere in the balance sheet of a bank, according to Swiss law. Yet, a $25 million figure, if reported correctly, would have invited an audit into the bank's commodity trading.

"The balance sheet was undeniably falsified," according to Max Studer, an auditor with Switzerland's Society for Bank Inspection. This auditing firm is an affiliate of Swiss Bank Corp., Basle, a situation permitted under Swiss law.

Erdman contends he didn't know the true position of the bank, and accepted Kummerli's word that everything could be put right. Kummerli contends Erdman did understand the situation.

"I realize now in retrospect that what I should have done was to call for an independent audit," says Erdman, today. "I was the decision maker, the top man."

But Erdman had a whiz-kid reputation. In his short acquaintance with UCB Los Angeles management, he had impressed some of the executives in the home office. There was talk of expanding UCB operations in Europe, of opening an operation in Luxembourg, and another in Zurich. Erdman was slated for bigger responsibilities. It wouldn't do him any good if he had to call on the home office for help in unraveling a commodity situation which seemed to be getting messier and messier.

No, this was something that he felt he had to sort out himself, with Kummerli's help. Kummerli was the only man in the bank who understood the many commodity transactions now outstanding. So, months went by.

"I was asking daily how we were doing. Kummerli was saying that everything was all right, and that it was unwinding itself," says Erdman.

Meanwhile, the cocoa market played against the bank. UCB Basle had plunged into the market at a time when cocoa was close to the highest level it was to see for some time. In November, 1969, the spot price of Ghana cocoa hit 48.57 cents a pound, then fell erratically to 29.74 cents in New York by June, 1970.

To compound the trouble, UCB Basle had another problem. Late in 1969, Kaltenbach, the bank's portfolio manager and number two in the bank, thought he had a winner in a company called Leasing Consultants Inc., a Roslyn, New York, company that financed and leased airplanes, industrial equipment, and computer equipment.

Shares had been recommended by a reputable Oslo market analyst. At Kaltenbach's urgings, the bank plunged heavily into Leasing Consultants' letter stock, purchased at $12 to $13 a share. The stock climbed to $28 a share. It seemed like a good buy for sure.

Then, on February 2, 1970, Leasing Consultants reported that it had overstated its 1969 earnings by $2 million. The stock plummeted to $7 a share. On August 19, 1970, the company filed a voluntary petition for protection under Chapter 11 of the U.S. Bankruptcy Act. UCB lost $2 million in that stock.

In early 1970, UCB Basle directors decided that the bank's capital should be expanded. In March, the bank issued a highly confidential prospectus for the benefit of would-be investors. Officials contend that the commodity problems had nothing to do with the recapitalization, and there is no reason for doubting this claim.

A perusal of that prospectus certainly indicates everybody thought the bank was on a sound foundation, though it actually was insolvent at the time. Erdman's own family subscribed to 250,000 Swiss francs' ($60,000) worth of the new shares on a loan of 7 percent.

Swiss law requires its banks to maintain a ratio of approximately ten to one between total deposits and capital plus open reserves. The capital plus open reserves of UCB Basle was listed at 24 million Swiss francs (nearly $6 million) at the end of 1969, insufficient for the size of its claimed assets. So it was felt necessary to inject another $3 million of new capital into the bank.

The prospectus certainly seemed to provide assurance for investors. A net profit of $125,000 was claimed for 1969. The prospectus said:

> The present situation, then, is that the bank is a sub-
> sidiary of United California Bank of Los Angeles, a bank
> with total assets of $5.2 billion at end of 1969. United Cali-
> fornia bank is, in turn, affiliated with Western Bancorp.,
> the world's largest bank holding company, embracing
> twenty-three full service commercial banks located in

eleven western states of the United States. United California bank, itself, is the full owner of an international bank in New York City, and has branches, representatives or affiliates in England, Belgium, Switzerland, Spain, Lebanon, Japan, Mexico and Greece.

The prospectus listed the bank's operations as involving commercial banking, investment banking, foreign exchange, and other activities. Not a line was said about commodities. Obviously, the S.E.C. would take after any corporation in America which issued a prospectus for a public issue of stock without mentioning essential details, such as $153 million worth of cocoa futures.

But this was a private issue in Switzerland.

Certainly, the prospectus stressed one evident point. It said: "No assurance can be given that the bank will continue to operate at a profit."

The prospectus also said: "From the beginning, the bank was conceived as a bridge between conservative Swiss banking, and modern corporate and financial management techniques, usually identified with the United States."

The recapitalization left UCB Los Angeles with 55 percent of the equity, bank management with 8 percent. Vesta Insurance Co., Oslo, Norway, was the largest outside stockholder.

UCB Basle might have seemed to be on its way to better things. Actually, it was slowly sinking. Those cocoa straddle positions should have been unwinding steadily. They weren't.

Still, Kummerli insisted that all he needed was more time, and everything would be all right. A bank audit in the spring of 1970 failed to show that much was wrong. UCB Los Angeles had a resident "watch dog" in Basle. He rang no alarm bells at the Swiss Banking Commission's headquarters in Bern. Nobody raised any questions about commodities at the official board meeting of the bank early in July, 1970. Erdman even felt constrained to guestimate that, though profits would "not be so hot" for 1970, the bank might just squeak through "with a mini-profit" for the year. Adds he, today: "I didn't make any mention of commodities and neither did anybody else."

He also says: "I still felt that we should and would solve our own problems in Basle."

The day that he was preparing for his vacation, Erdman did do something which he now terms "stupid." An abbreviated English translation of the official German language audit of the bank had been received from the Banking Commission. That audit contained a line listing 115 million francs ($25 million) as assets in commodity margins, foreign exchange, and a number of other things. That report was to go to the UCB Los Angeles' international department.

Erdman realized that nearly $25 million in commodity margins were outstanding, a figure which could flash warning signals for accountants in the States. They could ask questions. And Erdman wanted more time to remedy the situation himself.

In a statement filed with London City police, Erdman says: "I decided to buy some time in the following way. I instructed my secretary to retype the page dealing with commodities. In fact, it only contained one line, that line listing 115 million francs as assets and including commodity margins, foreign exchange and a number of other things. I told my secretary to change nothing, but to take out the commodity phrase and retype it and that was done."

Then, when on vacation in Marbella, Spain, he thought about that 25 million Swiss francs discrepancy in another account. On his return to Basle, his worst fears were realized. All the months of trying to recoup those cocoa losses had been futile.

In sworn testimony, Erdman said: "During my absence, another incident occurred. Mr. Helmuth Kramer, an assistant of Kummerli, wrote a letter to a manager of our bank called Dr. Victor Kruegle. Kruegle is a man that I hired in 1969 to add to our capability in the commercial banking and credit control areas. In his letter, Kramer accused Kummerli of having set up a series of fictitious deposits to hide the loss situation."

It is not a crime to lose money in stocks or commodities. It's done all the time. Kummerli insisted all along that UCB's troubles involved bum trading not theft. But in most countries, including Switzerland, it is illegal to doctor the books.

Kummerli was in London when the investigation into the

bank's position started in early August, 1970. As the story unfolded, it was evident that UCB Basle had serious problems. On August 11, Erdman hopped a plane to London for a confrontation with Kummerli at the Carlton Towers Hotel in West London. Erdman was told that it would take at least five years "to clean up" the commodity straddles in cocoa. Losses were estimated to total at least $20 million.

Erdman still hoped that the situation could be rectified, without calling in the authorities. He knew, though, that losses of the magnitude now becoming apparent certainly could not be concealed from the parent bank. Another audit was due for September 21. Home office cooperation had to be obtained for meeting this situation, and for keeping it a secret to avoid a disastrous run on the bank. No whiz kid would solve this one alone.

On Saturday, August 29, Erdman and his wife, Helly, arrived in Los Angeles at 7 P.M. via Air France. He proceeded directly to the Century Plaza Hotel where he met Neal Moore, UCB Los Angeles senior vice president. Erdman wasted no time reporting that the Basle bank had a loss of up to $20 million.

Next morning, at a 9 A.M. meeting in the Beverly Hilton Hotel, Erdman reported to the UCB Los Angeles hierarchy. Present were Frank King, board chairman, Clifford Tweter, vice chairman, Norman Barker, president, Neal Moore, senior vice president, Victor Rose, senior vice president, and Erdman.

Everybody listened as Erdman outlined the problem, a loss of up to $20 million in disastrous cocoa futures trading. The reaction was surprisingly tolerant. "One of the senior vice presidents," Erdman recalls, "said something about how you win some and lose some. Then, everybody agreed to keep this thing absolutely secret."

Adds Erdman: "I assumed responsibility for the loss. I offered my resignation, which was not then taken up."

It was agreed at the meeting that Neal Moore would head a team from Los Angeles which would immediately delve into books of UCB Basle. Norman Barker would supervise the task of working out a solution. Erdman was left with the impression that he would be continuing as vice chairman of UCB Basle, at least until that solution was reached.

When a bank gets in trouble, secrecy is a good thing, provided that it can be maintained. From the first, UCB Los Angeles realized its responsibility since its name was on the door of the Basle bank. From the first, UCB Los Angeles intended to see that depositors did not lose any money. So, secrecy here was aimed only at buying a little more time to avoid a run on the bank and much greater losses. It was not aimed at hiding affairs illegally.

On Wednesday, September 2, Neal Moore chaired a meeting of the bank's staff in Basle. He admitted the bank had "a little problem," adding that it was going to be solved immediately. Secrecy must be maintained. Erdman would continue as chief executive officer.

On Friday, September 4, Moore and Graham, the local "watch dog," estimated the bank's loss at 133 million Swiss francs, or $31.4 million. Subsequent events indicated this figure was correct. Additional losses which lifted the figure to nearly $50 million were incurred in the liquidation process.

This was the biggest such loss in Swiss banking history.

On Sunday afternoon, September 6, a special UCB Basle board of directors meeting was called at the Ambassador Hotel. The amount of the losses had stunned directors. Erdman's resignation was demanded and accepted by Chairman King.

On Monday, September 7, King and other directors reported the situation to the Swiss Banking Commission in Bern. From some accounts, it was a stormy meeting. The commission insisted that criminal charges had to be filed if there were any suspicions of law violations.

On Tuesday, September 8, Carl Wunderlin, the Basle city prosecutor, entered the case because of suspicions that Swiss bank laws may have been violated.

On Wednesday, September 9, the board preferred charges against Erdman, Kummerli, and Kaltenbach. The charge was suspicion of untrue management, falsification of documents, and suspicion of fraud in connection with the 1970 capital increase made in March, 1970. The three were jailed, immediately, to be joined by Beat Schweizer, Louis Thole, Helmuth Brutschi, and Victor Zuhrmuhle.

In Switzerland, there is no habeas corpus. Suspects may be

held almost indefinitely on suspicion that a crime has been committed, while the public prosecutor proceeds with his case. Switzerland's laws, of course, are based on Roman rather than Anglo-Saxon law. A court is much more interested in ascertaining the facts of a certain situation than it is in protecting the rights of the accused.

UCB Los Angeles immediately showed intention to wind up the affairs of its unfortunate subsidiary. It petitioned a Basle court for a moratorium permitting the bank to suspend payments while affairs were being wound up. The California bank put up a $40 million guarantee to protect depositors and creditors.

At the court hearing granting the moratorium, Max Studer, the official of the Society for Bank Inspection, told the court that he had "indisputable" proof that six or seven members of the business management plus a member of the board had "willfully deceived the inspection authority about a liability of 10 million" Swiss francs.

Louis Thole was the first of the charged bank team to be released on bail. Subsequently, he was to die in a Brussels apartment, victim of a leaky gas stove. One by one the others were released on bail, except for Kummerli. He remains in the seventeenth-century Basle city jail at this writing. Erdman was released on bail in late July, 1971.

August 1 is a major holiday in Switzerland, its independence day. Kids shoot firecrackers. There are parades, band concerts, and civic festivities. In Garone, a village high above Lake Lugano near the Italian border, there was a village barbecue and wine fest underway that evening in 1971.

Several score people sat at tables in the open air before the sixteenth-century church. Lights of Lugano flickered far below in the soft-summer night. A passenger boat moved on the serene waters of the lake, forming only a line of mobile lights in the darkness. Paul and Helly Erdman sat at one of the open air tables drinking Ticino wine with an American friend. It was Erdman's first outing after being held for over ten months in the Basle jail on suspicion of fraud in connection with the UCB Basle bank failure.

"I didn't get any money out of that, not one penny," said Erdman.

"If you didn't, who did?" asked the American, gently.

"I had a lot of time to think about that," Erdman quipped. He could still joke about his time in jail, denied bail, held without formal charge. Erdman laughed. "You know, when they were questioning me in jail, I told them that, the way every Swiss banker operates, he has one foot in jail. I guess I was the first Swiss banker to have both feet in jail."

He had been released on bail of $125,000, an amount painfully assembled by relatives and friends. Now he was taking a short vacation with his family in this mountain resort. A shadow crossed his face when asked what he might do.

"Finish my book, I guess."

"Your book?"

"Yeah. I started a fiction book about banking when in the jug. Naturally, I wanted to write about something I knew about, and I do know banking," said Erdman.

"Some people might dispute that," the American said.

"You can say that again." Erdman laughed. "But I do know banking even if I am a bum administrator."

A three-piece orchestra started to play on a makeshift stand established near the open air bar. Couples began dancing a polka with whoops and stomping of feet on the temporary board floor. Erdman poured another glass of the new Ticino red wine.

"So, where did the money go?" the American persisted. "Or do you think all of it was lost through legitimate bad trades?"

"I dunno. But I have some suspicions. Our commodity department was just a little bit too cozy with a cocoa house in London," said Erdman, "proving it, though, may be something else."

"Why don't you come to London if your bail permits it?" the American asked. "I know some people with Scotland Yard and with the Metropolitan Police. They'll be happy to hear what you have to say about any crookery which might involve a London cocoa trading house."

Erdman glanced up. "Could you arrange it?"

The American nodded.

"Okay. I have nothing to lose," Erdman said. He stood up,

a tall figure framed against the string of temporary lights around the town square. "But, come along now. I want you to read my book to see what you think of it."

Two weeks later, the American met Erdman again in an eleventh-floor apartment in Roebuck House, a high-rise apartment building overlooking St. James's Park in central London. Erdman had flown to London for a meeting already arranged with two detectives. The detectives tested their tape recording equipment prior to launching their interrogation.

One detective was a hard-bitten Yorkshireman who had battled his way to a plain clothes job in the tough competition of the London police force. The other was in his early thirties, a pleasant, mustached fellow of smooth manner, who exemplified the modern, educated police officer.

There were a few pleasantries, an explanation of the interrogation procedure which must conform to English court specifications. Then Erdman picked up the microphone of the recorder. For six hours the questioning and recording proceeded, with Erdman patiently telling the story of UCB Basle, its cocoa trading, the losses, the fraud charges now outstanding, and his suspicions about trades between UCB Basle and a certain named London cocoa house.

The story outlined Erdman's belief that at first the cocoa trading losses may have been legitimate. Then, at some point, certain people in the bank may have realized books never could be balanced and an attempt was made to shunt money into some pockets. In the statement he said: "Although, I don't know exactly how, I am convinced a good proportion of the money that the bank lost in 1970, namely twelve million dollars, was not in fact a loss, but money directed from the bank to persons identified with a London cocoa trading house."

Data presented to the detectives eventually reached Britain's Department of Trade and Industry, an agency which functions somewhat like the U.S. Securities and Exchange Commission where industry shenanigans are concerned. Shortly before Christmas, 1971, the Department launched an investigation into the curious trail of checks which had taken place between UCB Basle and this London cocoa house. Erdman carried on his personal crusade, hoping that any evidence of crookery turned up would help clear him of any charges of wrongdoing in the bank failure.

The Department of Trade and Industry is very secretive about its investigations. Still, it is known that some interesting bank checks have come to light, which bear explaining. In the spring of 1973 the investigation still was underway, in both London and in Basle.

A barrage of law suits is in the courts. Stockholders of UCB Los Angeles have filed a class complaint for damages in Los Angeles Superior Court, charging directors of the bank with "illegal and wrongful" acts. Stockholders aver directors should have paid closer attention to the Basle daughter company.

On September 30, 1971, UCB Basle had closed its doors after paying off most depositors and creditors in full. Some claims are still being argued.

The London *Financial Times*, in summarizing the case, said: "The closure of United California Bank in Basle AG with losses of $40 million (later raised to $50 million) has demolished two long standing myths: that U.S. banks exercise an iron control over their overseas operations, and that Switzerland is invariably a model of financial expertise."

PART III

CHAPTER XV

SWITZERLAND IN TRANSITION

In April, 1972, Pierre Graber, Swiss federal councillor responsible for foreign affairs, traveled to Paris on a state visit. Such visits may not seem unusual in this day, when summit meetings are part of the international scene, especially before elections. But Switzerland isn't a nation where politicians resort to Baedeker for votes and it doesn't indulge in summitry except when someone climbs one of its peaks.

This particular visit was the first such ever made by Councillor Graber. Its purpose was to promote Swiss interests in France at a time when Switzerland was negotiating for an association agreement with the Economic Communities, or Common Market. That Switzerland should take such an interest in its neighbor is significant, one might almost say historic.

Ever since the Napoleonic Wars, Switzerland has prized its neutrality. Usually this meant having as little to do with its neighbors on a political level as was possible without creating backlashes. No matter what happened in Europe, Switzerland always seemed insulated from it. This was a major reason why money poured into its banks from all parts of the troubled world.

Now Switzerland is being compelled to face changes which may be painful, yet which are vitally necessary if this little nation is to continue to prosper. Pressures come from several directions. The country's highly vaunted bank secrecy is under attack from outside the country, and possible revisions may have to be made. Expansion of the Common Market creates external problems, for little Switzerland cannot remain isolated from the rest of Europe. A revision of the liberal constitution promises to provide the federal government with economic controls which heretofore have been unknown in *laissez faire* Switzerland. And worldwide inflation spills into Switzerland on the crest of the flood of money which crosses its borders.

Where will all this take Switzerland? This is a question which involves Swiss money men directly. It also concerns anyone who is banking or who intends to bank with those Swiss money men.

When Dr. Alfred Schaefer, chairman of Union Bank, addressed stockholders at the annual meeting in Zurich, March 15, 1972, he chose an apt subject: "Changing Banks in a Changing World."

He said: "Structural adjustments, which used to stretch over decades, must today be realized in terms of years."

Of all the changes being experienced by Swiss banks, perhaps none engenders more bitterness than the pressure being exerted steadily and strongly by America to break down that wall of bank secrecy. The Howard R. Hughes book fraud case showed that bank secrecy is not 100 percent. That case, however, did focus a harsh spotlight on bank secrecy. When that fraud leaped into the headlines in early 1972, news publications around the world examined the bank secrecy question from all angles.

Many stories did emphasize how such secrecy sometimes cloaks nefarious activities. Clifford Irving certainly thought this was going to be so.

Checks of McGraw-Hill had been deposited into a mysterious account, No. 320 496, opened at Swiss Credit Bank, Zurich, by a German-speaking woman "of slim build, with long hair down to her shoulders." She signed her name as "H. R. Hughes."

Shortly after the bank cleared the checks, the woman appeared at the bank, signed her nom-de-plume and drained the account. She stuffed the wads of crisp Swiss franc notes into an airline overnight bag, and disappeared.

Amid the controversy enveloping that case, one point may be overlooked. Swiss Credit Bank opened its books to authorities in Zurich immediately after the case was presented to a city court for investigation. This illustrates one fact: Swiss bank secrecy is not absolute.

Clifford Irving certainly discovered this to his sorrow, when the confidence game he had devised was unmasked by Swiss Credit Bank's cooperation with the law. In no time at all, the whole world knew that the mysterious German-speaking H. R. Hughes was none other than Edith Irving participating in what ranks as one of the cleverest swindles to be concocted in many a day.

It certainly must have seemed foolproof when planned: fake an autobiography of mystery man Howard R. Hughes. Sell the book to a big publishing house. Collect a small fortune for it. Then hide the money behind the mask of Swiss bank secrecy. Mystery man Hughes would never appear in court to prove the autobiography was a fake. And the Swiss bank would guarantee that no one would ever be able to trace the checks and prove the swindle.

Sitting in his Zurich office, Dr. H. J. Mast, Swiss Credit Bank's economic adviser, scoffed at any suggestion that any reputable Swiss bank would allow bank secrecy to cover a fraud perpetrated through its bank. Dr. Mast doubles as the public relations officer for the bank. So, frequently, he has the task of being its voice. Usually this is for economic matters, an area where Dr. Mast is particularly well informed. The Irving fraud case found him explaining over and over again how Swiss bank secrecy works, and how it may be lifted, through a Swiss court.

Contrary to some of the newspaper reports published about this case, Swiss Credit Bank did not lift that bank secrecy merely at the unofficial request of McGraw-Hill, the publisher being bilked in this particular case. In all cases where fraud is an issue, the complaint must be filed through a Swiss court, which alone has the power to lift bank secrecy. The bank, or anybody hurt, may file that complaint.

"We certainly are always willing to cooperate with a Swiss court in any case where a crime has been committed," said Dr. Mast.

The sequence of events in this case are important, since they do provide an insight into Swiss bank secrecy and how it works, or perhaps it should be better to say in this instance, how it did not work to cover a fraud.

Those events, as detailed by Zurich's investigating magistrate, Peter Veleff, by Swiss Bank Corp.'s legal officer, Rudolph Hegetschweiler, by Dr. Mast and others, indicate that account number 320 496 was opened at the bank's Paradeplatz main bank April 15, 1971 when the swindle was in its infancy. The account was opened by a woman whom bank officials later remembered as blonde, with long hair down to her shoulders, about five feet three inches in height, wearing dark glasses. She identified herself with a Swiss passport issued to Helga R. Hughes, but she signed her name H. R. Hughes. This, of course, is the same signature as that of Howard R. Hughes.

She opened the account with $50,000. Apparently, this came from the advance which McGraw-Hill had paid Clifford Irving for writing the Hughes autobiography. On March 4, 1971, Irving claimed to have signed a letter of agreement with the elusive Hughes for Irving to do that book.

On May 27, a woman opened an account at the Winterthur branch of Swiss Bank Corp., not far from Zurich. This woman was described as about five foot three inches tall, with long blonde hair down to her shoulders and wearing dark glasses. She had a West German identity card issued to Hanna Rosenkranz, the family name of Edith Irving's former husband.

Irving employed the elusive nature of Howard Hughes to

convince McGraw-Hill that the industrial tycoon wanted to remain in the background. Hughes, Irving insisted, wanted to have his $650,000 payment for the autobiography to be banked at a Swiss account which Hughes had at Swiss Credit Bank. Checks were to be endorsed to H. R. Hughes in account number 320 496 at that bank.

Subsequently, $650,000 in checks were forwarded to that account for H. R. Hughes by McGraw-Hill. In December, 1971, "Helga Hughes" appeared at Swiss Credit Bank, and closed her account. She took the money in the form of 1,000 franc denomination bank notes, stuffing them into an airline flight bag. That same day, "Hanna Rosenkranz" appeared at the Winterthur Branch of Swiss Bank Corp., and banked $450,000. She asked that this be invested in a portfolio account for her, then disappeared.

Irving might have gotten away with it had he selected some individual who wasn't quite as newsworthy as Hughes. With Hughes, everybody wondered if he still were alive. He proceeded to prove that point in a way which became most embarrassing for Irving. Hughes instructed his lawyers to obtain a statement from Swiss Credit Bank to the effect that he did *not* have a bank account with that institution in Zurich.

Here, we come to an interesting area concerning Swiss bank secrecy. As written, the law is broad, i.e. whoever "violates the obligation of secrecy or of professional secrecy or who causes or attempts to cause its violation" shall be punished.

What secrecy? Which professional secrets? Does it refer only to bank customers, or to every single thing which a bank does? The law doesn't say, though practice and custom have established enough precedents to indicate what bank secrecy is.

In one federal court decision, the court said: "The duty of secrecy is a part of any contractual relation between a bank and its customer, the contract does not need to specify this clause. The violation of this privacy means a violation of a contractual duty overtaken, but at the same time a violation of the customer's right to observance of a secret as a consequence of his personal rights."

Another court decision said: "It is not essential if between the bank and its customer a special agreement has been concluded, as even without such agreements the bank is bound to keep the banking secrecy."

One report concerning bank secrecy in files of Swiss Bank Corp., Basle, says: "As the banking secrecy is a consequence of the general rules of the code of obligations concerning the contract, as well as of the articles 27 and 28 of the Civil Law which rules the personal rights, it was not necessary to give a specific description in the banking law. Therefore, this law contains only the aforementioned penal rules."

Whenever a law has been rather loosely defined, the safe thing is to assume that it covers everything. Swiss banks do just that, in effect making bank secrecy whatever the bank says it is.

That implication is contained in the following paragraph in that aforementioned Swiss Bank Corp. document: "The banks are bound to provide information if this is necessary in the superior interest of the collectivity. But, the banks do not have to judge themselves whether and when the secret has to be abolished. *In the first place it is their duty to keep the secret.* They are released from the obligation only if the text of the law explicitly signifies this disengagement." (Italics added.)

In other words, keep quiet until a court tells you to do differently.

Secrecy has been invoked at different times by banks to cover not only the shenanigans of bank officials but simple operational developments, too. The general public may be told only the barest facts about juicy scandals, even though details might be a matter of public concern. In the UCB Basle collapse, for instance, authorities have invoked bank secrecy to cover almost every aspect of investigations.

Certainly, there are some reasons for discretion. In a country where banking is one of the nation's most important industries, care must be taken to assure that the good name of the industry is not besmirched by careless publicity. Defendants in criminal cases should not be tried in the newspapers before their cases ever reach court.

But anyone who moves through the halls of Swiss banks in Zurich, Basle, and Geneva finds vast differences among banks concerning attitudes and beliefs about bank secrecy. All are reticent about accounts of customers. Some talk frankly about bank operations, clearly showing that secrecy does not shroud day-to-day activities. Others hesitate to even state the time of day, for that clock does hang on the wall in a bank, you know. And so bank secrecy must be applied.

Swiss Credit Bank is one of those institutions where almost any question within reason will be answered as long as it doesn't bear on the confidential relationships of clients, either individual or corporate. So, along comes the request from Hughes' attorneys for a bank statement to the effect that Howard Hughes does not have an account with the bank. First, bank officials satisfied themselves that the attorneys were making the request for Hughes.

"When we are satisfied that a particular individual is making a bona fide request for a statement to the effect that he has no account with us, we see no reason for withholding that statement," said Dr. Mast.

Here again, another phase of this complex bank secrecy question should be emphasized. If the client of a bank wants to talk about his account to an outsider, he has every right to do so. If a person wants a bank to talk about his non-account to an outsider, and if he signs a statement to that effect which evidently has not been obtained under duress, the bank may do so. Repeat, it *may* do so. The *may* depends upon whether or not the bank is absolutely convinced that the statement is obtained freely, without coercion.

When writing this book, this author obtained some information concerning a particular non-American client of a Swiss bank. That bank would only discuss this client's situation after a signed statement had been obtained from the depositor, even though he was sitting in front of the bank official when the request was made.

In the Hughes case, bank officials sensed early that something might be wrong with the H. R. Hughes account. So, the affidavit was given to Hughes' attorneys stating that the aviation tycoon did *not* have a bank account at Swiss Credit Bank.

The importance of this is clear. McGraw-Hill had paid $650,000 into the H. R. Hughes account at Swiss Credit Bank, believing that this amount belonged to Howard Hughes. Now from Hughes' attorneys they were presented with evidence which showed that Hughes did not have an account there.

A McGraw-Hill delegation flew to Zurich, sat down with the bank's lawyer, Hegetschweiler, on Wednesday, January 19, at bank headquarters. Hegetschweiler had no objections to confirming for that delegation that Hughes had no account at the bank. When McGraw-Hill officials asked who did open that account, Hegetschweiler referred them to the Swiss bank secrecy law. The bank could not divulge this information without a court order.

On Thursday, January 20, a complaint was filed before Magistrate Veleff, asking that bank secrecy be lifted because of a suspicion of fraud. Once the court order had been presented, Swiss Credit Bank revealed that the mysterious depositor was a Helga R. Hughes. Bank officials remembered enough about her to provide a description which most journalists in this case recognized almost immediately as someone who looked very much like Mrs. Irving.

So, how secret is Swiss bank secrecy? Before digging more deeply into this question, it may be wise to examine its limits as clearly defined by law and precedent. In cases involving inheritance and bankruptcy, secrecy may be lifted, as well as those cases where crimes have been committed. In the latter instances, however, the crimes must be crimes under Swiss law before this applies. Swiss authorities give no legal assistance to foreign governments in the case of political, military, fiscal, and foreign exchange offenses. Reason for this is that Switzerland has no laws of its own defining offenses in these areas as criminal matters.

If a punishable act has been committed, the bank is forced to provide information to authorities. Naturally, there may be examples where it is not readily possible to determine whether or not a punishable act has been committed. In theory and in legislative custom when litigation starts, penal law and penal procedure take precedence over bank secrecy.

Any analysis of bank secrecy seems to indicate that some erosion of that secrecy is underway in subtle ways which may not be noticeable immediately by the uninitiated. Some Swiss may claim that this is a matter of evolutionary progress, or may even deny it. This is a matter of opinion.

This erosion, or evolution, term it what you may, could have an important bearing on present or potential Swiss bank accounts. It certainly could affect anyone who opens such an account with the intention of defrauding the United States government in one way or another.

American and Swiss authorities have been probing dubious aspects of Swiss banking for the last two years. The I.O.S. crisis, the UCB scandal, and fraud cases involving secret accounts have bothered Swiss even as some of these matters have irritated the United States government. Four prongs to tighten bank secrecy and operations are emerging from these years of investigation and discussion.

These are:

—More active Swiss cooperation with law authorities at all levels.

—Possible initiation of a new Mutual Judicial Assistance Treaty between the U.S. and Switzerland.

—Tighter regulation of bank accounts on the American side through measures such as those contained in H.R. 15073, which concerns "Foreign Bank Secrecy and Bank Records."

—Tighter regulation of banks and mutual funds in Switzerland.

Swiss bank secrecy has posed problems for U.S. law enforcers for years. In 1968, negotiations were opened between the U.S. and Switzerland for a treaty which would establish closer relations between both countries. Switzerland already has legal assistance and mutual legal treaties with twenty-four countries, but not with the U.S. One reason for this is that American law is based on British Anglo-Saxon law. Switzerland's legal framework is based on the Napoleonic code.

The aim of this new treaty is to provide a foundation for close cooperation between Swiss and American authorities in criminal cases. The draft of that new treaty reads like something from a technical journal which can only be understood with the help of two dictionaries and a glossary. It is very precise when it defines terminology, for this is the first treaty in the legal assistance field ever negotiated by the United States with a nation operating under Roman (Napoleonic) law.

Though the treaty aims to supply authorities in both countries with the same privileges and degree of cooperation which exists for domestic authorities, Swiss are not ready yet to provide any cooperation where tax evasion alone is the crime being investigated by U.S. authorities. Switzerland takes a strong position on this.

"The bankers' association has made it very plain to the Swiss authorities that it would feel constrained to oppose any steps to institutionalize the exchange of information in tax matters in the proposed agreement," said Alfred Sarasin, president of the Swiss Bankers' Association. But he added: "On the other hand, there is apparently some readiness on the part of Switzerland to impart information about offenses coming under the heading of the fight against organized crime."

Because of this Swiss position on tax evasion, it might be easy to write off that treaty as a useless document. Not so. Even the years of negotiating concerning its features have given Swiss and Americans a better understanding of the problems each country has when it comes to law enforcement.

At the American Embassy in Bern, officials indicated some of the types of cases which may be cracked once this treaty is on file. There's the case of one New York industrialist who concocted a slick scheme to shift his assets beyond the reach of U.S. tax collectors. He "sold" his holdings in a series of transactions at bargain prices to a European concern, closing the deal through a Swiss bank. The U.S. government suspected that the "sale" merely represented a fraudulent transfer of assets to a dummy corporation for what was essentially a switch of those assets from one pocket to another. Loser, of course, would be the U.S. Internal Revenue since assets would be placed beyond American jurisdiction.

Investigative trails ended at the Swiss bank. Had the Mutual Judicial Assistance Treaty been in effect, American authorities feel they could have opened this case wide enough to convict that industrialist in an American court.

Then there's the case of the Los Angeles gambling interests which have been banking unreported profits in Swiss bank accounts. Money returns as "bank loans" to the American involved, and U.S. taxes are evaded. Again, Swiss bank secrecy barred U.S. investigators who sought to accumulate the evidence necessary for U.S. federal prosecution. But under the new treaty, Swiss would offer full cooperation in cases like this which fall under the category of the fight against organized crime.

As mentioned earlier, Swiss law provides for a lifting of bank secrecy in bankruptcy cases. This could have meaning for any American who shifted assets into a Swiss bank account, then filed for bankruptcy in the U.S.

That treaty would make it possible, too, for the U.S. federal government to call upon Swiss bankers as witnesses in certain cases. Swiss federal law exempts only medical doctors, lawyers, and clergymen from the necessity for serving as witnesses when requested to do so in a legal case. With bankers, the judge hearing a case determines whether or not the banker must provide information.

In penal cases, however, Swiss are very careful to confine any necessary testimony to the subject in hand. It is not permitted to extend information beyond the scope of that particular subject. Thus, any lifting of bank secrecy in one case can't be used as an excuse for a fishing expedition by authorities into another.

Over and over again, Swiss bankers do emphasize that tax evasion cases will not be covered by any moves toward cooperation with American law enforcers. As for U.S. taxes? It won't be so easy to evade these through a Swiss bank account, under the system being followed by America. On March 30, 1972, the U.S. Treasury announced that it was implementing on July 1 new rules concerning the reporting to the government of private money transfers of $5,000 and over. Authority for this was contained in H.R. 15073, a congressional bill aimed at tightening U.S. controls over foreign bank accounts. Some sources see this bill as a sly move by Congress to introduce currency controls in America.

Under this measure, U.S. taxpayers are compelled to report on form 1040 whether or not they have foreign bank accounts. If the answer is affirmative, then form 4683 must be used to describe them. Naturally, tax collectors will be doubly curious if bank accounts are listed, without taxes on interest, dividends, and capital gains being reported elsewhere among those myriad collections of paper which comprise a U.S. tax form.

The March 30 order was only one of the new battery of weapons of U.S. authorities for plugging bank account loopholes. Anyone taking or transmitting $5,000 or more in cash, foreign currency, travelers checks, money orders, or negotiable securities out of the country must report same to the U.S. Customs. Such sums being brought in also must be declared. With transfers by mail, reports must be filed within thirty days after dispatch of such transfers.

All private and institutional records of foreign bank accounts must be kept for five years. Banks and financial institutions must report all "unusual" money transfers abroad, plus all of those amounting to $10,000 or more each.

It is apparent what lies behind these directives. Some sources in the U.S. Internal Revenue Service believe that many Americans are using foreign bank accounts to evade taxes. With the above rules, it would be very difficult for any American to transfer money abroad without the U.S. government knowing about it.

However, U.S. government demands on banks are so onerous, claim banks, that a storm has been kicked up concerning this type of currency control. The constitutionality of the law is being challenged, by—of all groups—the American Civil Liberties Union, an organization which champions liberal causes more often than it does the right of a citizen to keep his financial dealings to himself.

In a suit, filed along with Security National Bank, Oakland, the ACLU termed Treasury demands a "chilling" threat to personal freedom. It appears that American citizens have not heard the last of the opposition to Treasury measures. Still, the trend is evident. Tax loopholes are likely to be tightened.

It should be emphasized once again, too, that nothing in legislation bars maintenance of foreign bank accounts. As long as U.S. citizens report and pay taxes on income from such accounts, they have no reason for concern. Tens of thousands of U.S. citizens do just that, for today there are Americans working abroad from London to Cape Town and from Dhahran to Buenos Aires. At the U.S. Embassy in Berne one official said: "I think everybody in the Embassy from the Ambassador on down has a Swiss bank account. How else can you handle your finances when you live here?"

Many Swiss bankers are happy that the U.S. is attacking its fiscal problems on its side of the Atlantic, instead of expecting that Swiss should act as policemen for America in tax evasion cases. F. W. Schulthess, Swiss Credit Bank chairman, said: "It remains to be said that it cannot be our function to act as public prosecutor for foreign countries."

Switzerland has tightened its own laws, too, in some respects, with more legislative revisions in the works. Writing in the January, 1972, issue of *The Banker*, a British monthly, Dr. Heinz Portmann, economics editor of the *Neue Zürcher Zeitung*, said: "Switzerland's financial scene has hardly ever undergone such far-reaching changes as in 1971. The revision of the antiquated and over-liberal banking legislation of 1934 has brought a new set of requirements and provisions for the foundation, take-over and management of both Swiss and foreign banks and financial institutions. It also has provided the Federal Banking Commission with additional supervisory powers. The new regulations shall lead to the elimination of doubtful banks and will therefore improve the creditor's protection."

The new bank law which took effect April 1, 1971, provides more powers to the Federal Banking Commission, increases reporting requirements of banks, and provides harsher penalties for violations of capital and reserve requirements of banks. Uniform account procedures are required for eurocurrency deposits.

Foreign banks require permission to open for business in Switzerland, and such permission will only be granted where reciprocity applies. If a Swiss bank can open a branch or subsidiary in a foreign nation, then foreigners from that country will be allowed to operate in Switzerland, provided that other requirements are met. The foreign bank coming to Switzerland must indicate in its title that it is not of Swiss character. It also must promise to abide by Switzerland's credit and monetary policies.

"We have been entirely too liberal in allowing foreign banks to establish operations in Switzerland," one Zurich banker bluntly said when discussing the new program. He added: "And perhaps we may see some of these foreign banks losing their permits to operate should they violate standards of good sense."

Foreign mutual funds now come under supervision of the Federal Banking Commission. To operate, these funds must have a representative bank in Switzerland, either Swiss or a branch of a foreign bank. The representative bank, which must be approved by the Commission, controls the investment policies of the fund. By law, that bank now is restricted to investments only in securities and real estate. Investments in commodities are specifically prohibited. Funds whose assets are partly made up of units of another fund under the same management or an associated management are no longer authorized to do business in Switzerland. Advertising is controlled by the representative bank, not by the mutual fund. Funds addressing themselves to the Swiss public must agree to redeem units at any time, to publish an annual report, and to have activities examined by an independent auditor. Funds making sales pitches outside Switzerland from a Swiss base must obtain Commission approval to even mention any Swiss addresses.

Regulations eliminate any chance of a return to the wheeler-dealer type of fund which flourished in the 1960's, the heyday of I.O.S. and its imitators.

One non-Swiss banker connected with one of the foreign banks in the country complained in late 1972 that "A hostile trend toward foreign banks has emerged at all levels of government in Switzerland."

The 1971 monetary crisis and its aftermath in 1973 has had a traumatic effect on little Switzerland, too. It showed that the country might be inundated by a flood of foreign currency in another such crisis. Even liberal bankers would prefer tight controls against foreign capital to monetary anarchy. So there has been a definite hardening of support for better control over money inflows.

This has increased support for a constitutional amendment under consideration in 1973. This would give the federal government broad power to influence economic cycles. Power to control prices, money flows, the volume of credit, and taxes would be vested in the federal council.

Inflation also is worrisome. Switzerland started 1972 with an inflationary rate of over 6 percent, a rate which hit 10 percent annually by year end.

"We don't like controls, but inflation is forcing us into applying them," one government official said in his office in Berne's Parliament. In the building, the two hundred-member Nationalrat was convening in a rose chamber facing a huge mural of Lake Lucerne. On the shores of this lake, the founders of Switzerland met in 1291.

Thumbing through a statistical tabulation, this official said: "Look, our consumer price index rose by 6.6 percent in 1971, compared with 5.4 percent in 1970 and 2.3 percent in 1969."

Fear may make traitors of the bravest. Inflationary fears may swing the staunchest economic liberal toward the controls he instinctively dislikes.

The direction Switzerland may take in the future will be determined outside the country as well as in. With the Common Market now nine nations instead of six, Switzerland no longer can ignore the political and economic combination which is forming around it. Even Austria, to the east, is associating with the Common Market. Switzerland sells 38 percent of its exports and purchases 59 percent of its imports from that Community. So, it has been forced to take cognizance of that developing EC, too, though it would prefer somehow to maintain absolute neutrality.

The monetary crisis convinced Central Bank officials that Switzerland should join the International Monetary Fund in order to participate in revamping the monetary system. The expansion of EC emphasized that Switzerland had to have an economic accommodation with that Common Market. Swiss hope that neither of these foreign entanglements will destroy political neutrality.

When Federal Councillor Graber traveled to Paris in April, 1972, it was to further this aim. He was received royally by French President Georges Pompidou, by Prime Minister Chaban-Delmas, and by Foreign Minister Schumann. Switzerland may need all the allies it can enlist in the Common Market.

Dr. Sicco Mansholt, when still president of the Common Market Commission, was once asked about his attitude toward neutral countries like Switzerland. Mansholt, a Socialist, bluntly said the Community could never provide Switzerland with the economic and financial position it enjoys today. Then

he added: "Switzerland is an island for certain capitalistic practices in the world, which seem to be very profitable for Switzerland. I must say it doesn't interest me that much. Let them find
their own way out."

Tough talk this. It provides Swiss with an inkling of what
may lie ahead. Mere association does not end Switzerland's
problems.

EC is an evolutionary entity which is progressing toward
what is hoped may be political as well as full economic and
monetary unity. At some time a few years hence, Switzerland
will be facing pressure to blend deeper into that Common Market, to tie its own money system to that of the Market. Currently, Swiss bankers shake their heads and say that Switzerland
will never give up its cherished money freedom for anything
which the Community might offer. The same bankers were
criticizing floating rates in 1971 and 1972, claiming that Switzerland never would adopt such a system. Yet at the end of January,
1973, Switzerland was floating its super strong franc.

Tomorrow and tomorrow and tomorrow all will be days of
change in Europe, and Switzerland is a part of Europe no matter
how much she would like to remain as only its money changer.

CHAPTER XVI

GOLD'S GLOWING TWILIGHT

In late March, 1972, the United States government frightened the free gold market. Word leaked that America might sell some of its dwindling gold hoard on the free market. The report was suspicious; it sounded like a trial balloon.

Still, gold traders worried. Where money is involved, sometimes cowardice is the best policy. In Zurich, traders anxiously watched the free market, then priced at $48.40 an ounce. They feared a bearish price reaction.

Instead, the gold price climbed.

Subsequently, the Nixon Administration denied the leak. The gold price rose still higher. By August, 1972, it had climbed to $70 an ounce. Gold was reacting very much like a precious commodity in short supply on a free market. Indications are that this situation is likely to persist. Developments provide little comfort for those who want to remove gold from the monetary scene.

Events in 1971–1973 provided more support for the gold positions of Swiss bankers than for the anti-gold lobby which is just as vehement in its way as is the lobby of right-wing gold bugs.

Few things raise more heat in monetary discussions than does the topic of gold. The gold standard, with its extreme rigidity, is denounced by liberals. They can cite events which followed the collapse of the gold standard in 1931 to justify all of their attacks on gold. Sound money advocates, on the other hand, see dangers in the printing-press money often endorsed at the other extreme of the monetary scale.

Gold raises such heat because it is much more than a yellow metal which glitters. It is the symbol of the conservative, sound money man, the sort of person you usually encounter when in a Swiss bank. Today, anti-gold lobbyists seem irritated because money trends and swings in the gold market just might bolster the debating positions of conservatives. Whereas not long ago they were claiming that the price of gold could be forced below $35 an ounce without monetary support, now they aver that gold is too valuable to use as a monetary metal.

Professor Robert Triffin, the Yale University economist, certainly knows how to denigrate gold in a non-intellectual manner, which is quite a feat for an intellectual of his caliber. He said a while ago: "Nobody could ever have conceived of a more absurd waste of human resources than to dig gold in distant corners of the earth for the sole purpose of transporting it and reburying it immediately afterwards in other deep holes, especially excavated to receive it and heavily guarded to protect it."

Granted! This is utterly ridiculous, almost as ridiculous as working for pieces of paper which may be green, with fancy engraved curlicues around a picture of George Washington. Who would be that stupid? Nearly everybody, of course. People feel there is something behind those pieces of paper, just as people also feel that gold has a value which will be retained through monetary upheavals, war, and the fierce debates ahead when the monetary system is reformed.

It is very easy to denigrate gold with witty remarks which bring knowing nods from the anti-gold lobby. Gold is the metal of the bloated capitalist, the cartoon character who smokes those awful cigars and never pays any taxes, though he needs a computer to tabulate his profits. Since there isn't enough gold to go around, the metal does raise problems when it is advanced as a monetary medium. Then, of course, there always is the fall-back position when besmirching gold: it is the principal product of those terrible South Africans.

John Maynard Keynes, the British economist, set the pattern for much of the economic thought in the post-World War II period when he termed gold "this barbarous relic." In this respect, his philosophy paralleled that of Lenin. Lenin claimed that in his socialist world gold would be used for lavatories.

George Bernard Shaw, a turn of the century left winger when radicalism was a novelty, had a few words to say about gold, too. One might have thought that he would damn the metal as a tool of capitalism. Not he. He understood politicians too well.

In *The Intelligent Woman's Guide to Socialism and Capitalism*, he addressed himself to voters as follows: "You have to choose between trusting to the natural stability of gold and the honesty and intelligence of members of the government. And, with due respects for these gentlemen, I advise you, as long as the capitalist system lasts, to vote for gold."

Trust politicians to spend and spend until the paper money in your pocket is reduced to a fraction of its original worth. It is impossible to do this where the currency is tied tightly to gold. Even when a nation merely uses gold to support its currency, that gold backing provides a disciplinary tool which frustrates free-spending politicians. When spending reaches the limit of the gold-backed currency, a country must either stop spending or remove the gold backing. Usually, it is the latter which becomes policy. But the mere act of removing the gold cover signifies political failure for those politicians, and may court political disaster.

It is no wonder that so many politicians are against gold. It is much easier to print money than to produce more gold.

There is no question where conservative Swiss bankers stand on the gold–sound money question. Dr. Max Iklé, former general manager, Swiss National Bank, Zurich, said: "We do not believe that gold will give up its role as a currency medium within the foreseeable future."

At Union Bank, Chairman Schaefer was asked if he thought gold would be demonetized. He answered: "If gold could be replaced by something else, a universally acceptable common denominator, my answer would be positive. Such as matters are now, I feel that gold will continue to play a major role in the international monetary system."

Switzerland always has been a conservative country where gold has been regarded as the ultimate medium for settlement of international payments. Some years ago Swiss citizens were asked to vote on an amendment to the constitution whereby the government's obligation to redeem paper money with gold would be abolished. Citizens refused to go along. Only when this amendment was changed to allow suspension of redemption in times of crisis would they certify it by ballot.

Many of the world's central bankers have a Swiss-like devotion to the yellow metal, too.

"The extreme view expressed by the United States is that gold should be demonetised," Dr. Milton Gilbert, economic adviser for the Bank for International Settlements, Basle, told the Swiss Institute of International Studies at a meeting in Zurich, December 6, 1971. "As the central banks hold over $40 billion of gold in their reserves, which they prize highly, this suggestion cannot be taken seriously. No doubt gold has been an irritant to the United States, and now that the dollar has been made inconvertible into gold, it may be appealing to take the further step of demonetisation so as to avoid all comparisons between gold and the dollar in the future. It is the first time in history that it has been proposed to confirm Gresham's Law by legislative enactment."

Gresham's Law, of course, says that bad money drives out good.

Gilbert happens to be an American himself, so his remarks

are not based on anti-American nitpicking. It has long been Gilbert's contention that a simple increase in the price of gold to a new equilibrium level would have solved many of the problems affecting the monetary system. His comments have weight since BIS is the central bankers' central bank, and their Basle-based club.

Any examination of monetary gold holdings shows that central banks have not lost their respect for gold because of U.S. attitudes. International Monetary Fund statistics listed total world official gold holdings by central banks and international agencies at about $44.5 billion (at $38 an ounce) in 1972.

Admittedly, there is a long-term trend toward a reduction of the volume of gold reserves in relationship to the total (gold, foreign exchange, and special drawing rights). These latter are the "paper gold" units created by IMF as a supplement to gold and an addition to world liquidity. They function as a form of official international money since only governments, not individuals, can spend or accept them.

Even the Russians love their gold, despite what Lenin had to say. Evidence indicates the Soviet Union has been hoarding its gold the last few years, probably anticipating higher world prices. Their stockpile early in 1972 was estimated at a little over $3 billion worth, computing at $38 an ounce. Perhaps they were fortunate in possessing that gold, for, as 1972 moved along, it became evident that the Soviet Union was having its worst farm crop for decades. That gold became a prime means of payment for enormous imports of grain into the Soviet Union.

In Moscow, at the bulky, granite block headquarters of Gosplan, the Soviet State Planning Agency, officials fend off questions about the Soviet Union's gold reserves, just as they do at Gosbank. The latter is the equivalent of Russia's central bank coupled with a giant savings bank. Russia's gold production and reserves are state secrets as closely guarded as are details of the Soviet Union's stockpile of atomic warheads.

"We are satisfied with our gold production," said one Gosbank executive as he sat at a green felt table, a pitcher of apple juice at his elbow. Since the Kremlin has ordered a crackdown on the drinking of alcoholic beverages, bureaucrats carefully refrain from alcoholic hospitality whether visitors are from inside or outside the country.

When they have gold to sell, which isn't often, they do it through BIS or through Swiss banks. It is gold which everybody likes to receive because it is refined to 999 parts per 1,000 purity, compared with 995 in most Western nations. Russians like Swiss banks because Swiss practice the discretion which Russians prefer.

The U.S. Central Intelligence Agency makes its own estimates of Russian gold production and reserves. CIA computations reportedly are based on a Communist Party Central Committee document which was photographed and transmitted to the West by Colonel Penkovsky, the Russian who spied for the West within the Kremlin. Projecting these figures from 1964 produces an estimated gold reserve of a little over $3 billion for the Soviet Union. Whatever the figure is, Russians hang on to their gold as avidly as do gold hoarders in India, only periodically selling some of it to purchase grain in bad crop years.

Paradoxically, the slowly declining position of gold in the overall total is a result of the strong demand for it, not because of any declining interest in the metal. Consumption of gold in industrial uses outruns supply. Meanwhile, demands of speculators and hoarders have been whittling away at the stocks of gold available for monetary uses. IMF figures show that monetary stocks have fallen by $2 billion since 1965. In Zurich, gold traders report that this total plus all the newly mined gold since 1965 have gone into hoarding, speculative holdings, and industrial uses.

At the end of 1971, IMF listed total reserves of all nations reporting to it at $119.6 billion, which means that the gold total amounted to 30 percent of the whole. In 1965, total international reserves amounted to $71 billion, with the gold portion accounting for over 60 percent of it.

Opponents of gold are right when they say the yellow metal is a diminishing asset. They neglect to say, however, that IMF figures at the end of 1971 still were based on a gold price of $35 an ounce. It is just as easy to increase assets by hiking the price of gold as it is to create assets from thin air, as was the case with SDR's. So the declining percentage of gold in international reserves might be used as an argument for a gold price hike rather than for demonetization.

Gold certainly is the most highly prized portion of central bank reserves. Foreign nations like to repay their debts with dollars, other foreign currencies, with SDR's, and with gold, in that order. When Britain repaid its debts then outstanding to IMF at the end of April, 1972, it would have liked to repay the entire amount with U.S. dollars. It was prevented from doing so because IMF already had so many dollars on hand that its rules barred it from accepting any more. Central banks have been hoarding their gold as avidly as any of the individual gold hoarders to be found today in many societies.

South Africa is the world's largest producer of gold, accounting for over three quarters of the world's newly mined supply. In 1972, its forty-five gold mines produced 29.39 million fine ounces, a 6.4 percent decline from the 1971 total. World output of gold amounted to under 39 million ounces in 1972, a decline from the record volume of 41.6 million ounces in 1970 and 40.4 million ounces in 1971.

In Johannesburg, the industrial city which has mine dumps like miniature mountains scattered through urban and industrial areas, mining moguls say that the country's gold production is on an economic plateau. It may hold there a few more years. Then, a slow, steady decline in production is anticipated, though any sharp jumps in the gold price could naturally delay that decline.

As production levels off, demand is expected to rise. So the free market price of gold finds itself in a classic free market situation. The price is likely to edge upward until demand and supply are in equilibrium. Gold producers claim that with relationships now existing, the price should rise on an average of 4 percent a year. A cautionary note is in order, however. In the winter of 1973 as gold soared to the $75 an ounce level, it seemed that bullish gold factors were being overestimated; there are some who believe periodic reactions in the price level will occur, even though the long-term trend is up.

Industrial demand for gold has been rising steadily through recent years, the main reason for market bullishness. Examinations of this demand have been made by two big London-based mining houses, Consolidated Goldfields Ltd. and Charter Consolidated Ltd. Both companies came to the same conclusion, that consumption is outrunning supply, with the gap widening.

One would expect gold mining companies to promote a higher gold price. But companies marshal some impressive data to support their contentions. The price of gold held at $35 an ounce from 1934 until the two-tier market was established in March, 1968. Meanwhile, prices of nearly everything else climbed, while wages and salaries soared. Many more people can afford gold bracelets, watches, and artifacts today than was the case in 1934. The jewelry market has grown and keeps growing, while gold production levels off.

Gold is where you find it, but it becomes ever harder to find. South Africa is mining gold as deep as 13,000 feet in the ground. This is so deep that the pressure of the rock sometimes leads to rock bursts. Rock in a tunnel will explode like a detonating hand grenade, spewing deadly fragments in all directions.

Consolidated Goldfields studies of new production coupled with sales to the West from the Communist bloc show the following picture when measured against consumption for industrial uses. All figures are in millions of fine ounces:

	1965	1969	1970	1971
New Supplies	52.6	41.2	41.3	41.
Consumption	36.2	40.2	43.7	42.

In 1965 that surplus of supply over consumption went into monetary uses. Today, no gold is going from new production into coffers of central banks for monetary purposes. Gold is being demonetized by attrition rather than by political fiat. But it may take another score of years to phase it out completely from the monetary system at the present pace. Truly, gold is becoming too valuable to use for money, though a substantial hike in the monetary price could change that situation in a hurry.

Projections made by Consolidated Goldfields to 1980 indicate that, even if the Soviet Union sells surplus gold on the Western market, consumption should outrun new available supplies from now on.

One report, "Gold 1972," written by P. D. Fells, a Con-solidated economist, says: "Mine production in the Western world is already exceeded by demand, and it is tending to fall rather than rise. In almost all areas outside South Africa, the output of gold from mines in which it is a principal product has been falling for a number of years, and there is no prospect of a reversal in this trend within the foreseeable future. South African production reached an all time peak in 1970 and dropped slightly since. There may be marginal increases from time to time, but it seems extremely unlikely that total Western world gold production will be higher in 1980 than at the present time, and it could well be considerably lower."

So, Fells is bullish about gold. He says: "It is evident that, quite apart from its role as an international monetary asset, gold has an assured future as a commodity."

When the gold industry speaks of "industrial uses," it really means gold which is fabricated into something, whether it be a spoon or a wristwatch casing. In 1971, jewelry absorbed 74.9 percent of gold going to industrial use worldwide, 60 percent of total consumption in the U.S. Italy, with its many craftsmen, is the leading jewelry producer in the West, with many of its plants on an assembly-line basis. Ballestra at Bassano del Gruppa, for instance, has five hundred machines producing gold chain alone. Not surprisingly, Italy is where you may expect to find the best gold jewelry bargains. India is the leading jewelry producer in Asia.

Jewelry markups are so steep that it is useless to purchase such items as inflation hedges. Most of the price is based on the skill and artistry of the designer and fabricator, coupled with the bargaining power of the salesman merchandising pieces. On average, gold jewelry wholesaled at $24 will retail in France for $76, in Switzerland for $72, in West Germany for $60, and in Italy for $48.

Electronics accounted for 6.5 percent of gold use in 1971 worldwide. In the U.S. electronics accounted for a fifth of its gold consumption. Dentistry took 5.4 percent globally, 9 per-cent in the U.S. Other industrial and decorative uses consumed 5.3 percent worldwide, about 11 percent in the U.S. in 1971.

In fabrication, gold's strength, resistance to corrosion, and its high melting point plus high electrical conductivity are important selling points. Gold can be beaten so thinly that one ounce can make a sheet one hundred feet square. A gold coating of only 0.000004 of an inch thick helps to protect men and equipment in space ships from the heat generated by rocket engines. Some jet aircraft have windshields impregnated with a thin layer of gold one fifth of a millionth of an inch thick. The layer does not interfere with vision. Yet it provides the medium for electrically heating and de-icing the windshields.

Gold alloy connectors are helping to extend lives of voltage regulators in automobiles. At a cost of about forty-eight cents a square foot, a building may be covered with a super-thin layer of gold leaf. The gold cover reflects the sun and results in savings in air conditioning costs in hot climates. Microcircuits on the Boeing 747 Jumbo Jet contain gold wires half the thickness of a human hair.

Coins and medallions account for the remainder of the yellow metal being put to industrial uses. Hoarding and speculative demand for gold adds to the overall demand.

Perhaps another word of caution is necessary here. Gold demand has an elasticity related to its price. Industrial demand at $40 an ounce is much stronger than when the free market price rises to $70 an ounce. Gold traders may find that substitutes encroach on gold's market if the price rises too sharply.

Take jewelry, for instance. Pure gold is twenty-four carats, but this is seldom used with jewelry because of the softness of the metal. Pieces would wear quickly. In Western Europe, eighteen-carat gold is preferred (75 percent purity). In the U.S. most jewelry is in the ten- to fourteen-carat (42 to 58 percent purity) range. In Britain, nine-carat gold (37.5 percent) is popular. By dropping the amount of pure gold in jewelry, craftsmen may stretch the metal much further than the consumption rate of today. This provides the entire jewelry industry with some protection against too high a free market price for gold.

Still, there are a lot of bulls in gold in the present climate. One of the most bullish is Harry Schultz, who seldom misses a chance to plug gold in his *International Harry Schultz Letter*, which is put together in London. He opened the year in January, 1972, by predicting: "We are going to see gold at least at $70 an ounce within two or three years, maybe much sooner. Right now is the time to plan for it."

How? By buying gold or gold mining stocks, according to Schultz. Of course, his prediction about a $70 price came much sooner than even he had anticipated. Now, he still is bullish on gold, long term, but warns that the price may run ahead of itself at times.

Ultimately, gold will have to be replaced in the monetary system by something else, unless nations are willing to price the metal at $100 to $150 an ounce. It would require a price in that order if the U.S. is to return to the gold convertibility of its dollar to justify that now dead claim that "the dollar is as good as gold."

A review of the history of the gold standard provides some clues as to why the U.S. tries to demonetize gold. Gold has been with us since the dawn of history, but seldom in quantity large enough to allow a full gold standard.

Spaniards discovered their El Dorado in the New World in the sixteenth century. Gold flowed into the channels of commerce as never before. More discoveries came in succeeding centuries, in Brazil, in California in 1849, in Australia, in South Africa. In the nineteenth century alone more gold was produced than had been mined in the preceding five thousand years, says one report made by gold producer Union Corp., Johannesburg, South Africa.

This influx of gold into Europe enabled Britain to go on the gold standard in 1816. One by one other major European nations followed. The U.S., which had a strong silver lobby in its western states, continued on the silver-gold standard until 1900.

The gold standard is perhaps the simplest of all monetary systems. There is a fixed price for gold in the currency of the home country. Gold coins circulate, along with paper money which is freely convertible into the appropriate coin on demand. Import and export of gold are permitted. Gold is used to settle international obligations.

Thus, a nation which has gold in its treasury imports the products of other lands, making payment in gold. Meanwhile, it earns more gold from the sales of its products to other countries. As long as the trade is in balance, commerce may continue indefinitely. But if a nation spends more of its gold than it earns, it must reduce its imports, or increase exports, to earn enough to bring its books into balance again.

Since the internal volume of currency is established by the amount of gold in a country's treasury, the state of a nation's reserves also decides the level of economic activity within the country. If gold is flowing outward because of a trade deficit, the volume of money within the country will contract. This automatically disciplines the country, through recession. Prices come down. Imports are cut back. Factories lay off people. Manufacturers seek to increase productivity and to make their products more competitive in markets.

As exports become more competitive again, gold again starts to flow back into the country. The expansion of the money supply stimulates more economic activity and prosperity is resumed.

The gold bullion standard operates in about the same way, except that gold coins don't circulate. But paper money may be redeemed for bullion bars, if one has enough of the currency for such redemptions.

Weaknesses of the gold standard are evident to anyone who believes in full employment. The gold standard fosters depressions and booms, with the likelihood that they alternate. From the human standpoint, it is a ruthless system, geared to maintaining the stability of money instead of the well-being of citizens.

Of course, hard money advocates contend that stable money is the best instrument which politicians can provide to assure the well being of citizens. The gold standard does prevent politicians from printing paper money to the point where the currency becomes worthless. Nevertheless, in the final analysis, there is little chance that the world ever again will return to a full gold standard.

Through Britain's empire-building of the nineteenth century, the United Kingdom lived by the gold standard. Its gold-backed pound sterling became the key currency around the globe. Every second week, stately bankers in The City, London's financial district, set foreign exchange quotations, decreeing how other currencies would relate to that pound. There was no rush to dispatch such quotations to the far corners of the world. Figures didn't change that much. Most foreign exchange dealers could depend upon newspapers to set their quotations.

World War I knocked the gold standard off the world trade rails. In 1919, Britain officially went off that standard and tried vainly to maintain a gold bullion standard for the six years from 1925 to 1931. One by one other nations went off gold. Switzerland still sticks to the gold standard in theory, if not in fact. The U.S. went off that standard in 1933, establishing the gold-dollar standard in 1934.

Under this system, gold does not circulate. Dollars are supposed to be redeemed in gold when international debts are settled. This system became the non-socialist world standard in 1944, when monetary experts from Allied countries so decided at Bretton Woods, New Hampshire. It was to continue until August 15, 1971, though in its last years America had so many hedges around its promise to redeem dollars for gold that the system really was dead on its feet when President Nixon kicked it over.

The system might still be in effect were it not that the U.S. undertook far more obligations in the postwar period than it could bear: foreign aid, defense of the Western world, expansion of a corporate empire abroad. Nothing seemed beyond the power of the U.S. But at $35 an ounce, there wasn't enough gold to finance demands successive Administrations placed on the U.S. Treasury.

Still, Bretton Woods had provided the U.S. with a reserves mint, the ability to create international dollars simply by printing more dollars. The dollar was as good as gold. It could be used to settle foreign accounts much more conveniently than might 1/35 of an ounce of gold for each dollar of debt. Year after year, the U.S. produced deficits in its foreign accounts. Dollars flowed out to settle in reserves of central banks abroad.

As far back as October, 1960, there were warnings of danger. A speculative gold rush started and the price of the metal soared to $40 an ounce. Rumors had developed that the U.S. meant to increase gold's price. Reports proved false. The upsurge subsided. The new Kennedy Administration ignored the warning signal.

In America, perhaps more than in any other country in the world, an antipathy to gold developed over the years. It is difficult to support the doctrine of full employment, and still believe in gold as a weapon for monetary discipline. Americans hadn't owned gold for so long that many people hardly knew what it looked like. The country had never experienced the catastrophic inflations and the nation-smashing wars which periodically hit Europe. There was no gold mystique with its song like the voice of the turtle in the land.

It was easy to believe that flowers would appear on the earth and "the time of the singing of birds" would come if only gold could be buried as a monetary tool. The dollar or some other man-made instrument could do the job much better. Gone would be the threat of restricting the U.S. economy and reducing employment because of the discipline of gold. After all, any new monetary instrument would be handled by the IMF, and the U.S. controlled that organization. Or did.

Not for nothing did France make certain that Common Market nations together obtained a veto within IMF. This was a tip-off that European nations did not want to replace the gold-dollar standard with a paper gold-dollar system. Through the decade of the 1960's and into the 1970's, France frequently seemed to be anti-American, always on the other side where American policies were concerned. It would be an oversimplification to say that this was basically a gold versus anti-gold argument. Yet it isn't far from the truth, though General de Gaulle's pique went deeper.

French citizens hold more than $6 billion worth of gold in their hoards. Their respect for gold is so strong that no French government can ignore it, even if it wished. None does.

General de Gaulle realized early that the gold-dollar standard was degenerating into a gold versus dollar question which could determine the hegemony of the world. He adopted some of the ideas of that venerable resident of the Left Bank in Paris, Jacques Rueff, the octogenarian economist with a mustache as gray as what little hair he has left on his head. For years, Rueff argued that monetary problems could be eased through a simple increase in the price of gold. But de Gaulle was more anti-dollar than pro-gold. America's gold position played right into his hands. By promoting gold, he could strike at the dollar, for he knew the U.S. wouldn't take the gold-price-increase step which would have defused him and added more life to the dollar-gold standard.

In the early 1960's, when a gold price increase of moderate proportions might have provided decades of monetary peace, the U.S. scoffed at the idea. Numerous arguments were presented by the U.S. anti-gold lobby to "prove" that the idea was stupid and an absolute non-starter. Wicked South Africa and Communist Russia would be the big gainers, they said. (This was one of the few points which united America's liberals, and its Far Right.) The lobby criticized a system whereby the monetary base allegedly was tied to South Africa's gold mines. This overlooked the fact that nearly half of the 80,000 metric tons of gold mined since the dawn of time are in vaults of central banks. A quarter of that monetary gold is in America. Governments, not South Africa, control the world's monetary gold, though South Africa does control three fourths of the new supply—under one thousand tons a year.

The anti-gold lobby contended also that wild inflation would stem from any gold price hike. They also said that it would be mechanically impossible to introduce. Every other nation would revise its currency in relationship to gold, and the exchange rate structure would be unchanged.

So what happened? The U.S. delayed any gold hike until May 8, 1972, and experienced one of the wildest inflations in its history prior to that date. Wicked South Africa and the Soviet Union still are around, policies unaffected by the U.S. gold position. In Washington, December 18, 1971, the Group of Ten (and Switzerland) proved the falseness of that argument about the mechanics of change. For the first time in history, major nations arranged a multinational realignment of currency parities along with a small increase in gold's price. (It didn't become official until Congress passed a bill, and the president signed it May 8, 1972.)

The U.S. almost succeeded in persuading the world to adopt willingly the dollar standard. For the last few years, the world has been on just such a standard without much light being focused on that fact. Had the economic might of the U.S. been properly managed, America might have kept the world on the dollar standard by the sheer weight of all that power. Some sources say it still might succeed should Washington put its mind to the job.

Two factors weakened the dollar standard in the 1960's. One was the Vietnam war, which drained money, man-power, and moral strength from the richest and most powerful nation on earth at a rate that even America could not bear.

The second factor was the closing of the Technical Gap which once worried Europeans so much. A few years ago, the U.S. seemed so far ahead of the rest of the world in space, computer, electronics, and other technologies, and in manufacturing know-how, that Europe seemed condemned to being a serf society for the technological masters in America. Then, Europe and Japan developed their industrial capacities to the point where they challenged America.

These two factors destroyed what control the U.S. had over its balance of payments deficits. Dollars poured outward in a flood, destroying the stability of that materializing dollar standard.

A third factor probably should be mentioned, too. Interest rate differentials sometimes have been sharp as each nation developed its own program for control of its national economy. Higher rates in Europe tended to draw money from America to Europe.

In recent years, economic theorists have leaned toward controls over the money supply as a means of regulating economies. Trouble develops, however, where monetarist doctrine is uncoordinated internationally. Interest rates may be a percentage point or two higher in one country than in another. This might be permissible with floating exchange rates globally, for any movement of funds to capitalize on the better rate would hike the particular exchange rate of the money-receiving country until the higher interest rate was neutralized. Most money men in the business of handling foreign exchange don't like floating exchange rates. What experience the world gleaned from them on a mass basis in the August 15 to December 18, 1971 period was not encouraging.

In any case, uncoordinated monetary policies certainly

played a part in undercutting the dollar standard. In the process, gold gained new stature, much to the embarrassment of the anti-gold lobby. This should not be surprising. In any period of monetary unrest, when nothing better than gold is being offered as a standard of value, gold develops an attraction of its own.

Having muffed the opportunity to make the dollar as good as gold at one-fiftieth, or one-seventieth or even one one-hundredth of an ounce of gold to the dollar, it remains to be seen if America has lost control of gold. Dollar devaluations of 1971 and 1973 were forced by events, not by policy switches carefully prepared to further long-range compaigns to put the world on a dollar standard, an SDR standard, or anything else.

Gold has so many political overtones that Switzerland has remained very much in the background insofar as the gold-dollar argument has gone. There is no question where it stands —on the side of a sound currency, whether that happens to be gold or the dollar.

The anti-gold lobby has very cleverly handled their propaganda to imply that anyone who supports gold in the argument is a "gold nut" or a "gold bug" or some sort of escapee from an insane asylum. In this, they are sometimes assisted by the more rabid of the gold lovers, who indeed do sometimes sound as if they have deified gold.

Yet, it isn't gold itself that is the crux of this argument. It is sound money, money that doesn't lose 5 or 6 percent of its value every year because of inflation, money that will guarantee you some purchasing power in the pension for which you have worked all your life. There would be no need for gold as a monetary metal if governments devised paper instruments which provide the sound money which has become only a magnificent illusion in most countries in the post World War II period.

Miracles don't happen easily, which is why gold sold for $75 an ounce in 1973, with all signs indicating that its price a few years hence may be higher. As the leading retailers of gold, Swiss bankers happily reflected that gold may be in its twilight. But it is a glowing twilight in the monetary muddle which confronts the world.

CHAPTER XVII

THE MONETARY MUDDLE

In late April, 1972, Dr. Edwin Stopper, president of the Swiss National Bank, revealed that Switzerland may seek membership in the International Monetary Fund. Switzerland wants a voice in the reorganization of the world monetary system which is slowly getting underway.

With so much of its future depending upon monetary matters, this little nation may seem to have a bigger stake than most in the monetary system. Actually, nearly everybody in the industrial world is affected. The monetary troubles of recent years emphasize that money is a commodity with a price that is fixed in the market places of the world. Stabilizing money prices is what the monetary system is all about.

America's future will be determined by those negotiations concerning its dollar. America's ability or inability to spend dollars abroad depends on them. There can be no more Vietnams with a weak dollar, which probably is one favorable factor stemming from dollar weakness. But the U.S. will to provide a military shield for Europe is based on the same factors.

In the sixteenth century Rabelais said: "The strength of a war waged without monetary reserves is as fleeting as a breath. Money is the sinews of battle." Peace, without monetary reserves, has no strength, either. Certainly, the dollar's strength, or lack of it, may determine whether the U.S. remains a first-class power. Swiss are more aware of this than are Americans.

In one monetary discussion, not long ago, Dr. Nicolas Bär, partner in Julius Bär & Co., Zurich, said: "Even in large cities like Detroit or Boston in the United States, it often is difficult to obtain a foreign exchange rate at a bank. You ask at a counter concerning the spot and forward rates for the Swiss franc or the German mark that day and you receive a blank stare. The person behind the counter may not even understand the question, and there may be only a couple of people upstairs who do. In Switzerland, even the messenger of a bank will know the day's foreign exchange rates. We think in foreign exchange terms."

This is understandable when you consider that a continental European may cross three national borders on a trip of a few hours. The much-traveled European may carry the currencies of a half dozen countries in his pocketbook. He not only will know the quotations of the dollar against the Swiss franc, the pound, or the DM, he also will know the cross rates: how many Swiss francs to the pound, or how many Italian lire to the German mark.

Often, during money crises, massive movements of money will occur. Newspapers report movements. What may not be emphasized is that, when money moves from one nation to another, it doesn't just disappear. It goes into investments of some kind. Anyone who understands international finance enough to transfer money from here to there will have some place to put that money when it gets there. Such investments affect stock prices, interest rates, bond demand, and other markets. Moreover, they may affect trends in either a positive or a negative manner.

Immediately after the December 18, 1971, currency realignment, Wall Street became euphoric. Belief spread that a flood of money would pour into the U.S. from Europe, with Wall Street attracting a lot of it. This, claimed some brokers, might push the Dow Jones Average over the thousand mark early in the year. It didn't happen because of monetary developments abroad. Investors who had transferred funds to Europe decided that the dollar still wasn't healthy enough to merit shifting of funds from Switzerland, Germany, and Japan to America.

Monetary factors may affect individual share prices, too, for U.S. companies are going global through their networks of plants, mines, oil fields, and other installations abroad. One study based on 1970 figures shows that Exxon Corporation was obtaining 50 percent of its $16.6 billion sales and 52 percent of its $1.3 billion net income from abroad. Figures for International Business Machines Corp. were 39 percent of its $7.5 billion sales and 50 percent of its $1 billion net profit. CPC International claimed 50 percent of its $1.4 billion sales and 51 percent of its $61 million net from foreign operations. International Telephone & Telegraph gained 42 percent of its $6.4 billion sales and 35 percent of its $353 million net (excluding Canada) from abroad.

That same story comes from scores of other companies. In Switzerland, bankers say that monetary stability and free currency convertibility are key factors in determining profits of multinational corporations. Thus, anyone holding shares in MNCs has a reason for wanting something akin to the monetary system which served the world so well for twenty-eight years.

Union Bank of Switzerland's 1971 annual report said: "The Washington compromise [of December 18, 1971] represents, of course, only an initial step toward the consolidation of the monetary situation." Another step was the 1973 devaluation.

Dollar devaluations settled little. They merely purchased time for a reorganization of the monetary system which may take several years to effect. The IMF is expected to play a major role in that reorganization, which is why Switzerland looks to joining it.

Dr. Stopper's desire to lead Switzerland into IMF is not

fully supported. Both Union Bank and Swiss Bank Corp. feel that IMF is too hasty in expanding the world's SDR total. Once in IMF, Switzerland would have to participate in the SDR scheme, along with everybody else. Swiss bankers feel that these man-made instruments are about as solid as the thin air from which they were created.

If you don't understand exactly what an SDR is, imagine a penny-ante poker game which is starting. Somebody notices the chips have been mislaid.

"Never mind," says the host. "We will use matches for chips."

So matches are divided on the basis of what each player has in the "kitty." In effect, artificial chips have been created. SDRs are parallel on a giant scale, except that, instead of matches, the scorekeeper (the IMF) marks down on paper the number of SDRs issued to each "player" in the game of international finance. In the poker game, there would be an ultimate settlement when matches are redeemed for cash. The game of international finance is a never-ending one, where there isn't any final game-end settlement.

SDRs, like matches, are good only among the international "players" and can't be used as cash by ordinary citizens. SDRs may be used, though, like dollars or gold when settling the debts of those "players." This is why they also are called "paper gold."

The SDR is viewed with suspicion by Swiss bankers because, in the final analysis, there isn't anything but mutual cooperation behind them.

"We need something more substantial than SDRs as the final media for settlement of accounts," said F. W. Schulthess, chairman, Swiss Credit Bank. In an interview in his office he added: "I may be an arch-conservative and somewhat old-fashioned, but I believe gold is the best medium to fulfill that role." In other words, the poker players shouldn't use matches, but should stick to cash, even though there might not be enough small change to go around.

Other sources hail the SDR as the greatest invention since paper money appeared. These differences show the gap which must be closed before agreement can be reached concerning monetary reform. When the Group of Ten realigned parities in December, 1971, the communiqué said:

> The ministers and governors agreed that discussions should be promptly undertaken, particularly in the framework of the International Monetary Fund, to consider reform of the international monetary system over the longer term. It was agreed that attention should be directed to the appropriate monetary means and division of responsibilities for defending stable exchange rates and for insuring a proper degree of convertibility of the system; to the proper role of gold, of reserve currencies, and of special drawing rights in the operation of the system; to the appropriate volume of liquidity; to reexamination of the permissible margins of fluctuation around established exchange rates and other means of establishing a suitable degree of flexibility; and to other measures dealing with movements of liquid capital. It is recognized that decisions in each of these areas are closely linked.

They are closely linked, not only to each other, but to the economic well-being of nations and individuals around the world. Some factors reach into the bones of nations. This makes for tough negotiations.

Until the U.S. has corrected its balance of payments deficits, it is highly unlikely that any new system can be introduced. Without dollar convertibility, it is difficult to see how anything can be implemented. Convertibility is manifestly impossible with the massive deficits that the U.S. has been having.

The situation is complicated because some foreign nations suspect that the U.S. really doesn't want to create a new monetary system. They think America wants to push the world onto a dollar standard, come what may. Such a system could result by default if foreign nations continued to accept any dollars which poured outward from the U.S. because of the latter's deficits.

These fears lie behind the speed with which Common Market nations closed ranks to work toward a monetary union. They had talked for years, hounded by Raymond Barre, the polished and intense ex-vice president of the Commission of EC who is godfather of the Common Market monetary union. Barre, an urbane Frenchman from the remote island of Réunion in the Indian Ocean, is a brilliant and persistent technocrat. He uses opposition as a whetstone to sharpen his arguments for the trend toward a common currency which he feels is irreversible.

His optimism is unbounded, anyone realizes who examines the obstacles before monetary union. Nevertheless, first steps in that direction were taken April 24, 1972. Common Market nations narrowed the bands separating currencies to 2.25 percent from the 4.5 percent established at the December 18 realignment in Washington. Currencies move up or down in relationship to market demand, of course. But central banks may control movements by manipulating currencies.

In effect the central banks of the Common Market are cooperating so that national currencies in the nine-nation bloc are not pushed any further apart by market forces than 2.25 percent, or by 1.125 percent on either side of the average of all the currencies in the bloc.

Difficulties of the task were emphasized shortly after this step was taken, however, when Britain floated its pound sterling, removing itself from the narrow bank scheme. Under Barre's prodding, other nations agreed to push forward, with Britain returning to the fold after its parity problem is sorted out. Then Italy floated its lira to complicate matters.

EC has a long way to go before it can reach its goal of establishing one common European currency which might become a competitor of the dollar. In any case, with its own monetary union started, EC has a bargaining ploy in future monetary reform discussions. If things don't go its way, it can claim the right to work toward a European currency without regard for other sensibilities.

"If the United States drags its feet in the creation of a new monetary order, we may find that the world divides into competitive monetary blocs," warned one Swiss banker who spent part of his career in the U.S. "This is not one of those one-sided situations where all of the power lies on a side of the table."

René Larre, BIS general manager, warned in the bank's 1972 annual report that "The United States should have a constructive approach in this matter as permanent dollar inconvertibility could split the world into restrictive monetary blocs."

Perhaps Europe's suspicions of American intentions may be unfounded. At the annual convention of the International Monetary Fund in Washington in late September 1972, U.S. Treasury Secretary Shultz sought to allay fears of American intentions. He sketched a broad outline of a new monetary order built upon SDRs, with provisions for automatic adjustments if a country ran a surplus or a deficit. Since details were lacking, however, the plan really is a statement of bargaining intention at the present time, rather than the blueprint for constructing a new monetary order.

Bargaining certainly is in order. America has said it wants a reorganization of trade patterns along with any new monetary system. Trade concessions are expected from Europe, Japan, and Canada, by American reasoning. Thus, there are opportunities for bargaining, better trade deals to help American exports coupled with U.S. concessions toward monetary reform.

With years of negotiations probably ahead, it is possible to visualize three possible routes which the world may take:

1. THE DOLLAR ROUTE. America pays lip service to monetary reform, as it tries to keep the world on a dollar standard. If everybody goes along, then the dollar will be the reserve currency, the trading currency, the intervention currency, and the standard of value, just as it has been in reality recently.

2. A TWO-BLOC SYSTEM. Europe establishes a monetary bloc to counter the above, with the non-socialist world dividing into two blocs, the dollar bloc and the European currency-gold bloc. In this case, currencies of the European bloc would float together against the dollar, with narrow margins existing among intra-European currencies as the trend toward monetary union proceeds.

3. A NEW MONETARY SYSTEM. This involves a cooperative international reform of the system.

Because the EC moved so fast to launch its monetary union (Route 2 above), chances are that Route 3 may become the goal. With EC threatening to march forward toward its monetary union, it will be harder for the U.S. to try the dollar route. Yet, creating that monetary union is not going to be an easy matter for EC, either. So both America and Europe have reasons for taking Route 3.

Merely establishing this as a goal does not mean that the end will be reached. Differences are wide. Should negotiations break down at some point in 1973 or 1974, or later, the world still could revert to Routes 1 or 2.

In actual fact, the world has been on a shaky dollar standard ever since August 15, 1971. This has been accepted because nearly everybody has been insisting that this is "temporary." But, then, the French like to say that nothing is more permanent than the temporary.

The full dollar standard has many advantages for America, which may become apparent to U.S. congressmen, senators, government officials, and negotiators as talks toward reform proceed. This is what worries some Swiss money men. Swiss fear being asked to choose between a dollar bloc and a European bloc. The latter probably would be the choice, but at a heavy price to Switzerland's banking empire.

A full dollar standard could raise problems of its own, too. William McChesney Martin, Jr., former chairman of the Federal Reserve Board, asked a troubled question when encountered in the executive suite of Dow Jones & Co. in New York. "If we tried to maintain a dollar standard on our own what would this do to international cooperation? I'm afraid that such cooperation on a grand scale might be finished."

Such worries are shared widely enough to guarantee that monetary reform negotiations will be launched.

It is easy to sketch the bare bones of possible reform, more difficult to ink in details. Initially, something must be done to reduce the huge dollar overhang. In early 1973 foreign central banks and international agencies held $70 billion worth of U.S. dollars in their vaults, a doubling of the total in a year and a half. Since the U.S. no longer exchanges gold for dollars, those central banks wonder what they are supposed to do with those dollars.

Linked with this question is the matter of dollar convertibility. When the dollar was convertible into gold on demands of central banks, it was more than a piece of paper. Today, the dollar has the U.S. economy behind it, but doubts about the strength of that economy are transferred to the dollar which, after all, is only a symbol of the America behind it.

Before convertibility can be reestablished, an important question must be answered: convertible into what? Into gold? Into something else?

Any new reserve unit must be created, or adapted from the SDR. Will this replace gold as well as the U.S. dollar? Questions such as these haven't even moved beyond the stage of initial sparring, that stage when statesmen utter weighty remarks to cover their own ignorance of which way future diplomatic winds will blow.

Agreement must be reached, too, on the intervention currency which will help control money markets. Will this be the dollar as has been the case since the Bretton Woods agreement? If not, then what will do the task? Rules for market intervention must be established. The place of floating currencies and fixed parities must be determined. Something must be done to control short-term money movements without destroying the freedom of currency flows which is so necessary for development of commerce.

This is quite a package, and only highlights have been hit. It took the major nations two full years to create the SDR when this reserve tool was advanced as a means of increasing world liquidity. In 1972, nations spent most of the year arguing over the type of forum which would be used for negotiating the reform, not about the substance of the reform. A Committee of Twenty, a grouping of twenty nations is handling the job, with IMF support.

The General Agreement on Tariffs and Trade, Geneva, is viewed by most sources as the best forum for negotiating trade topics which are certain to rate attention, along with the monetary. GATT has been in existence since 1947. It already has a long list of "bindings," or trade liberalizing agreements, on its books, bindings which would come apart if GATT were permitted to die.

It has a competent team led by Olivier Long, the courtly Swiss diplomat who was Switzerland's ambassador to Britain before moving to the GATT secretary generalship. It already has made a start on many of the technical details, such as the relationship of different tariffs.

In his Geneva office, GATT Chieftain Long displays eager-
ness for the task. He is a trim, handsome man with silvery hair
who has the right word for the right situation, without ever
sounding over-aggressive about it.

Mere establishment of forums for the necessary negotiations does not mean that anything will get done, or get done fast
if success is attained. There isn't even agreement yet concerning
how reform should be focused: toward a revamp of the old
system, or toward creating a completely new monetary order.
One suspects, however, any final product will be a revamp
rather than something startlingly new. There are too many
elements of the IMF which are worth saving. But past history
leaves little ground for believing that solutions will be found
easily. Monetary experts have proved only too human in the
past, and all humans err easily, and admit it only with difficulty.
Any errors built into the mechanism of a monetary machine
may compound troubles.

Take floating exchange rates. For years, proponents have
argued that they were a remedy to solve parity change difficulties. Learned paper after learned paper appeared plugging floating rates as a means whereby free market forces would set parities for currencies in trouble. The more imaginative even
pictured all currencies floating happily on free enterprise tides.
If people didn't want a currency, its price and parity would go
down. If they did want it, the price would rise.

So what happened? After President Nixon's August 15, 1971,
bombshell, all currencies floated against the dollar, by necessity
rather than choice. After only four months of that float, it was
difficult to find anyone in the business of banking or foreign
exchange in Europe who had a good word to say for currency
floats. The exceptions usually were journalists, or non-industry
economists.

Ironically, the floating rate proponents seldom seem to realize that their arguments for the float are very similar to those
advanced by proponents of the gold standard. In both cases, it
is the market which establishes policies for employment, investments, and other economic matters. On the surface, this sounds
fine to the true believer in free enterprise, i.e. let the market
decide. In one case, it is the amount of gold earned in a market;
in the other, it is the market for currencies which is decisive.

But neither standard can work well today. Voters are un-likely to accept the rigidities of the gold standard. Meanwhile, they are unlikely to surrender certain other rigidities which defy the free float of all currencies. The way a currency moves may decide the employment level, rates of pay, social security benefits, and various other aspects within a country. Which worker wants to accept a pay cut? How do you lay off people in certain industries? If the market decides that a saloon on the corner is better than a children's park, should the market make the decision? And what if an internationally organized free-floating money market decides that investments in Britain should be shunned, while those in Germany should be in-creased? Should Britain go meekly along, or should it hoard its own resources for the benefit of its own people?

If a nation like Britain decided to drop out of the free float, then it would affect the whole system. Other nations would have to take measures to protect themselves against repercussions.

Pierre-Paul Schweitzer, managing director of IMF, is among the most vocal opponents of floats. Said he: "The exter-nal value of a country's currency exerts an important influence on its aggregate output and expenditure, as well as on the alloca-tion of its resources. For this reason, national governments will not find it possible to avoid intervening in the foreign exchange market. But such intervention will, in turn, affect the exchange rates of other currencies and thereby other currencies."

Unquestionably, social and political strains would be enor-mous under any free-floating money system. Arguments may be advanced to claim that, ultimately, changes would benefit every-body. But it is highly doubtful that most governments would surrender capacities for intervening in markets, allowing com-pletely free markets to set wage levels, employment totals, popu-lation distribution, and other such factors.

Dr. Alfred Schaefer, chairman of Union Bank, said at the time of the 1971 general float: "The general uncertainty with regard to floating exchange rates weighs heavily on world mar-kets, particularly where profit margins are customarily low. Hedging costs have soared up to 5 or 6 percent per annum in certain currencies, which is more than twice as much as in 'normal' times."

One survey made in Europe in early December, 1971, covering fifty leading bankers, foreign exchange dealers, and others directly in business, found only three willing to say anything good about floating rates. Even those three wouldn't endorse them, merely saying that perhaps more time might be necessary to form a sound judgment. That experience in 1971, of course, provides many more answers than are possible with one-country floats such as that of Canada, Britain, and West Germany at various times. The answers have not been encouraging.

Indications are that, when the choice is made, there will be more support for fixed parities than for floating rates in any new monetary system. But it probably will be much easier to adjust those fixed rates under the new system, than was the case in the past.

Everybody pays lip service to the fight against inflation, too. But one wonders if monetary reformers will have the courage to create and introduce a system which will be anti-inflationary, since it is so much easier to spend money than to save it.

Consider the SDR, for example. Few people now seem to want to remember that this was created, not to replace the dollar, but to increase world liquidity. Yes. To increase world liquidity, just at a time when the world was facing an enormous inflationary binge.

Today the SDR, quite rightly, is being viewed as an extremely useful instrument for application in any monetary reform. Yet one can conclude that monetary experts aren't so bright after all, if they create inflationary instruments to expand liquidity even as their own governments ostensibly are trying to dampen inflation.

World liquidity, which was supposed to be in such short supply, increased by over 18 percent in 1970, with 4 percentage points coming from newly created SDRs. In 1971, world liquidity jumped by an inflation bolstering 26.7 percent, with a 3-percentage-point boost from SDRs.

Questions could be asked, too, about the massive increase in national IMF quotas which came with activation of the first round of SDRs. In one swoop, IMF quotas, which decide how much nations may borrow from the Fund in time of need, were raised 35 percent to over $28 billion.

With this background, one wonders how much attention will be paid to inflation as the system is reformed. Will new instruments be created atop all the liquidity now existing?

If you happen to have investments in stocks, bonds, or anything else, it will be worth your while to pay attention to the way monetary reformers increase world liquidity, and how other monetary actions may affect inflation. Their actions may have a direct bearing upon what happens to your investments.

One remembers a conversation with Dr. Karl Blessing, the kindly late president of the German Bundesbank, shortly after he had retired. Dr. Blessing, a long-time Unilever executive and devotee of the theatre, spent the last years of his life fighting inflation. He preached the doctrine of a sound mark so avidly that he filled his countrymen with a rabid fear of inflation.

"Our monetary system is a perfect inflationary machine," he said after analyzing the effects of the creation of a new batch of SDRs. "It creates liquidity when we don't need it, then creates some more as if ignorant of the damage which is being done."

This is something to think about as monetary experts ponder how to reform the system. If misjudgments could be made about liquidity, what sort of errors may be expected in the future when experts are looking at the entire system.

In the light of current developments, it can now be said, of course, that creation of the SDR was a major achievement. Had distribution been delayed, the idea might have been quietly shelved. As it is, they do provide one of the tools necessary should any new monetary system emerge from the present muddle. The present SDR, however, is not the reserve instrument for becoming the focal point of any new system. It will require a super-SDR for that, and perhaps a new type of IMF deposit. Surplus dollars of foreign central banks, for instance, might be deposited with IMF to increase drawing rights of holding nations, while removing the dollars from the system. Perhaps there may be a combination of SDRs, super-SDRs, deposits, and drawing rights in this new system.

The tasks of monetary reformers will be complicated by attempts to inject foreign aid concepts into the question of monetary reform. Developing nations view the present as an opportunity to institutionalize the role of foreign aid by constructing an automatic handout program into the new system. They overlook the fact that the best guarantee for continued foreign aid is prosperity in developed nations. A sound monetary system may promote that. Only delay may result from attempts to create a jerry-built monetary system based on the idea of taking from the haves to give to the have-nots. If competition for trade intensifies during that delay, beggar-my-neighbor policies would hit poor nations first.

Poor nations certainly should not be forgotten, while money problems of the rich take precedence. Ingenious schemes could be established to handle the dollar overhang, that huge volume of dollars now in the hands of central banks and of private individuals overseas. Interest on any funding of these dollars might be shunted into aid reservoirs, a joint contribution of the U.S., which would be doing the interest paying, and of foreign nations like West Germany which would be surrendering the interest payments. But this is far different from using any central reserve instrument—a super-SDR—as a medium for disbursement of foreign aid. Above all, any new monetary system must be strong and sound if it is to survive. There is nothing more soulless and impersonal than money. Money has a built-in radar which automatically leads it to the man of ability or the nation with the soundest financial policies, not to men or places which are most in need. Failure to recognize this simple fact when creating the mechanics of a new monetary system could be disastrous.

In launching their deliberations, monetary reformers must pay heed to causes of the collapse of the Bretton Woods system. These causes have been discussed so many times over the last dozen years that most participants can cite them by rote. They include: the U.S. balance of payments deficit; ability of the U.S. to create reserves through those deficits; inability of the U.S. to revise easily the dollar's parity; political opposition to currency revaluations in Europe; failure of the U.S. to adjust to the hard-money conditions requisite for maintenance of its dollar as a reserve currency; unwillingness of foreign nations to reduce surpluses; neurotic opposition to a gold price increase; interest rate and monetary policy differentials among nations; huge short-term capital movements; and a marked preference for excess liquidity over even a remote chance of liquidity shortages. The list easily could be extended.

Causes provide grounds for bitter controversy. Take the matter of those U.S. deficits, for instance. Dollars went abroad because the U.S. was spending more than it was earning overseas. But on the other side of the Atlantic and Pacific, Europe and Japan waited eagerly for the rain of dollars. They paid only lip service to pleas that they should reduce their dollar surpluses. So who was to blame for America's deficits?

Negotiations certainly won't be a simple matter of pointing the finger at the U.S. and expecting America to make all the sacrifices. Should negotiations take that turn, we might see the U.S. opting for a dollar standard, letting the SDRs fall where they may.

Already it appears that money asymmetry may be another area of strong controversy. Webster defines asymmetry as "want of proportion between the parts of a thing." A big boy and a little boy, or a rich man and a poor man are asymmetrical. The United States has been so much more powerful than any other single nation that Bretton Woods took this into account, as do most international organizations. The United Nations was an exception. Here, desire for symmetry led to the incongruous "one nation one vote" principle. So now we have a situation where the U.S., with a population of 210 million and the mightiest economy on earth, has one vote in the U.N. General Assembly. So does tiny Sierra Leone.

Now, European nations insist that more symmetry should be introduced into any new system. If France can't create reserves through deficits, then the U.S. shouldn't be allowed to do so either. The U.S. views asymmetry differently. It claims it is unfair that every other nation in the system easily can devalue or revalue; yet it is extremely difficult for the U.S. to do so unilaterally.

Other currencies are computed against the dollar, i.e. so many marks to the dollar, so many Swiss francs to the dollar. The dollar, as the kingpin currency, had been pegged to gold at one dollar is equal to 1/35 of an ounce. (Now, one forty-second, on paper, anyway.) So the dollar had always remained steady while other currencies moved up or down as a nation's policy directors decided.

The U.S. position on asymmetry ignores the fact that the U.S. could have revised the dollar value by changing the price of gold. This could have been done either through a uniform change in IMF par values, or more hopefully, through a change in the American valuation alone. Obviously this would have required international agreement. The December 18, 1971, parity realignment in Washington proved that such agreement was possible. The February, 1973, devaluation did likewise.

That asymmetry question will be difficult to solve. Symmetry is almost impossible in monetary matters when nations of vastly different power are brought together. Common Market nations realize this, which is why they are joining together to operate as a bloc.

Today the world is on a dollar standard. This is a one-sided asymmetrical standard because the world is one sided. The dollar dominates because no other nation comes close to the U.S. in economic power. This nation has a trillion-dollar gross national product, nearly double that of the entire expanded Nine Nation Common Market. Its national energy production is double that of the Community. Its 75,000-plus computer total in operation is triple that of EC. This is why the dollar dominates, not because of any conniving by Washington or by the Gnomes of Zurich.

The dollar became the world's intervention currency because other nations found it convenient for the job. The dollar became the standard of value for measuring other currencies again because it was convenient and because it had a tie to gold. The dollar became a reserve currency for the same latter two reasons. Because the dollar was used for all of the above purposes, it became the favored trading currency, too.

If you open an international airlines guide, you will find the fares quoted in dollars. Most contracts of shipping conferences are cited the same way. As mentioned earlier, even the duty-free shops in the Soviet Union use dollars in their quotations. The dollar was and still is an important currency because the U.S. is an important country. With the right policies, the dollar can regain strength and be not only an important currency but a strong one as well.

It is not certain yet whether or not the American people are willing to work hard enough to keep the dollar strong. What's needed is a little upsurge in productivity without rises in costs; more control of inflation; more willingness by people to accept what they have, rather than to pine endlessly for more; and more frugality on the part of both citizens and government.

The formula sounds like a Swiss banker preaching a monetary sermon. With that formula, of course, America may be tempted to keep the dollar strong and to press for a dollar standard. Such temptation won't come only from the U.S. either. Should the dollar become robust again, a lot of foreign nations will be eager to have it.

It may be an illusion, however, for America to think that it could force a dollar system onto the world. Nationalism runs strong in Europe. Any U.S. moves in this direction could stimulate the Common Market to expedite its own monetary union as a competitor rather than as a cooperative partner with the U.S.

Should any new system emerge, then rules of the game must be drawn, too. What rules should apply if a nation intervenes in its own money market? And what should be done to control short-term money movements? How can these rules be applied without hurting multinational companies, most of them American?

Controls may be aimed at the eurodollar market, too. Then there is the question of how parities may be changed in the future without causing disruptions to the system. Monetary experts seem to agree that more flexibility is needed. Parity changes should come oftener, in small packages, they say. Still, past history shows that if speculators are taught to expect parity changes, they will gear operations for it. In that case, the mere expectation of parity changes might bring them about. So how could this tendency be controlled under the new rules?

The more one studies monetary reform, the more it is evident that there can be no hurry in finding solutions to all of the questions which are sure to be raised. Any investor, however, would be wise to study essential developments as they take place, so that he has a basic understanding of them. Perhaps at no time in history have monetary matters been of such importance to investments.

This is why Swiss bank accounts have proved so attractive to tens of thousands of people who live far from that mountainous little country. This is why those Swiss bank accounts may continue to be popular, but maybe not for everybody.

CHAPTER XVIII

FINAL ACCOUNTING

A diplomatic and banking scandal rocked Switzerland in March, 1972. It caused some embarrassment in London's White-hall, seat of the British government, and much more than embarrassment to certain British citizens who held Swiss bank accounts. British Treasury agents had bribed employees of a Geneva bank to pass along detailed information about British bank accounts. The bank was the small Société Financière Mire-lis S.A.

The story broke when holders of those accounts in Britain were called to Treasury offices. Not only were tax matters involved, but it was illegal in Britain to transfer money to foreign accounts without authorization from the government. Swiss fumed at this intrusion into Swiss affairs.

Some Britishers gloated, as only Englishmen can when neighbors are caught committing sins which nearly everyone wishes he could commit undetected, himself. A tax man is unloved when knocking on your door, an ingenious fellow when catching that neighbor up the street who has been getting away with it for so long.

This illustrates that it all depends on whose bank box is being gored. If you have a Swiss bank account, you may sympathize with the Swiss. If you believe all the stories about crooks hiding loot in Switzerland, you may sympathize with the British. If you are simply a person who would like to know more about Swiss bank accounts, then you should understand all sides. And for you, this may be a many-sided matter.

The snoopiness of those British tax men shows that Swiss bank accounts are not super-secret. It only took $2,000 in bribes for British Treasury agents to crack those accounts. The U.S. government can afford to spend a lot more than that.

The erosion of Swiss bank account impermeability comes from pressure from, or developments in, several countries. The most important insofar as you are concerned involves the United States and Switzerland. Tax procedures of the former are being tightened enough to affect a good many present and potential American holders of Swiss bank accounts.

Switzerland itself shows signs of irritation concerning the abuses of its banking liberality. Bankers are tightening some of their own practices and procedures. You may now find it difficult to open a bank account if you try to shield your identity. Some banks won't even accept your application. And if you fake your identity as did Mrs. Clifford Irving, and find yourself involved in a fraud, you may discover to your discomfiture that your account has no secrecy at all.

Negative interest rates are not palatable, either. In 1972, because of heavy inflows of money, Switzerland had an 8 percent annual negative interest rate on foreign deposits switched into Swiss francs. This applied on accounts first of $13,000 and up then of $26,000 and up in mid-summer, with some bankers saying it might be revised to apply only to very big accounts. Moreover, there wasn't anything to stop a person from having several different accounts. And if you kept your money in dollars, the negative rate didn't apply.

There are numerous reasons other than U.S. taxes why an American might prefer a secret bank account as far from home as possible. Relatives, for instance. It is simple to withdraw assets from your bank account in Switzerland. It can be made to sound very difficult to the uninformed. Attachments in civil cases may make a Swiss account attractive. If a husband wants a secret bank account to keep funds from an avaricious ex-wife, the Swiss are right there to help. This doesn't work in reverse, however, for a husband sometimes can obtain a court order to inspect a wife's account, though a wife can't do the same concerning her husband's account.

If you are interested in investing internationally, a Swiss account might be useful. You don't absolutely need a Swiss account for that. But those Swiss do view money as a global commodity. What the United Nations does for the good neighborliness of nations, Swiss money men do internationally for individual pocketbooks. The state of the U.S. dollar and the monetary situation does mean that the international situation could affect your pocketbook.

Today, there are two schools of thought concerning the dollar, one pessimistic, the other optimistic. The first contends that the devaluation of late 1971, followed by that of February 12, 1973, won't correct the dollar's ills. In two or three years, the dollar may again weaken, and another devaluation may become necessary. If this scenario is correct, then it may be wise to have some savings in a hard-currency country, not to evade U.S. income taxes, but for the same reason that American multinational corporations may invest some of their funds abroad: to protect the capital itself. Switzerland certainly is a hard-money country.

As of December 31, 1972, the Swiss National Bank had 11.88 billion Swiss francs ($3.1 billion) in gold and 12.3 billion francs in foreign exchange ($3.2 billion) for a total of 24.2 billion francs ($6.3 billion). That was a 9 percent rise in monetary reserves from the total at the end of 1971. In addition, the bank held 4.3 billion francs worth of other foreign assets ($1.1 billion). Against these reserves, Switzerland had a monetary base of 26 billion francs ($6.8 billion) in bank notes in circulation, demand deposits, and minimum reserves of banks.

That pessimistic school is exemplified by one corpulent Swiss banker in Germanic Zurich, that lakeside city which is surrounded by green hills and, more often than not, by fog. Sitting in an office on Bahnhofstrasse, this banker voiced his monetary fears over a cup of coffee.

"The dollar is sick because America is sick," he said, with that condescending air Europeans sometimes reserve for visiting Americans.

He fingered one of Elliot Janeway's letters predicting that the Dow Jones average would slide down to five hundred, and his manner was as depressing as the thin fog which enveloped the lime trees along the busy avenue outside. Zurich on a damp day has all the grayness of Navy battleship paint, a grayness which becomes solid enough to taste and cold enough to chill as the day wears away. Nothing is more apt to deject the spirit of an American than a wet day in Zurich with a Swiss banker ridiculing the dollar.

"We are correcting our problem," said the visitor. Dollar devaluations of nearly 18 percent are substantial."

"Surface treatment. Surface treatment," he said.

"The American economy still is tremendously powerful." The visitor had a sense of fighting a rearguard action in deep snow.

"I am afraid America will continue to spend more abroad and to import too much," he said. "Your deficits will continue. Then the dollar again will go kaput."

The last word was spoken with abrupt finality. It seemed, too, to be the last word about the dollar, uttered with the finality of one who already sees the dollar on its way to perdition.

The second, optimistic school among Swiss money men in this international playlet contends that the 1972 devaluations will correct the ills of the dollar. It may take a few years for those correctives to show. During that time there may be precarious times which could cause problems for the dollar. But with wise management in Washington, the dollar should emerge among the strong currencies of the world.

The world would then move onto a freely convertible international investment stage. Americans in Paducah or Oshkosh and elsewhere may be investing legally, and without interest equalization taxes, in Australian mining shares, in Ghana cocoa plantations, in Japanese electronics companies, and in other profitable overseas situations. Meanwhile, overseas investors would be finding America to be a fertile field for some of their capital.

In such a world, Swiss banks, with their international connections, might be good places for maintaining some accounts. But, then, American banks and brokerage houses with international networks might do just as well for you, too. And don't forget those American Depository Receipts even now when thinking of international investment. Many major foreign companies have these ADRs listed on U.S. exchanges. Shares may be purchased without worrying about the interest equalization tax which is payable on direct foreign purchases of shares.

In short, Swiss banks are not a panacea for everybody. They are geared for the big investor, not the small. They are universal banks, again something appreciated more by the wealthy investor than the little guy who can't diversify.

The Swiss banker is a master in the handling of fixed interest securities. He has a natural affinity for bonds and for interest-bearing paper of sound companies. When it comes to stocks, he can purchase shares for you in any of the world's markets whether it be New York, Tokyo, London, Frankfurt, Paris, Milan, Johannesburg, Amsterdam, or elsewhere. Swiss low-interest rates are an advantage when using margin trading for leverage. Time deposits are handy when you want to switch into strong currency cash. (Here, the low Swiss interest rates are a disadvantage, though.)

Of course, Swiss bank deposits may be switched from one currency to another as you see fit. This is one way of "playing" the foreign exchange situation with almost no risks. (That is, provided that you show a minimum of sense in selecting the right currencies to hold in your account.) You will find Big Three banks not much interested in handling your foreign exchange speculation through short selling, unless you happen to be wealthy enough to operate as a corporation in your own right. Smaller banks may not be that particular once they are acquainted with you.

Swiss bankers remove emotions from their dealings with

currencies. They believe there is little difference between dumping a weak currency and selling shares of a company hit by adverse developments, or conversely between buying a strong currency and jumping onto a sound company which looks as if its shares may take off.

The optimistic school concerning the dollar is found at banks like that of Julius Bär & Co., also in Zurich. In his office, Dr. Nicolas Bär, partner in the firm, said: "I'm not a pessimist insofar as the dollar is concerned. I do realize that there are some troubles in the monetary system which must be corrected. But that realignments were very substantial. It will take time, but I feel that America will solve its problems."

Swiss bankers do agree, however, that monetary developments promise to play a more active role in investments in the future. Monetary reform, for instance, is expected to involve rules which may make it easier for nations to devalue or revalue their currencies. Moreover, there are indications that currency parity revisions may become an economic tool in bags of government planners. Should exports decline and recession threaten, a nation may be quick to devalue its currency by a small margin. Should domestic inflation threaten at the height of a boom, a nation may quickly revalue its currency. It is vital for investors and bankers to know what this means to them.

This situation led to the creation in 1972 of the International Center for Monetary and Banking Studies in Geneva. Founding fathers were Nicolas Krul, Lombard, Odier's chief researcher, Pierre Keller, a Lombard, Odier partner, and Alexander Swoboda, an economics professor at Geneva's Graduate Institute of International Studies. Support is being given by major Swiss and continental banks.

"This is proof of the greater interest in fundamental research, an interest which is much stronger than we originally expected," said Krul, when outlining goals of the new organization.

A project outline emphasizes those goals. It says: "The Center is devoted to the scientific study of monetary, financial and banking problems in their international context through collaboration among specialists from central banks, international organizations, the private sector and the academic community."

Focus will be on research, on the exchange of information, and on training. Hope is that this Center will encourage a coordinated approach to the international aspects of problems which are too often studied only at the national level.

IMF is well aware of the importance of monetary developments. One confidential document circulated within IMF says: "The most important cause of disruptive capital flows, especially in recent years, is of course to be found in the emergence, from time to time, of expectations of imminent appreciation or depreciation of particular currencies."

Past history shows there's money to be made (and lost) during periods of "disruptive capital flows." Swiss bankers are among the most astute in the world in assuring that the profits of such transactions outrun the losses when the final accounting is made.

What are some of the other things Swiss bankers say about the future in the investment area? The list is lengthy. But here are a few of the main points they emphasize:

—Economic growth will continue to be pressed, despite complaints of ecologists that growth should give way to "quality of life."

—Ecology, however, will become a more important force, not only in the United States but in the rest of the world, too.

—Expansion of the European Common Market broadens investment opportunities in this area. Mergers will be stimulated, producing chances for merger speculation by investors. Aggressive firms will seize sales opportunities, while weaker firms will grow weaker.

—Japan will be moving overseas with plants and facilities. There may be some listings of Japanese firms on overseas markets, while direct investments in Japan will be made easier through expansions of Japanese brokerage houses and banks abroad.

—Cyclical stocks always will provide opportunities for long or short sales in America. But investors should watch for those companies which introduce new techniques for slashing service costs. These firms may be the Xeroxes and the Polaroids of the future.

—The trend toward a service industry society, which is so

noticeable in America, is appearing in Europe, too. Wise investors are seeking to apply knowledge of that trend gained in America to investments in Europe.

—Economic controls may be a much more important part of the world scene in the future than free enterprisers would like. Such controls will affect investment opportunities in various nations, probably adversely.

—Capital may be tight in the period ahead as demands come from all sides for funds to expand industry and to develop nations. Thus, interest rates are apt to tend toward the high side, rather than the low, over the long term.

—Currencies such as the German mark, the pound sterling, the Dutch guilder, and the Japanese yen will play a more important role in the euromarket, though the dollar may still be the key currency for some while.

—Multinational companies will grow at a faster rate than domestic-bound competitors, offering more profit opportunities for investors.

—Energy shortages will enhance the power of oil-producing nations in bargaining with international oil companies. The latter must adjust to earn more profit from downstream operations and from diversification. Companies with crude-oil deficiencies will suffer, as will those unable to adjust to the new political atmosphere. Companies which do adjust should do well in an era of energy shortages.

Growth still seems well ahead in the ecological struggle it now faces. Early in 1972, Swiss Credit organized a meeting of prominent economic people from various nations. The speaker was Professor Herman Kahn, the futurologist of Hudson Institute, New York. He predicted that the 1970 Gross World Product of $3.4 trillion will grow by 1980 to $5.6 trillion (1970 dollars). Then the U.S. and Japan would be the two largest exporting nations, dividing about 25 percent of the world export market. The sales of America's own MNCs, however, will continue to dwarf U.S. exports, futurologist Kahn said.

Kahn is a huge man who spills over both sides of his chair when he sits down. He looks like a living Buddha when he stares owlishly through his spectacles. Sometimes he presents figures and complex economic formulas so fast that a companion needs a tape recorder to obtain all the information. Unquestionably, he dominates his audiences, both physically and intellectually.

His views about multinational corporations are widely shared by Swiss bankers, too. Those American operations abroad promise to play a vital role in the position of the U.S. in the future, adding to its strength, providing a substantial plus factor in its balance of payments. America may be slipping in the world trade parade. But it would be deceptive to conclude that America itself is slipping as far as the trade figures might seem to indicate.

In investing, of course, it is not enough to know the overall trends which may be underway. What counts is the position of a specific company in its industry and its relationship to trends. Here, homework is required on your part. And, if you bank in Switzerland, you should be getting some assistance from your Swiss banker, else there's no point in dealing with him.

Considerable information is available about the international investment scene, economic trends in various countries, monetary factors, and the outlook for industries and individual companies within countries. Markets abroad, however, are thin compared to those in the U.S. The total market value of equities in the U.S., for instance, at the start of 1972 was estimated at $780 billion. In Britain, equity values totaled $106 billion. In Japan, the figure was $57 billion. It was $34 billion in Germany, $23 billion in France, $18 billion in Australia, $13 billion in Switzerland, and $10.5 billion in Italy.

The American market is overwhelmingly larger than all the other equity markets put together. This means that a like volume of money can be much more upsetting to a market in Australia or Germany than would be the case in the U.S. So one needs to know what is going on in foreign countries before putting any money there.

Swiss banks issue a considerable amount of market analysis material. All major banks and many of the big private banks publish monthly stock and bond lists. These same banks issue monthly economic and market letters, in French and German, and in some cases, in English.

Union Bank of Switzerland, Bahnhofstrasse 45, Zurich, has its monthly "Business Facts and Figures" which is in English.

The February, 1972, issue starts by reporting a world-wide decline in interest rates. A second article discusses Swiss foreign trade. Others examine appreciation records of two of the bank's funds, Bond-Invest International Bond Investment Trust and Helvetinvest-Investment Trust for Swiss Fixed-Interest Securities; the state of the gold, silver, platinum, and palladium markets; and the state of the world's monetary reserves.

Swiss Bank Corp., Aeschenvorstadt 1, Basle, publishes its bimonthly "Prospects" in English. Often, the lead article will consist of a speech by the chairman, or by another bank official. Swiss affairs are well covered. Tabulations of Switzerland's economic statistics provide capsules of how the economy is going.

Swiss Credit Bank, which frequently terms itself Credit Suisse even in its English publications, is located at Paradeplatz, Zurich. Its "Bulletin" is a comprehensive economic magazine which appears monthly in French and German, quarterly in English and Italian, and semi-annually in Spanish. The March, 1972, issue contains a personalized account of a trip through South Africa by R. H. Lutz, one of the bank's general managers. Another article goes into detail concerning investment possibilities in South Africa.

The "interesting" investment possibilities are: Anglo American Corp. of South Africa Ltd.; De Beers Consolidated Mines Ltd.; Greaterman's Stores Ltd.; South African Breweries Ltd.; Tiger Oats & National Milling Co., Ltd.; and Vaal Reefs Exploration & Mining Co., Ltd. The bulletin also contains a comprehensive securities list ranging from Latin American power companies to Australian industrial and mining shares.

All the Big Three banks issue pamphlets at different times outlining philosophies concerning topics of interest to investors. Private banks also publish much investment literature, though they are more inclined to reserve distribution to clients rather than to the general public.

Capital International SA, 15 rue du Cendrier, 1201 Geneva, Switzerland, one of the Capital Group companies, sells a detailed equity list, "Capital International Perspective," in English, French, and German. The monthly publication lists the top one hundred shares on major non-American markets in the preceding month, with percentage gains recorded by these companies in the last month, three months, six months, and twelve months. The same coverage is given to the one hundred companies making the worst records on international exchanges. This report also details valuation and performance of shares in specific countries. Its comparisons end with industry breakdowns so that comparisons may be made among companies in particular industries regardless of geographic locations.

Swiss bankers and finance companies aren't alone in covering trends in international investing. All the big continental and British banks offer services of this kind to customers, and sometimes to the general public. Big American banks do the same thing. Then, of course, there are the international investing newsletters which you can buy on both sides of the Atlantic. Prices are steep, and the advice is slanted toward the fellow who invests in chunks of $10,000 or $25,000 and up, not for the odd-lot trader.

All in all there is a considerable amount of information available concerning the securities of companies in the international investment field. Remember, though, there is no S.E.C. to compel foreign firms to reveal all information which might be desired by stockholders, present or potential.

Not so long ago, American investors became aware of the peculiar accounting of some of the U.S. conglomerates. It became evident that annual and quarterly reports did not always provide the true picture (or at least not in the way that the average shareholder could discover without an accountant at his elbow). In Europe and other parts of the world, those conglomerate accounts would be criticized by managements for being too revealing.

Foreign companies have hidden reserves and unreported obligations which often keep stockholders in the dark. Philips Lamp, for instance, is extremely conservative with its accounting practices, so conservative in fact that one Dutch analyst estimates profits in recent years might have been 30 to 40 percent higher on company reports had American methods been employed. But for every Philips there are other companies padding their earnings to look better than they are.

Nearly all companies are super-secret about operations and profits by American standards. Fortunately, foreign security analysts become better at ferreting information necessary to determine what is really happening. In Switzerland, Swiss bankers serve on boards of major companies. So banks certainly know better than analysts concerning Swiss happenings. Generally, European companies are more prone to talk to bankers than they are to others. And Swiss bankers do circulate, not only around Europe, but around the world talking to company officials about loans, about floating issues, about putting funds to work. Some of that information often helps portfolio managers in the handling of their jobs.

A Swiss bank client should realize that there is no deposit insurance in the country. The big banks certainly are solid. This can be said about most of the private banks belonging to the Swiss Private Bankers' Association, too. And, of course, the foreign banks are just as strong as the First National City's, the Bank of America's, or whatever else lies behind Swiss branches.

Still, absence of government insurance may be a handicap in the foreign field. This is what many American investors now are discovering after being lured by allegedly high interest rates to put money into phony banks in the Bahamas and in various Caribbean islands. Some of these banks collapsed just as soon as a few million dollars had been collected from gullible investors, many of them American.

Low and even negative Swiss interest rates certainly are a drawback. It may be argued that it is better to have your money in a sound currency at low interest rates than in a weak currency at high rates. This isn't always true. If the rate of return in a weak currency more than compensates for the devaluation possibility, then it may be a worthwhile risk to put some money into the weak currency, at least for speculative accounts.

There may be language difficulties with your Swiss account, too. Visit Switzerland and you most certainly will be greeted by a banking official who speaks English fluently. However, the paper work of banks is in German and French. Computers occasionally have intellectual indigestion in Switzerland, the same as anywhere else. So you may find communications arriving in German or French. And you will encounter foul-ups.

Swiss banks are encountering mammoth labor shortages.

There are a million foreign workers in the country doing most of the dirty and menial work. So, many of the less-educated Swiss who, under normal circumstances, might be swinging picks and shovels, now are working in Swiss banks. It's a splendid example of how the proletariat of a specific country may be upgraded by the importation of foreign serfs to do the dirty work.

Those proletariat may be handling your account. Inefficient labor is aggravated by the fact that banks have had an avalanche of new business because of monetary upheavals. Between 1966 and 1970, the Swiss gross national product rose by 35 percent. In that same period, the paper work at banks soared by 70 percent.

One Union Bank report covering this same period notes that the number of cash payment transactions (excluding savings account transactions and foreign currency sales) increased by 77 percent, while the size of the bank's staff climbed by 71 percent. This report adds: "The fact that the speed and accuracy of the services provided by the Swiss banks have suffered, and that mistakes and delays occur more frequently is regrettable, but understandable."

The decline in staff efficiency at banks affects some portfolio managements, too. The ratio of service from a Swiss bank rises in proportion to the amount in an account. One certainly can't expect to receive the same management care and foresight with a $50,000 account as would be the case with one involving $5 million. This is one of those facts of life which the $50,000 investor may consider unjust. Nevertheless, as portfolio management efficiency declines, it is the smaller investor who is most apt to feel it.

Small and medium-sized investors should teach themselves how to make some of their own decisions. If that rich investor didn't inherit all his money, he probably made it in just this way.

Remember, too, that Swiss banks are in the banking business to make money. That sounds axiomatic. The fact is that Swiss banks charge for many of the services which might be free at an American bank. In Switzerland there will be a debiting fee, a crediting fee, a charge for this, a charge for that.

One British banker connected with a bank in Geneva quips: "If you leave your money long enough with a Swiss bank, the charges will eat it up."

This is an exaggeration. Generally, you get the service you pay for anywhere. Like the French waiter, however, the Swiss banker will have an answer for every charge you may find listed on one of your accountings. After UCB Basle folded, all deposits were frozen for a year pending audits. The bank assessed "handling charges" on all accounts, even though depositors were unable to withdraw their money.

Swiss banks do withhold a 30 percent tax on dividends and interest payments in most cases. This doesn't apply if holdings in eurobonds or certificates of deposit are offered through bank subsidiaries outside Switzerland. Since there is a double tax agreement, Americans may claim refunds on such payments when filing American tax reports. Your Swiss bank will give you all the details of transactions for your taxes. It will not offer any help at all with a tax problem.

So suppose you have evaluated some of the advantages and the disadvantages of a Swiss bank account. You decide you will open one. The matter of geography does seem to create another disadvantage. Perhaps. But the world grows smaller. Every year, Europe is cluttered with Americans who have not been daunted by distance.

If you do happen to visit Europe, you can visit one of those banks mentioned earlier and do your own evaluating. Accounts may be opened by mail, too. Swiss bank desire for your account rises with the size of the deposit you are considering. As mentioned earlier, many of the private banks have minimums of from $50,000 to $100,000. Even where a private bank does not have minimums, it is unlikely to become excited about an overseas account lower than that.

Don't be misled by recent moves involving negative interest rates, either. In the summer of 1972 these applied to amounts of $26,000 and up transferred to Switzerland from outside for deposit *in Swiss francs.* They did not apply to bank accounts in dollars, pounds, marks, or any other currency. Moreover, bankers were claiming that measures were temporary, with the likelihood that the barrier level might be raised much higher, or eliminated altogether.

You will find, however, that the customer selectivity at banks has been increasing as the volume of money under banking control has been rising. There is no enthusiasm, either, for the American who might be seeking to evade U.S. taxes.

J. Vontobel and Co., the big Zurich private bank, has a notice which it presents to American clients who are opening an account with them. It reads:

> In view of the friendly relations between the United States and Switzerland, we attach great importance to the fact that our American clients do not violate American regulations when they effect their transactions through our private bank. Although Swiss banks neither have to render account nor give particulars at any time to Swiss and/or foreign authorities concerning their clients' transactions, for the above-mentioned reason we nevertheless ask you to take into consideration the following points:
>
> 1. The securities purchased from us for the account of American citizens and residents are liable to taxation in the United States.
>
> 2. Purchases of non-American securities by American citizens are subject to the American Interest Equalization Tax (save in exceptional cases).
>
> 3. On the occasion of general meetings—save in cases of justified exceptions—we do not vote against the proposals of the Board of Directors of the company concerned.
>
> 4. We do not buy or hold any gold bullion for the account of American citizens.
>
> 5. When American citizens make use of credits on securities, we endeavor to observe the margin requirements of the competent American authorities.

Many Swiss banks give like notices to American clients. Julius Bär, for instance, tells prospective American clients that it will dispatch all mail involving the account to the customer's home address. This alone is enough to discourage citizens opening accounts with the hope of cheating the U.S. government. There's no point in trying to cheat the Internal Revenue Service if a mail trail leads directly from a Swiss bank to the home of the taxpayer in the U.S.

Numbered accounts are extremely difficult for Americans to get in Switzerland right now, too. So you had better have a good excuse if you seek one of them.

In summary, a Swiss bank account is not for everyone. It is a business and financial tool which could be useful to the American abroad, to the American with enough money to want some diversification into foreign markets, to the person who frequently vacations abroad, and to the investor who is thoroughly convinced that the best investment opportunities exist abroad. American expansion in the second half of the nineteenth century depended upon European capital, which nobody resented. There should be no resentment if some American capital goes abroad now.

Neither the Swiss nor U.S. tax men are going to be very helpful if any Swiss bank account involves breaking any American laws.

Perhaps the individual should take a few hints from the big, multinational corporations which are growing fat in international markets, not by breaking any laws, but simply by taking advantage of opportunities which exist abroad. Dow Chemical Co., the Midland, Michigan, giant, is a multinational firm which generally is regarded as one of the most astute when it comes to operating abroad, so astute in fact that it has been able to open a bank which thrives on the home ground of Swiss money men.

C. A. Gerstacker, Dow Chemical chairman, in one recent speech said: "In the Seventies, money must float and flow from country to country and from continent to continent, so that the best qualified companies can take advantage of the various capital markets. The real problems are going to be costs and timing: which currency to borrow, when."

The individual investor easily could paraphrase that last sentence as follows: "the real problems are going to be costs and timing; which stocks to buy, at what price, and when."

Swiss banks may help in finding the answers to those questions.

INDEX